Living Free in 5D

Embodying your Multidimensional Self

Vidya Frazier

First Edition Design Publishing
Sarasota, Florida USA

Living Fee in 5D
Embodying your Multidimensional Self

Copyright ©2022 Vidya Frazier

ISBN 978-1506-910-76-5 PBK
ISBN 978-1506-910-77-2 EBK

LCCN 2022TBD

November 2022

Published and Distributed by
First Edition Design Publishing, Inc.
P.O. Box 17646, Sarasota, FL 34276-3217
www.firsteditiondesignpublishing.com

ALL RIGHTS RESERVED. No part of this book publication may be reproduced, stored in a retrieval system, or transmitted in any form or by any means — electronic, mechanical, photo-copy, recording, or any other — except brief quotation in reviews, without the prior permission of the author or publisher.

Table of Contents

Introduction

Chapter 1: Humanity's Ascension into the Fifth Dimension 3
- The Dimensional Shift 4
- The Fifth Dimension 4
- Two Pathways 5
- Negotiating the Ascension Path 6
- An Unexpected Monkey Wrench in the Ascension Process ... 7
- This Book 8

Chapter 2: Negative Forces Impeding Our Evolution 11
- World Leaders and the Deep State 12
- Manipulation through Humantarian Ideals 13
- Feeling Helpless against the Powers-That-Be 14
- Even Darker Realities 14
- Hostile Off-World Beings 15
- Implants 16
- Infiltration of Religious and Spiritual Teachings 18
- Controlled Reincarnation System 19
- Blaming Humanity 20
- Trust Your Own Inner Guidance 21
- The Good News: They Can't Go with Us 21
- The Earth Alliance 22
- Staying Positive 24
- End Notes 25

Chapter 3: Birth of a New Identity 29
- Death of Your 3D Self 30
- Descension is Also Occurring 30
- Puzzling Periods of Peace amidst the Chaos 31
- Deeper Inquiry into Who you Are 32
- Discovering Your 5D Self 33

Understanding the Shift from 3D to 5D Consciousness

Chapter 4: Understanding the 3D Self 37
- What Exactly is the 3D Self? 37
- Letting Go of Your Identification with Your 3D Self 38
- 3D Emotions and Beliefs 39
- Feeling Disconnected from Source 40
- 3D Relationships 40
- Believing You are What you Do 41

    3D Belief about Happiness 41
    The Cause of Suffering 43
    3D Self-Help Practices 44

Chapter 5: Understanding the 5D Self 45
    What is the 5D Self? 45
    Full Embodiment of 5D Consciousness.. 47
    5D Mood and Emotions 48
    Your Expanded and Open Heart... 48
    5D Relationships... 49
    Openness to the "Impossible" Happening 49
    5D Focus... 49

Chapter 6: Experiencing your 5D Self 51
    Glimpses You Can Miss... 52
    Prolonging the Glimpse 54
    Once the Glimpse has Passed 55
    Attracting 5D Glimpses into your Life 57
    Who Am I? 58
    Centering Your Awareness in your Pineal Gland 58
    Meditation... 59
    Shifting your Identity from your 3D Self 60
    Detachment... 61
    Spiritual Polarization... 61
    The Next Step 62

Letting Go of 3D Identification

Chapter 7: Shifting Your Identification from the Roles You Play 65
    Rules and Expectations in Roles 65
    Remembering that Roles Aren't Who You Are 67
    Detaching from your Roles.. 67
    Needing to be a "Good" Person... 69
    Going the Step Beyond 70
    Becoming the Observer 70

Chapter 8: Shifting Your Identification from Your Body 75
    The Body Elemental 75
    You are Not Your Body 76
    Ways in Which We Suffer Due to Body Identification.......................... 77
    Altering the Body Itself... 78
    Changing your Beliefs about your Body 79
    Accepting your Body as it Is.. 80

Chapter 9: Living Free with Health Issues **83**
    Freeing Yourself from Identification with your Body 85
    Surrendering to the Pain 86
    Having Compassion for Your Body 87
    Dealing with Severe or Chronic Illness and Pain 88

Chapter 10: When You don't Like your Body Image **91**
    Releasing Judgments about Your Body Image 92
    Exercise: Releasing Negative Judgments about Your Body 92
    Detaching from Identifying with your Body 94
    Exercise: Observing Your Body 94
    Exercise: All Bodies are an Expression of the One Self 95

Chapter 11: Facing the Fear of Death **99**
    Dealing with Death through Denial 99
    Turning to Religion 100
    New Age Teachings about Death 100
    Reincarnation 101
    Resolving the Fear 102
    Exercise: Plunging into the Fear 102
    Exercise: Body Expansion 106
    A Complex Task 108

Chapter 12: Shifting Your Identification from Your Emotions **111**
    The Worship of Emotions 112
    Focusing on Negative Emotions 113
    Focusing on Positive Emotions 115
    Remembering about the Inner-Critic Implant 116

Chapter 13: Experiencing Emotional Freedom **119**
    Freeing Yourself from Emotional Attachment 119

Chapter 14: When Emotions Overwhelm You **135**
    Embracing the Pain 136
    Surrendering to the Emotion 139
    An Experience with the Surrendering to the Emotion Exercise 140
    Emotions as Gateways into your 5D Self 144

Chapter 15: Letting Go of Your 3D Story of Suffering **147**
    Motivations for Keeping the Story Going 148
    Trying to Fix the Story 149
    Do You Really Want to Let it Go? 150
    Exercise: Letting Go of the Story 150
    Starving Your 3D Story 152
    Ashley's Story 153

Observing a Story of Suffering 156
Developing Boredom with your Story 157

Chapter 16: Surviving Relationship Challenges in the 4th Dimension .. 159
Change Must Occur 160
Positive Aspects of the 5D Frequencies on Relationships 160
Ending of Karmic Contracts 161
Different Paths of Ascension 162
Finding New Relationships 163
New Phase of Ascension 163

Chapter 17: Experiencing Freedom in Intimate Relationships 165
"Good" and "Healthy" Relationships 165
One Catch that Cannot be Avoided in Relationships 166
Addressing the Real Issue 167
An Attempt to Improve a Relationship 168
Your 3D Self Cannot Give You the Fulfillment You Seek 169
Commitment Agreements 171
Moving into a 5D Relationship 172
The True Value of Relationships 180

Chapter 18: Shifting your Identity from your Mind 181
Confusing the Mind with 5D Consciousness 182
The Mind Creates the Illusion of Duality 184
The Mind Gets Caught in Time 185
Exercise: Accessing Timelessness 186
The Mind Claims Spiritual Experiences as Its Own 187
Thinking with your Heart 188

Chapter 19: Stilling the Chattering Monkey 191
Learning to Quiet the Mind 192
Redirecting the Mind 194
Experiencing the Silence Within 196

Chapter 20: Rejecting the 3D Self's Game Plan for Happiness 199
Understanding the Nature of Desire 200
Finding Freedom from Desire 201
Exercise: Experiencing the Feeling of Desire 201
Becoming Fully Aware of Your Desires 202
Exercise: *If Only* 202
Exercise: What Do You Really Want? 203
Are you Effectively Pursuing What you Really Long for? 204
Exercise: Looking for the Block 205
Exercise: Observing Your Desires 208

Redirecting Energy From Desires 208
It Takes Some Time 210

Chapter 21: Releasing Your Identity from your "Spiritual Self" 213
The Trap of Spiritual Identification 213
An Even More Subtle Trap 214
Differences between 4D and 5D Identification 215

Surrendering to 5D

Chapter 22: Learning to Completely Trust Source to Guide You 219
Accepting Yourself Just as You Are 220
Exercise: Practicing Acceptance of Yourself 220
Accepting your Life as it is – Just for Now 222
Letting Go of Trying to Control Your Life 222
Learning to Trust your 5D Self 224
Feeling for the Flow 224
Exercise: Finding the Flow 225
Bypassing the Traps of the Mind 226
Taking "Baby Steps" 228
Floating Down the River 229
Surrender Doesn't Mean Doing Nothing 230
Staying in the Now 231
The Process of Surrender is On-Going 232

Chapter 23: Embodying 5D 233
Paradoxical Experiences 234
Experiencing Bliss 234
Riding the Waves of 3D Dissolution 235
The World is Still in 3D 237

Chapter 24: Keeping Focused on 5D Consciousness 239
Staying Vigilant 239
Focusing on Being 240
Seeing Everything as Yourself 240
Who is Experiencing This? 241
Listening to the Silence 241
Staying Connected to the Earth 241
Living Fully in 5D – Free 241

Introduction

Chapter 1

Humanity's Ascension into the Fifth Dimension

A new reality on Earth is dawning. Due to high-frequency waves of light now streaming onto the planet, humanity is poised to make a monumental evolutionary leap in consciousness. And because of this, a whole new world is coming into being, one filled with love, harmony, joy, peace and unity. Some have called this glorious new world the *Fifth Dimension.*

Of course, this new world is not yet very apparent. Although there are already some signs of its emergence, most people are not aware of them. There is obviously still a great deal of chaos, fear and division occurring, more than anyone of us has ever known before.

In fact, humanity is generally anxious, confused, angry and depressed. Old familiar institutions are collapsing around us. There are threats of nuclear war and an escalation of conflict between a number of countries. Unprecedented numbers of people are sick and dying. And governments around the world are continuing to tighten their control over populations through fear and manipulation.

And yet, as horrific as all this is, it is actually to be expected. What is occurring is a death of an old world, an old reality that has been playing out on planet Earth for many thousands of years. According to the teachings of the spiritual paradigm known as *Ascension*, we are simply in the midst of navigating our way through what has been called the "Transitional Times" – a period of time in which humanity is being compelled to make an enormous shift into a much higher consciousness.

Because this leap is so immense and is happening at such a rapid rate, our experience of this transitional period has become a very dark and rocky one. It's easy to get caught in fear with all that is occurring. But in understanding the full picture of what's going on through this lens of Ascension, it's easier to keep focused on where we are headed – and to understand that we are now securely on a positive timeline toward the Fifth

Dimension reality. Even in our lifetimes, we will be witnessing and contributing to a magnificent new world that is now already emerging.

The Dimensional Shift

Prophesies about these times have existed for thousands of years in a wide variety of cultures and spiritual traditions throughout the world. All have made reference to this evolutionary shift, indicating that humanity has been living for millennia in a reality that Ascension teachings have called the *Third Dimension*, one that has been filled with fear, separation, war, hatred, suffering and poverty.

They have further predicted that a shift would be occurring during these current times we are in now in which humanity would be evolving very rapidly into a much higher consciousness, thus creating a reality sometimes known as the *Sat Yuga* or the *Aquarian Age* – or, within the Ascension paradigm, as the *Fifth Dimension*. The tumultuous transitional period – where we've now been since December of 2012 – has been called the *Fourth Dimension*.

The Fifth Dimension

But what exactly is the Fifth Dimension? First of all, it's important to understand that it's not a place; we're not going anywhere. We will still be on Earth – but our experience of it and of ourselves will be very different. Like all dimensions, the Fifth Dimension is a structure of reality that is created by the consciousness we are holding.

Specifically, according to Ascension teachings, the Fifth Dimension is a reality in which we will finally awaken into full consciousness of who we are as truly powerful Beings, aware on multiple dimensions of reality. We will be blessed with a true knowing of the oneness of all that exists, and we will live in a consciousness of unconditional love, inner peace, joy, harmony, kindness and reverence.

In essence, we will enjoy an on-going freedom from fear, shame, judgment and separation. Cooperation, co-creation, and collaboration will come naturally to us as we work, play and create together. Hunger, poverty and crime will all be obsolete, and there will be equality, justice, respect and abundance for all.

The Fifth Dimension is described as a reality without limitations; all positive possibilities are available. As we progress through the levels of this dimension, our full DNA will gradually be activated, and the 90% of our brain that's been dormant for thousands of years will be turned on again. Physical density as we know it now will be very different. Form will be dynamic and physical bodies will have morphed into more of a crystalline structure.

For many of us, the Fifth Dimension is a state of being that will feel like "Home". It is a reality we once existed in many thousands of years ago, before the advent of what's known as the "Fall of Consciousness", a time when we began descending into the lower vibrational field of the Third Dimension. When we finally make the shift into the higher reality of 5D again, it will feel as if we are returning Home after eons of existing elsewhere, with only a sense of longing and dreams of this Home sustaining us.

Many of the Ascension teachings and the age-old prophesies indicate that this dimensional shift has happened a number of times before in the past, about every 26,000 years, while the Earth has traveled through a very powerful section in the galaxy in which high-frequency waves of light exist. It is said that each time the Earth has passed through this section of the galaxy and has been immersed in these waves of light, there has existed an opportunity for all life on the planet to make a huge leap in evolution. And that is what humanity is currently experiencing – and will continue to experience until the Earth eventually, once again, passes out of the section of the galaxy where these high frequencies exist.

However, again, because the shift is so immense and rapid, there is naturally a great deal of chaos and disruption, as well as a collapsing of all systems and structures in the world that do not resonate with the higher-frequency energies now streaming onto the Earth. Much of what now exists in the world must be swept away.

Even though it may look as if injustice, greed, war, manipulation and control are prevalent and becoming stronger in the world today, in actuality, it has all been here for many millennia. It is simply being revealed much more clearly at this point. And, very importantly, these forces will eventually not survive in the world into which we are heading. When the Earth has finally shifted into the Fifth Dimension, only compassion, justice, harmony and unity will eventually survive in the world and our personal affairs.

Of course, this New Earth will take some time to fully manifest; it cannot appear overnight. But we can focus on those things that are already now beginning to manifest and help to energetically bring them into form.

Two Pathways

As may be clear, not everyone currently on the planet will be surviving this immense shift of consciousness. A great many people alive today will not be able to make the journey into the Fifth Dimension reality; as Souls, they are not yet ready to do so. At some point, before the planet makes its final shift, they will be leaving to be incarnated in another solar system, one that still offers experiences for their further evolution in the Third and Fourth Dimensions.

Indeed, as time goes on, it is already possible to see this bifurcation occurring within humanity. The two pathways are quite plain: very simply, one is focused on love, the other on fear. Some people – those headed for the Fifth Dimension – are busy consciously raising their frequencies and focusing on creating a new Earth they'd like to live in. As a reader of this book, you are likely part of this group. Others seem fast asleep, still enmeshed in the vibrations of separation, fear, hatred and desperation, and continuing on blindly in their ever-more-restricted lives.

A third group is somewhere in between: they are not yet quite awake to what is occurring, but neither are they caught up in the rampant negativity that exists among other people. They will follow the first group into the Fifth Dimension – just somewhat later.

Negotiating the Ascension Path

And yet, even for those who are destined to make the shift into 5D, it won't necessarily be a fast or easy journey. It will take some time – perhaps a few more years for most – before fully entering the Fifth Dimension reality is possible. Shifting into 5D consciousness is the doorway into the new 5D reality; it is what creates it.

If you have been aware of Ascension for a while, you have probably noticed that, until early 2020, the path forward was already becoming somewhat difficult for you. Both psychological and physical Ascension symptoms were showing up, as the 5D frequencies coming onto the planet became more intense. Perhaps, among other things, old, unresolved traumas were surfacing, along with challenges in relationships, a sense of disorientation, and confusing physical symptoms.

Loss may have also been a theme for a while in your life. Maybe you'd lost your career and/or your means of livelihood. You might have had to move from a home you'd lived in for years. Perhaps new health issues had arisen, preventing you from being able to do things you once had, or old ones had been exacerbated. Perhaps you'd even lost loved ones to death – or were torn apart from them over political or other issues.

Nonetheless, if you were conscientious in wishing to ascend as quickly and effectively as possible, you knew you could still do your inner work and spiritual practices and feel you were being successful in raising your frequency. You could feel you were shedding old, low-vibrational patterns, and you could experience a greater sense of light within your being.

In addition, you likely began discovering delightful p
pening in your life, as well. Despite the new challenges y
encing, perhaps synchronicities and what felt like magic se
up out of nowhere. Experiences of profound joy might sud
you, or your heart would fill with a profound love you'd never before experienced. Or perhaps deep peace might overcome you at the most improbable times.

All of these kinds of experiences had probably been increasing for some time, ever since the high-frequency waves of light began to fully stream onto the Earth, beginning in 2012, as the 5D bandwidth they were creating was becoming more and more available for you to tune into.

An Unexpected Monkey Wrench in the Ascension Process

But then Covid-19 and all the mandate craziness showed up, perhaps creating fear, anger, anxiety and confusion in you, as all life as you knew it began to collapse. This understandably might have thrown a monkey-wrench into the whole process of your Ascension healing work, upping the ante and requiring a huge amount of increased awareness of what was going on both in the outer world and in your inner world. Greater focus was now required on external circumstances. You had to be careful how you maneuvered your way out in public, how you related to family and friends, and what you could physically do or not do.

You may have discovered that the covid mandates also surprisingly created some unexpected gifts for you, such as the ability to spend more time with family and friends, more clarity on what's really important in your life, more inner strength to really say and do what is right for you, and maybe even more money from the state. These were important benefits that few people anticipated. And yet, the situation in the world with all the unknowns, still likely made it much more difficult to focus on the positive aspects of Ascension that had been previously happening for you. The world's situation had suddenly become very dark, and, to one degree or another, you were pulled into that darkness.

For that reason, you've probably discovered that the Ascension journey now requires a great deal more effort, courage and trust. And, if you're someone who knows you are here to help create a New Earth, you're understanding that you are serving as a wayshower on this path. And this may bring an even deeper feeling of importance to your own awakening. You are becoming more aware of just how unknown and sometimes frightening this path of Ascension can be.

In particular, you may have discovered that Ascension is now a two-pronged path. First it is necessary to wake up to the truth of humanity's ndition, and to understand how the current heart-wrenching state of affairs on the planet has come about. Going through this particular aspect of the awakening process often demands a lot of courage and a great deal of self-nurturing. But without this understanding of humanity's evolutionary condition, it is next to impossible to fully step into the vast spaciousness and power of fifth-dimensional consciousness.

The second aspect of the Ascension path involves releasing your sense of identity that has been based in third-dimensional misconceptions, misidentifications, and lies you've been told throughout your life, and discovering who you truly are as a multidimensional Being of Light. After lifetimes of living in 3D on this planet, there is a lot of "deprogramming" that needs to occur in order to shift your habitual identity from your 3D self to your 5D Self.

This Book

In the next chapter, we will briefly explore the first aspect of Ascension awakening: humanity's evolutionary trajectory at this point. This will provide an understanding of the bigger picture within which your personal Ascension is occurring.

Following that, the main focus in this book will be on the second aspect: discovering who you essentially are as an eternal, powerful multidimensional Being of Light, one who has until now mistakenly identified yourself to be an inherently imperfect and limited third-dimensional form of body and consciousness.

In the final chapters, the focus will turn to learning how to shed this mistaken 3D identity and fully embody the true essential YOU in order to begin living fully in fifth-dimensional consciousness.

In my previous books on Ascension and the Fifth Dimension, I have discussed the many ways in which you can shift lower-dimensional reactions in life to conscious, positive responses, in order to raise your vibration. I have given information, exercises and examples of how to respond to the huge variety of programmed patterns you have likely developed while living in the limited and controlled 3D world. Focusing on these responses is very important when doing initial inner work on the Ascension path, as it can strengthen your connection to your higher consciousness.

However, although this kind of work can assist you in becoming aware of your third-dimensional tendencies in order to change them to a higher frequency, eventually, there is still a final step in making the transition into 5D consciousness. And that is to experience a shift of your entire sense of identity into 5D – a complete, embodied knowing of who you are, beyond your personal self and the story of your life. It involves a shift from believing you are your body, your emotions and your mind – and even what you've come to believe is your "spiritual self", no matter how enlightened this self may seem to you. It is, in the end, a radical transformation of your whole experience of yourself.

The path of shifting your identity from 3D to 5D can be difficult and confusing, especially during these times of turmoil and disruption in the world. There is hard work involved. But it need not be painful or overwhelming. I have therefore attempted in this book to also emphasize the joy, the excitement, and the peace that is inherent in this journey into the glorious freedom that exists when living within fifth-dimensional consciousness.

I wish to also emphasize the importance of your presence on the planet during these times. As a rapidly-awakening Soul now alive in 3D form, you are contributing your light and awareness to the collective consciousness of humanity. Indeed, you are very much needed for the Ascension process of all humans who are destined to ascend into the Fifth Dimension.

Never under-estimate yourself or the impact you are having on the planet's awakening. Even if you can't outwardly see what you are contributing at this point, know that energetically, simply because you are alive now, you are having an important impact on the collective human consciousness. You are anchoring these new high frequencies, making it possible for others to awaken more easily. And, probably, in the not-so-distant future, you will be seeing much more that you will be able to do.

So, let us explore all the different ways in which you can become more aware of this sacred mission you've come to fulfill – and how you can continue to awaken to who you really are as a powerful multidimensional Being. We will initially look briefly at the first element of awakening that is necessary for Ascension: the discovery of the reasons as to why the process of spiritual awakening is so fraught with pain and confusion. We will explore how humanity has been trapped in the illusions of the Third Dimension by hidden forces on this planet that have essentially held back humanity's spiritual evolution for thousands of years.

Once this is understood, you will see how it serves as a backdrop for the personal issues you've been struggling with, perhaps for many, many decades, as you've attempted to spiritually awaken to the true Essence of who you are.

Chapter 2

Negative Forces Impeding Our Evolution

You may be familiar with the information this chapter spells out; if so, see it as a review. But if this information is new to you, it's understandable if it reads like conspiracy theory; it can certainly initially sound that way.

Yet I encourage you to continue reading. It may help you to understand the deeper reasons for the events that are now occurring across the planet – and also why you have had to work so hard to fully awaken to who you are as a multidimensional Being of Light. It may at times even help to simply keep you sane. Indeed, it explains why all humans have suffered so greatly during *all* the millennia they have been living in the Third Dimension.

What you will discover in the information presented here is that there *has* in fact been a global conspiracy that dates far back in history created by a small elite group of people on the planet. The power of these people is currently greatly diminishing, now that the frequency of the Earth and humanity is rapidly rising. But it's important to understand that these people have committed monumental crimes against humanity throughout history in order to consistently stay in power and hoard the wealth on the planet. And that, behind them, giving them their power, are hostile non-human sources hidden in the lower Fourth Dimension.

What I present is but a brief overview of the information as it pertains to the general purpose of this book. But if you wish to research the subject yourself, you can find there are numerous and varied sources both in books and on the internet that further explain and document the information. In the End Notes at the conclusion of this chapter, you will find a great many sources to get you started. My book, *Triumph of the Light*, is also an in-depth exploration of the whole subject.

However far you go in your own research, hopefully you will achieve a deeper understanding of what has occurred on this planet for thousands of years. At that point, you will be able to decide for yourself what makes sense and feels accurate to you.

World Leaders and the Deep State

Let's start by looking at the world leaders and those people in power behind the scenes on the planet today. As you are probably aware, most politicians do not seem to have humanity's best interests in mind. They have taken information – and often "their marching orders" – from corrupt heads of Big Pharma, Big Tech, Big Finance, and certain aspects of the military and three-letter agencies – groups of people often referred to as the *Cabal* or the *Deep State*. A number of these powerful people making decisions that affect the world are unelected and hold no accountability for what they do. And yet, those elected in our governmental bodies have created mandates based on intentionally false information given to them from these nefarious sources.

Even more chilling is the fact that these political leaders and members of the Cabal are, in turn, controlled by even more powerful people behind the scenes. Called the *Illuminati* or the *Shadow Controllers*, these people are part of the super-wealthy elitist families on the planet, including those who are members of the royal bloodline families, those pulling the strings from within the global financial structures, and those who rule from deep within the Vatican.

These people not only control the wealth on the planet but have also infiltrated all of our social institutions and religions, the mainstream media, social media platforms, the entertainment industry, health institutions, global politics, the militaries of the world, and most all educational systems. They are the ones who have throughout history created wars, and then financed both sides. For many years, they have poisoned our air, food, water and soil and controlled our weather, creating droughts, floods and hurricanes. They have started huge, devastating fires. They have exercised mind control on various parts of the population, arranged numerous assassinations, and committed egregious crimes, especially in regard to children. They were responsible for causing 9/11 and Fukushima.

In addition, they conduct thriving businesses in human and drug trafficking. They have held back advanced healing technologies from the public for many decades, including what have been called "medbeds" which could give incredible healing to alleviate all diseases humanity suffers from. They have used advanced AI technology to negatively impact and control people's minds. Over and over again, they have been responsible for creating the huge crises that occur in the world – and then offering the solutions to them which have served to greatly increase their profits and further tighten their control over humanity.

This has never been so obvious as it is now. If you have really gone down the proverbial rabbit hole about the covid pandemic, you have likely learned from numerous renowned scientists and doctors not only about the lab origin of the virus, but also about how lethal the vaccines have been to many thousands of people. You don't have to dig far to discover the huge numbers of deaths the vaccines have caused, as well as the monumental numbers of serious injuries and illnesses they have caused across the planet. Nor does it take much digging to learn of the massive profits the manufacturers of the vaccines have made over the past couple of years.

In addition, you may have read or heard about the plans certain world leaders who are part of the World Economic Forum have for depopulating the world. There are speeches you can hear online in which they are very open about this and how their plans have been working, most lately through the vaccines. It can be terrifying to hear these speeches, so blatant in what they reveal, and how smug the people giving them are in pulling off what they have.

Manipulation through Humantarian Ideals

Perhaps you also understand that the agenda of these people has created suffering in multiple other ways, as well, such as through turning certain groups of people against other groups in order to weaken them both. You may realize that they've managed to create scenarios in which certain groups would be ostracized and ridiculed – all in the name of encouraging us to do the "right" thing for society, the "good" thing for our fellow humans. They are expert in knowing how to manipulate and program us to not only turn against each other, but to also create guilt in us for being "selfish".

They are especially masterful in encouraging us to follow humanitarian ideals we can't help but want to uphold, such as doing things that are "good for the environment", "good for racial justice", "good for helping to alleviate suffering of our fellow humans", or actions that will "help feed more people". We're also encouraged to do things to "bring democratic ideals" to other populations in the world.

How can we argue against anything that sounds so good and right? Little do most people realize that these kinds of clever and manipulative campaigns only serve to tighten the Cabal's control over us.

In their insidiously effective way, through these campaigns, they somehow sell us on war in the name of creating peace. They justify the loss of humanitarian rights, freedom and truth in the name of safety and duty.

And they manage to convince us that hatred, division, political correctness and judgment will bring about equality and inclusion.

Feeling Helpless against the Powers-That-Be

And yet, even in realizing this, perhaps like most people, you feel rather helpless. You have simply accepted that these corrupt leaders and controllers behind the scenes are just part of this world. We are essentially powerless to do anything about them. They've always been here, they always will be. And maybe you don't stop to realize that, after so many centuries, humanity has simply become accustomed to living in an oppressive society in which abuse is inbuilt – that we are, in effect, long-term survivors of trauma and injustice, having endured a heightened level of suffering, poverty and control for as long as anyone can remember.

And yet, even if you have realized all this, maybe you've still reasoned that all that most of us can do, really, is accept this reality as it is. Significant changes never truly happen, no matter who is elected or placed into power and no matter how many protests may occur. Corruption, abuse, control and manipulation by the powerful and wealthy elite will just always continue on – along with the wars, financial collapses and pandemics they create.

What you've maybe never really considered is just how small and ineffective you and most of humanity have been rendered by living in this world. You may have times of rage or depression when certain things occur – especially in current times, when the control of humanity has become so apparent. Perhaps you've joined protests and maybe even brought about certain small victories. But, in the end, because you have felt powerless to change anything of real significance, you've probably just gone back to trying to live your own life as well as you can.

This has been the fate of humanity for many thousands of years while living in the Third Dimension – and you have likely lived numerous lifetimes on Earth under these conditions – so, it is no wonder if they feel normal and inevitable and simply need to be lived with.

Even Darker Realities

But have you ever wondered how this relatively tiny group of humans (the proverbial "one percent") has managed to keep such a powerful hold on all the rest of humanity for so long? Why haven't more people awakened enough to see the reality of what's been going on and wrested control from such a small group of individuals?

It's important for your Ascension process to understand the answer to these questions. The answer is that there is something that is even darker and more powerful than these controlling human groups on this planet. There is a malevolent force that has existed invisibly in the lower Fourth Dimension for thousands of years, and that force has been controlling the Illuminati, the Deep State players and most of the world leaders throughout time to achieve their own negative agenda with the human race.

Again, if this information is new to you, it may understandably sound like crazy conspiracy theory – something dredged up by people who have watched too much science fiction. But, if you research the subject, you will discover that the ideas in most of these types of dark science fiction movies have been given to Hollywood writers and directors by CIA agents in secret space programs who have been behind the scenes for a number of decades. In these sci-fi movies, there is a great deal of disclosure of what is actually going on in the world that most people just dismiss, believing it to be fantasy or science fiction.

Yet that is the purpose behind these movies: to keep the information that gets leaked out by whistleblowers from within the secret space programs and three-letter agencies from being accepted by the public as real. Because these movies are described as "science fiction", people are led to believe the existence of dark extraterrestrial forces is just fantasy.

But, in reality, there *are* powerful extraterrestrial beings living on and even within the planet, many of them hostile to humanity – and they have been here for eons of time. There are now multiple whistleblowers from within these secret space programs who have described this phenomenon at length. Even NASA has recently disclosed some of this information on its website. There are also a number of highly-credible people who describe physical contact they have had over the years with malevolent extraterrestrial beings.

Hostile Off-World Beings

At any rate, one piece of information a number of insider reports give is that it is known that many thousands of years ago, there were actually a great number of off-world beings who frequently visited Earth to do experiments with what they found here. And part of what they found was a developing race of human beings. Many of these visitors were highly-evolved Beings who wished to assist humanity to evolve more quickly. Others were not especially benevolent, simply curious.

And then there were those who were actually not interested in assisting humanity at all. They only wanted to do experiments that would benefit their own race and agendas. There was one extremely powerful group, in particular – sometimes referred to as the *Archons* – that eventually took control of the main experiments being done on the human race.

Unfortunately, although they were very highly-evolved technologically – and with AI, in particular, especially in working with DNA – they were not at all evolved spiritually. They gathered to them a number of other off-planet races here who were also hostile to humanity to assist them in their endeavors to control this human race they'd found on Earth. Some of these races have been called the *Dracos*, the *Reptiles*, the *Greys*, the *Annunaki* and the *Chimera*.

All of these hostile races have had one main thing in common: they've wanted the DNA they found in human beings for their own use. We humans are evidently seen by other galactic races as "royalty" within the universe, due to the fact that we have DNA given to us by 22 different races who tinkered with our DNA over the initial millennia of humanity's existence.

However, the Archons were not only not interested in helping to develop humanity's DNA to upgrade it for humanity's evolution. They also took measures to essentially deactivate 90% of humanity's DNA, in order to weaken humanity's spiritual abilities and powers. Not understanding this, scientists today have labeled this DNA "junk DNA".

In addition, the Archons also discovered they needed to produce food for themselves while on this foreign planet. And what they found was that they thrived most on the energy produced by humanity's suffering – fear, anger, anxiety, depression. They realized they needed this energy, something that has been called "loosh", in order to ensure their own survival here. Therefore, they needed to create weakness and suffering in humanity, in order to produce the food they themselves needed.

All this is especially important information if you wish to understand why humanity has suffered so dreadfully all through the millennia of existing in the Third Dimension. It explains why there seems to be no end to wars, pandemics, famines and poverty, and why we human beings have had such difficulty in knowing who we inherently are as powerful multidimensional Beings. It makes it clear why there are humans who have been seduced, bribed and blackmailed into taking advantage of humanity from positions of power in the world: There exists this even darker hidden force that has been controlling humanity *through* these people, our so-called "leaders" and "politicians".

Implants

One of the critical achievements these darks beings pulled off to ensure their necessary "loosh" was their creation of a variety of AI implants that they spliced into humanity's DNA. These implants were designed to not only create suffering and weakness in people, but to also impair their connection to Source. The most powerful of these was an implant they attached to the frontal lobes of the human brain on the etheric level. It is programmed to create fear, shame, guilt, self-judgment and self-doubt within a person.

Every human being since then has this implant in their brain. It has mistakenly been considered a natural part of the human blueprint and has been called the *inner critic* or the *superego*. But it is not natural to the human race. And, unfortunately, it has greatly hindered humanity's spiritual evolution throughout time. In causing inordinate pain and suffering, this implant has exacerbated the third-dimensional experience, turning it from a somewhat limited but interesting existence into something of terrible confusion and pain. If left free, humanity could have evolved out of the third-dimensional experience a long time ago.

Another mind-boggling aspect of this implant is that it has created a programmed reality for us to live in that is actually a very subtle AI simulation. Remember *The Matrix*? Although many of the details involved in that film are apparently not accurate, there is a great deal of truth in it that was disclosed: the reality we've been living in is indeed a simulation that has created an experience of life that has felt real, but is actually an AI program that serves to keep us trapped in a false and unempowered sense of existence.

Think about all this. Contemplate all the long years and difficult work you've had to do in trying to heal yourself and awaken to who you really are as a spiritual Being, and how you have so often been hindered and blocked. The shame and guilt, the self-doubt and dysfunction you've experienced and attempted to heal have been caused by something that is not even a part of who you naturally are. And, importantly, neither has any sense of separation from Source you've felt been natural to you – it has all been an artificial condition imposed on you.

As if this weren't enough to deal with, there is a second powerful implant that all of humanity has also carried around in the pelvic region, thanks to the Archons: one designed to weaken intimate relationships through creating sexual and emotional conflict between men and women. The implant in women causes them, to one degree or another, to automatically bond emotionally with men they are engaging in sex with. Whereas the implant in men does not have this same effect; they are generally able to have sex with multiple women and not feel an emotional attachment. Their heart and sexual organs are not connected in the same way women's are.

Fortunately, the effect of both these implants is beginning to fade, as the power of the Archons continues to diminish during these times of transition. At some point, both implants will eventually be totally deactivated. But until then, it is important to keep these implants and their effects in mind, so you don't overly stress about what you think you need to "fix" in yourself or in a sexual relationship you may have. Remember that there are impediments causing misunderstanding and conflict that have nothing to do with who you are.

Infiltration of Religious and Spiritual Teachings

In addition, the Archons did not stop with implants. Throughout the centuries, all religions that have sprung up within humanity have been infiltrated, as well, by the technology of these off-world beings. They have even *created* religions for certain vulnerable groups, distorting all ideas about who or what God is. They created the idea of original sin and hell and invented teachings that create pain, guilt, and shame, as well as division among peoples. We're all aware of the religions that teach that God will punish you if you're bad, immoral, or not suffering enough for your own imperfections. Then, when you think about all the religious wars that have occurred throughout history – and, to some extent, continue on today – it all begins to make sense.

But what may especially dismay you is learning that even many of the new age spirituality teachings have been based on distorted and incorrect information about reality, as they too have been infiltrated by the insidious interference of these beings who have attempted to suppress humanity's spiritual awakening.

This news can be very disheartening. Those of us who have been exposed to new age teachings have been fortunate, in that many of these teachings at least tend to be much more supportive and embracing of our true spiritual nature than many traditional religions on the planet. However, although we may generally learn from spiritual teachings that we are inherently divine beings, free of "original sin", there is still usually a subscript that there is something wrong with us. So often, teachings imply that, in order to evolve and become enlightened, we need to work very, very hard, probably for many lifetimes, in order to be free.

Further, there is the perfidious implication that we are somehow to blame if we suffer, because we are "creating our own reality". It becomes our fault if we don't have positive thoughts and emotions, if we can't form nurturing relationships, or if we can't find our way out of poverty. In general, there's the insinuation that we have to sacrifice and suffer, if we are to purify ourselves. There are even teachings that tell us we have to become vegetarians or vegans, or that we must be celebate or give up our wealth and basic comforts in order to become "pure".

In addition, have you ever wondered why, if you are an extension of Source, a spark of its very Essence, as most new age teachings claim, you have to constantly remind yourself of this when you're feeling depressed or afraid? Why you have to meditate and pray over and over again to get back in touch with it? These teachings generally tell us we need to do these things in order to connect with Source; somehow, because we're naturally flawed, most of us can't seem to keep ourselves fully connected to Source all the time. Again, we are to be blamed.

Then, to top it all off, you will also often find in many new age teachings the encouragement that you should only ever focus on love and light – or that "evil" doesn't actually exist. There is the assurance that, if you simply focus on only positive emotions in yourself, you will finally become enlightened or evolve into 5D reality.

This can perhaps sound and even feel good at first. But if you're like most people and you're honest, you have probably discovered that all you manage to do in trying to follow this philosophy is to stuff all negative emotions and thoughts that occur within you down into your subconscious. And then you discover, much to your chagrin and shame, that they eventually rise the surface again, often at inappropriate times. You may at that point find yourself asking the age-old question, "What's wrong with me?" It's important to realize there's nothing wrong with you when you feel disconnected from Source; your natural connection has simply been tampered with.

Controlled Reincarnation System

Perhaps you feel that because certain new age teachings have explained about reincarnation and the karmic wheel, they have helped you to at least better understand the broader view of humanity's suffering. And, indeed, these are ideas new age teachings describe quite well; they make sense of many mysteries in our lives.

However, what is generally not understood is that the Wheel of Karma is something the Archons created so that human Souls would continue on, over and over again, providing them with the "loosh" they thrive on – the energy of suffering. The reincarnation system has never been "fair" or truly helpful to humanity. It has essentially been a system that has kept human Souls recycling over and over again in ignorance, for the benefit of these beings living in the lower Fourth Dimension.

And because of this controlled reincarnation system, humans have only been able to evolve and awaken very, very slowly. It's been especially difficult, since most people have no recollection of their past lives and what they experienced or learned in them, and they've therefore tended to make the same mistakes, life after life. If reincarnation were a benevolent process, wouldn't it make sense that we would remember our past lives so we could learn what we needed to learn and get off the Wheel as quickly as possible?

In addition, what is generally not understood is that many evolved Souls have not only brought forward their own personal karma to solve in each lifetime – they have also been saddled with the unresolved karma of their ancestors. It's just part of how the system has been set up.

Blaming Humanity

What can be especially perplexing in most new age teachings is that they essentially tell us that God is all-loving and benevolent. And yet, it is never truly explained why God would then allow such traumatic suffering in people's lives to occur, or why such insidious events like the Holocaust could happen. It's never really explained why innocent people are killed in war or why suffering seems so necessary and pervasive.

Instead, these things are generally all blamed on humanity's imperfections. All we're told is there is something inherently wrong and imperfect about us as human beings. Again, we somehow have to work hard on ourselves in order to wake up, heal ourselves and overcome all our imperfections.

Of course, this doesn't mean that we are not here to evolve and continue awakening to who we are. Of course, we are here to do this – and sometimes, this entails a lot of work. This is our agreement as Souls on a path of evolution in this Universe. And, it doesn't mean that we shouldn't strive to create positive thoughts or work on our relationships or learn to create abundance in our life. Focusing on these things will definitely assist us in waking up to who we truly are and eventually help lift our frequency into fifth-dimensional consciousness.

But the point to understand is that we have generally been led to believe that our imperfections are inherently our fault, that they are part of who we *are,* rather than energies and patterns we have picked up while living many lifetimes in a controlled third-dimensional reality. It's to realize why it is often so hard to wake up spiritually – and how we need to have a tremendous amount of compassion and appreciation for ourselves. This controlled reality has made our evolution extremely difficult; it is not the environment that was initially designed for humanity.

So, if you are weary from trying to heal one negative pattern after another within yourself, perhaps the reason is now more clear. You have been hindered, held back, and slammed by many hidden forces throughout your sojourn on planet Earth in the Third Dimension. In essence, you have been prevented from knowing that you are *already* Love, you are *already* Light – that you don't need to change yourself in order to hold more of these qualities. You *already* exist as a powerful multidimensional Being – you don't need to *become* one. What you need to do, as you continue to heal yourself, is shrug off all beliefs you've adopted about yourself as a being who is inherently flawed, along with any guilt or shame you feel about this.

Trust Your Own Inner Guidance

At the same time, this is not to say that all principles and teachings in the new age literature are contaminated or false. Of course, many of them contain much wisdom and beautiful guidance. They can definitely help sustain you through the worst of these transitional times. It's just important to begin truly questioning the beliefs you hold – especially those for which you've never had any personal validation. It's wise to be discerning with all the teachings you've accepted as truth just because someone put them out there as such.

Trust your heart and gut and your own experience. If a teaching doesn't truly resonate with your inner knowing, perhaps question it and put it aside for now. You may eventually go back to it, having had it confirmed somehow through your own experience. But if not, then perhaps it was a teaching that was tainted by other forces not truly interested in your spiritual awakening and freedom.

And, very importantly, keep remembering that you can overcome the dark constraints that have been put on your healing and your spiritual awakening. You can simply do this by recognizing that these constraints have been programmed into you, hindering your natural evolution and causing unnecessary physical and emotional suffering. They aren't natural to you. Realize that your whole sense of identification has been skewed by implants causing you to experience yourself primarily as a simple physical form with a mind and by cutting off your awareness of who you actually are as a magnificent and powerful Being of Light. Knowing this, you have the power to wake up to the reality of who you really are.

The Good News: They Can't Go with Us

And finally, remember: the good news is that the times of bondage are ending. The invisible malevolent forces are increasingly losing their power. The Earth and humanity are currently rising rapidly in frequency, and these hostile beings are feeling greatly threatened. They know they will not be able to continue with us as Ascension continues to occur, because they cannot raise their frequency any higher than the Fourth Dimension. In fact, at this point, many of them are already gone, leaving their Deep State human actors without leadership and without the power they once had.

For this reason, the actions of these Cabal members are now becoming extreme in their last attempts to control and destroy humanity's freedom and to create suffering and death in every way possible. They are desperately pushing back hard at this point, knowing they can't hold on much longer. It may take a while, but the darkness that has reigned on Earth for so long is finally being addressed and countered.

The Earth Alliance

Indeed, you may be aware that there have been whistleblower reports for at least a decade on alternative internet sites about a group of planetary "white hats" called the "Earth Alliance". These are sincere and passionately dedicated people in power positions in the world who have formed an alliance for the purpose of taking the Cabal down. It is reported that those in this Alliance have been focused ever since the early 1960s on gathering intelligence about the Deep State players in order to eventually make mass arrests around the world. There have been photographs online of the prison in Guantanamo Bay ("Gitmo") that show huge additions that have been constructed over the last few years, reportedly in preparation for housing those who will be arrested.

Of course, it is difficult to know how much of this disclosure information is accurate. There is so much misinformation now in all news media – in alternative sources as well as mainstream. The Cabal has very cleverly infiltrated it all. And, there has also been an inordinate amount of censorship of whistleblowers, independent journalists, doctors and scientists that has gone on, both by blocking them online and by condemning them as "conspiracy theorists" – so it can be hard to even know they exist.

Yet many of them have survived on Rumble and Bitchute, and also on other uncensored platforms and sites that use alternate languaging to avoid being blocked. So, with some determination, you can find that there have been many different sources over the years who have given intel on this Alliance and what they are accomplishing. You can't help but conclude that at least some of it must be accurate.

At any rate, there are reports as of this writing in early Fall of 2022 confirming that almost everything is in place for these arrests to finally take place. It has been said that, along with the arrests, there will be

Nuremburg-type trials in different parts of the world of those who have caused for many, many decades the poverty, death, and destruction that humanity and the planet have suffered from.

Some reports tell us that these arrests will all take place during "ten days of darkness", which apparently refers to the shutdown of all internet services across the planet for a time. Also that an emergency broadcast system will be in place to inform people of what is occurring and to tell them not to panic. Many whistleblowers have cautioned people to stock up on 2-3 weeks of food and other essentials to protect them from temporary breakdowns that will likely take place in the systems that deliver these necessities.

It is said that, during the trials, much will eventually be revealed about the deaths that have been caused by the Cabal throughout the years in creating wars, pandemics and false vaccines, droughts, floods, fires and hurricanes, food shortages, and a plethora of other phenomena that have also caused humanity to experience poverty and illness. Many of the most egregious crimes to be revealed will be those that have been done against children.

Apparently, also to be revealed will be their take-over of the vast majority of the major media companies in recent decades to control the news. In addition, 9-11 will be exposed as an inside job; and widespread election fraud that has occurred for many, many decades will also come to light. Misinformation about climate change and chemtrails will further be revealed. In other words, the World Economic Forum's whole plan of major genocide of 90% of the world's population will finally be exposed to the public, and all those involved in this plan will be arrested and tried – and likely put to death.

In addition, reports have come out that, during this period, the entire global financial system, long-controlled by the Cabal, will also be shut down temporarily. During this time, a vastly different system called the Quantum Financial System will be turned on to replace it – a system that ensures the safety and privacy of all funds within it. This switch will be accompanied by huge humanitarian changes that will take place, in which great wealth will be returned to the populations of the world through a plan referred to as GESARA – the Global Economic Security and Reformation Act.

In the US, this act is known as NESARA. It is a document that was signed into law by President Clinton at the end of his term (some say at gunpoint), ordering this act to be implemented in the US on September 11, 2001. We all know what happened instead to stop this.

If all this is new to you, details can be found on the internet and by linking to references offered at the end of this chapter.

The news about events planned for the near future is very exciting to those who have been waiting impatiently many years for these arrests and trials to take place. As can be imagined, huge operations have had to take place to prepare for these arrests, and so it has taken a good deal of time and great effort for all plans to be implemented. In addition, all efforts on the part of the Cabal, such as the attempts to start nuclear wars, the sabotaging of pipelines, the creation of new pandemic scares, and attempts to further take over the financial control they already hold, have created delays and postponements of the Alliance's plans. Some have described what's been going on as an undeclared World War III.

Because of all this, many throughout the years have lost faith that the mass arrests would ever occur. However, according to some recent reports, these arrests may soon finally occur in late 2022 and early 2023. Again, it is difficult to predict, because of all the misinformation that has been fed into both the mainstream and alternative news over the years, but it may actually finally happen. It is said the whole process is "event-driven", so exact timing cannot be predicted. Still, even if things don't move as quickly as any of us might like, we can at least know that valiant efforts are being made in the right direction.

In any case, when the arrests finally do begin happening, it will be wise to be prepared. There will understandably be huge confusion, angst, and rage that will likely occur among those in the world population who have been totally blind to all that has gone on by the Deep State over the years. It will be a huge "red pill" event. Those who have had their eyes open to it all and who have already gone through their own reactions to it will be greatly needed at that time to help calm and educate the traumatized newly-awakened people.

Staying Positive

The really good news, however, will be to realize that, when all the dark forces are finally gone, huge changes will be taking place – even aside from the prosperity and humanitarian projects GESARA and NESARA will bring. There are predictions about a solar flash event that will eventually occur to clear the planet further of negative energy and assist humanity in its ascension.

There will also be the opportunity for people to start building the New Earth through creating new institutions based on love, cooperation, compassion and caring for all of humanity. New highly-advanced healing technology will be available to the public, along with other technology, such as individual units for each household that create free energy. So there is a lot of reason to stay positive and optimistic, even as we experience all the chaos and disruption that will likely continue for a while.

In addition, it's been reported by many that benevolent and highly-evolved Galactic Beings from numerous other civilizations within the universe will begin landing here, inviting humanity to join galactic federations designed to bring greater joy and cooperation among all Beings, everywhere. There are many reports, even now, about these Galactic Beings assisting the Alliance in defeating the dark forces out in space.

It will take a while, of course, for all this to occur. But meanwhile, what you can focus on is how you can help the forces of light that are working to free humanity at this time. If nothing else, you can do your best to not fall into despair. You can be a clear and determined frequency holder of Light and maintain a powerful flame of love in your heart. You can say prayers for the Earth. You can be there for others with compassion and understanding.

All these kinds of energetic actions by individuals are powerful in helping to raise the vibration of humanity and thus determining how quickly this momentous spiritual war on Earth will be over. Keep in mind that the Earth and humanity are securely on a positive timeline now. But you can assist in making the journey as smooth and rapid as possible.

In addition, know that being conscientious in wanting to assist humanity on this momentous journey into 5D reality will assist you in shifting into 5D consciousness yourself more quickly. As you concentrate on your own healing and awakening process, you can also focus on how extremely exciting it is that you are here now during these times when humanity across the planet is in a phase of momentous awakening into freedom. What an amazing time it is to be alive!

End Notes

To help you research more deeply into the information presented in Chapter 2, below are links to websites and videos of intel providers within the alternative news community. You can also find many of their videos on Rumble (https://rumble.com/), and Bitchute (https://ground.news/ interest/ united-states_b67315).

I offer these sources, not because I believe everything they report is absolutely true. It's important to always be alert to the fact that there is probably misinformation and disinformation within all these alternative news sites. Because millions of people now read and listen to these sources, it's common sense to suspect they've all been infiltrated by the Deep State to one degree or another.

However, these links do seem to generally offer information that rings much truer than any of the mainstream sources at this time. And when you read the same kind of information from many, many different sources who approach the news from a variety of angles, using different intel sources, certain things start to make sense and ring true.

Still, it is important to always use your own discretion and intuition to decide what may seem true for you.

Please note that all sources are listed in alphabetical order, not in order of importance.

Information about World Leaders & the Deep State

1. Charlie Ward - https://drcharlieward.com/
2. Children's Defense Fund - https://childrenshealthdefense.org/
3. Del Bigtree - https://thehighwire.com/watch/
4. Foster Gamble - https://www.thriveon.com/media/welcome-to-thrive-ii
5. Gene DeCode - https://rumble.com/search/video?q=gene%20decode
6. Jacqueline Hobbs - https://youtu.be/mobYvKtIt7A - https://www.oraclegirl.org/
7. Juan O'Savin - https://rumble.com/search/video?q=juan%20o%27savin
8. Michael Jaco - https://rumble.com/search/video?q=jaco
9. Nicholas Veniamen - https://rumble.com/search/video?q=nicholas%20veniamen
10. Nino Rodriguez - https://rumble.com/search/video?q=nino%20rodriguez
11. Prepare for Change - https://prepareforchange.net/
12. Robert Malone, MD - https://rumble.com/search/video?q=robert%20malone
13. Sacha Stone - https://lazarusinitiative.com/happenings/
14. Simon Parkes - https://www.simonparkes.org/blog
15. Stew Peters - https://rumble.com/search/video?q=stew%20peters-
16. Stillness in the Storm - https://stillnessinthestorm.com/
17. Will Barney - https://rumble.com/v1mkf6s-global-affairs-update-with-will-barney-2022-09-29-the-acceleration-of-the-p.html

Information about Even Darker Realities – Hostile Non-Human Beings

1. Alex Collier - https://www.alexcollier.org/
2. Cobra - https://2012portal.blogspot.com/

3. Corey Goode - https://coreygoode.com/
4. David Wilcock - https://divinecosmos.com/blog/
5. Ismael Perez - https://aprojectionofyou.com/2022/03/04/ismael-perez/
6. Jacqueline Hobbs - https://www.youtube.com/watch?v=TjWB_i5VwiU
7. Michael Salla - https://exopoliticstoday.com/
8. Nicholas Veniaman - https://rumble.com/search/video?q=nicholas%20veniamen
9. Paul Levy - https://www.awakeninthedream.com/articles/wetiko-in-a-nutshell

Chapter 3

Birth of a New Identity

Now that we've explored the bigger picture of what is occurring on the planet at this time and how humanity has been held back on its evolutionary path, let us turn to the aspect of Ascension that is more immediate to you – your personal shift into fifth-dimensional consciousness. In a certain way, individual Ascension is a microcosm of the Ascension occurring on the planet: the old is dying, and the new is being born.

As mentioned earlier, fully embodying 5D consciousness involves more than simply learning how to respond in more positive ways to challenges in life and strengthening your spiritual awareness. These are very important to begin with. But, in the end, it involves an actual shift in your whole sense of identity – to a full and embodied knowing of the eternal Essence that you are, beyond your personal self and the story of your life. It entails a shift from believing you are your body, your emotions and your mind, or even what you've come to believe is your "spiritual self". It is a radical transformation of your whole sense of yourself, experienced continuously in your everyday life.

This, of course, is a tall order to accomplish during these times of great disruption and chaos in the world. Perhaps, on top of all you were already experiencing on your Ascension path, once the covid madness hit the planet, you began experiencing further divisions with family members and friends over decisions of how to respond to the mandates forced on you. Heart-breaking arguments and separations may have occurred with loved ones, causing despair and hopelessness. And perhaps you have experienced all this while still dealing with old issues and unresolved traumas that had already been arising within you, even before all this came about. It can be overwhelming, causing ongoing anxiety and fear.

And perhaps even more distressing might be the experience of realizing that spiritual practices and teachings that have served you for many years no longer seem to give you the kind of support and solace you need. And, especially after reading the last chapter, you might really be questioning your spiritual beliefs as a whole. You might even feel a sense of loss about what you believed your spiritual mission in life to be; maybe it no longer feels important or workable to you.

Death of Your 3D Self

However, perhaps the most basic challenge that can occur during these times of Ascension is that of somehow losing your old familiar sense of identity. With so much change and loss, your very sense of who you are may seem eerily unfamiliar to you. Certain parts of yourself may feel like they've been disabled or are nowhere to be found anymore – except in your quickly-fading memory. Once-exciting pursuits and passions have perhaps become dull and uninteresting to you. Your life as a whole may have become something almost alien to you.

If any of this has been happening for you, understand that what is occurring can be seen as the process of death of an old version of yourself. In the past, this type of experience might have been called a "dark night of the soul". But this is different, in that a radical shift of your core sense of identity is occurring. It's an experience of spiritual awakening intense enough to cause a great deal of fear and confusion. In the Ascension paradigm, it could be called the "death of your 3D self".

Even if you are someone who has known for some time about the dimensional shift occurring, it may still take you by surprise in seeing how increasingly dramatic the changes happening in your life are. The interim period between letting go of your old 3D identity and shifting into your new 5D identity can be very challenging. You are passing through the Fourth Dimension, a space where great transformation is taking place, in which both death and birth are occurring simultaneously.

Descension is Also Occurring

In addition, as if the Ascension process weren't confusing enough, what you are likely also experiencing is what could be called *Descension*. On the one hand, you are *ascending* in your consciousness into a higher frequency, which, due to the unknown territory through which you are passing, can feel confusing and even frightening. You're having to learn what works in this new high-vibrational landscape and what does not.

And yet, at the same time, 5D frequencies are also *descending* into your body, clearing space for your higher multidimensional Self to anchor itself more and more securely into your body. These higher frequencies are causing numerous uncomfortable, even temporarily painful, physical and emotional changes. As these lower energies are forcibly released, old traumas to the body and unresolved emotional patterns tend to get activated again. In addition, your DNA is reactivating, your brain is being rewired, and all systems in your body are attempting to adjust to all of this.

It can feel as if your old, familiar consciousness is fading very quickly; and 5D consciousness has not yet totally shown up and established itself. You're still in the process of letting go of all the old identifications and the psychological debris of your older self, and you are only somewhat aware of the newer energies of your 5D Self. You're in what I've called the "Ascension Void". There's a sensation of emptiness in this state, as well as a feeling of aloneness and vulnerability.

And yet, if you are feeling these emotions and sensations, know that this is exactly what needs to happen for a while: all your old unhealthy 3D habits, thoughts, emotions, fears and ways of operating need to be left behind. Your 3D identities cannot go with you into the Fifth Dimension. It's time to focus as best you can on letting them go, so you can see what might be coming in to take their place.

Puzzling Periods of Peace amidst the Chaos

To add to the confusion you may be experiencing, another puzzling phenomenon can also occur: Even when you are having some of the worst days of your life, you may find that suddenly you are experiencing days – even weeks – in which all seems to be proceeding along very smoothly. You're feeling calm, even happy and unaffected by all that is happening out in the world. Your life, although greatly altered and restricted in certain ways, seems to be filled with a simple sense of contentment and even excitement. You feel free, floating along peacefully and joyfully, enjoying your simplified life.

This is also something that can happen due to the high-frequency energies of light that are now flooding the Earth. It is possible to tune into them and shift for periods of time into 5D consciousness. And you may be fooled into thinking you're past the "worst of it", that you're finally out the other side of the challenging shift occurring within you. However, if you're like most people, these periods tend to eventually come to an end, and difficulties return, along with a shift back into a lower vibration. This is because, if you are not yet established in the higher frequency of 5D, there is the tendency to eventually slip back into 4D and even 3D consciousness for a while again. It can all be very confusing and unsettling.

And yet, if you are experiencing all this, the good news is that it means you are totally on track on your path into the Fifth Dimension. It's an indication that you are deep into your process of Ascension and you are awakening very rapidly. This type of both inner and outer chaos is what occurs when you are passing through the higher Fourth Dimension. You are well on your way in making the transition into fifth-dimensional consciousness; you are experiencing a rebirth into a whole new dimension.

Deeper Inquiry into Who you Are

Perhaps the greatest benefit of feeling lost and confused during this transitional period is that it inevitably leads you to a deeper inquiry into who you actually are – and who you are not. If you have come to this point of feeling a loss of identity, you now have the opportunity for deeper spiritual investigation as to who you are at the core of your being.

In feeling a loss of familiar identity, your first response may be a strenuous and seemingly urgent attempt to work as hard as possible to *create a new identity*. You may decide to change external elements of your life – like your work, your home, your friends, your meditation practice. Or perhaps you take on new higher-frequency goals. Maybe you commit to creating new emotional responses to life or new mental habits and beliefs through healing programs or new spiritual practices. Or perhaps you create a new "story" about who you are now, trying to give your life some meaning.

You might also seek out good astrologers or channels who can see things about you that you can't. Or you begin reading books that describe characteristics of people based on metaphysical principles – all in an attempt to figure out who you now are on a deeper spiritual level. Perhaps you've enrolled in classes so you can become a healer or rediscover metaphysical abilities that are latent within you.

Doing these kinds of things can certainly be helpful. They can assist you in sloughing off old habits and bring new energies into your life. They can keep your mind focused and help you feel like you're moving ahead and that you've entered into a higher energy field. In fact, despite all that is happening in the world, you may be having increasingly deeper experiences of living in a much higher consciousness in which you feel more joy and love than ever before. You may feel as if you're finally creating a life you've always wanted.

But then, you may also find that something unexpected happens and you find yourself back in your old familiar 3D self again, unhappy, impatient, in pain and dissatisfied with your life. And you may finally realize that none of your efforts to "ascend yourself" are enough. You're still dealing with issues in your life, old stuff keeps coming up for resolution, relationships continue to be somewhat bumpy, and you are still subject to deep emotional suffering.

No matter how hard you strive to change yourself and your life, many of the same emotional and mental challenges continue to arise. It can be confusing and extremely frustrating. And, of course, in reading the last chapter, you understand the main reason that all these efforts have met with so little change is that your path to higher consciousness has been greatly impeded – so you probably feel even more discouraged.

And yet, even with all that going on, what you can discover is that your inability to truly change yourself is also due to the fact that you are still unknowingly identifying with your 3D self – your body-mind self, your ego-personality self. And this self is doing what it's always done: attempting to define itself with new and important things you're doing and feeling, and with new beliefs and decisions you've made. It's trying to create a new self – a better self – that could hopefully become your 5D Self.

If you've tried any of this, you may have realized that all you've really been doing is "rearranging the furniture" of your 3D self. You've attempted to somehow reinvent yourself.

But the truth is you cannot create your 5D Self – you can only discover it. It is already there within you; it has always been there, just not fully recognized.

Discovering Your 5D Self

What is needed is a complete shift out of identifying with this 3D version of yourself to discover something much deeper within you that has next to nothing to do with what you do, feel or think. It lives in an alternate reality, one you have likely yearned for your entire life. Your 5D Self is so different from your 3D self, it is so magnificent, that it is difficult to imagine. And yet, it is so close, so familiar to you, you may have never really recognized it, even when it's come into your awareness.

In the following chapters, as a step in learning how to make the shift into 5D consciousness, we will explore the nature of both the 3D self and the 5D Self to help you understand better the differences between the two. The chapters following those will further explore steps you can take to actually make the shift into 5D and remain there.

Understanding the Shift
from 3D to 5D Consciousness

Chapter 4

Understanding the 3D Self

So how can you start to make the shift into 5D consciousness and begin living your life as this new Self? How can you step free of the fear, the anger, the despair – and all the other emotional and mental suffering you've experienced while identified as your 3D self?

It's true, you cannot create your 5D Self. It already exists, and it must simply be discovered. But you *can* focus on this discovery and call it into your experience. You can recognize your 5D Self when it does appear – such as when you have sudden, unexpected and profound experiences of peace or love or joy. And then, through that recognition, you can begin to discover pathways into this expansive space inside you. You can also clear away old 3D identifications to make those pathways more clear.

Before I begin describing the 3D self, I wish to say that, in using the terms "3D self" and "5D Self", I am not indicating that these are fixed entities – or that everyone's experiences of these selves is exactly the same. Of course, we are all complex and fluid Beings, and we each have our own unique experiences when identified with either 3D or 5D consciousness. I simply use the terms as a matter of convenience, to indicate that when you're identified with either 3D or 5D consciousness, you are identifying with two very different perceptions and experiences of who you are.

What Exactly is the 3D Self?

So what exactly is the 3D self? In one way, this self could also be called the "ego self". But this term has been used over the years to mean many different things. In particular, people often use this term to refer to that part of themselves they consider bad or unacceptable – their negative emotions and thoughts, their arrogance, lust, greed, and ignorance – or whatever else they consider "unspiritual". I consider these negative qualities to be just one part of the 3D self – a part disliked by another part; both these parts reside within the 3D self.

When I use the term "3D self", I refer not just to these aspects of the personality, but to much more: it's your identification with your entire personal, separate sense of self. This includes your identification with your body and all its sensations; your mind and all its thoughts, beliefs, judgments, and desires; and your emotions – along with the memories of all of these. It also includes your identification with all roles you play in your life, your work, and your relationships. In addition, it includes your understanding about the world and about reality, itself. It may even include your spiritual beliefs. In other words, it is your identification with your entire separate personal "me", living in the story of your life.

Another way the 3D self can be described is as a *conditioned consciousness*. It is consciousness that has been influenced and distorted by your particular upbringing and by the culture to which you've been exposed. It has also been created by both the personal and ancestral karma you've been compelled to carry.

In addition, very importantly, it has been conditioned – and, in some ways, has actually been created – by the energies of the dark forces that have infiltrated humanity's evolution throughout the ages. Therefore, if you continue to identify yourself as the limited and distorted consciousness these forces have helped you develop, you are necessarily living with a highly unstable, constantly changing, and insecure sense of self.

Letting Go of Your Identification with Your 3D Self

Letting go of your identification with your 3D self is obviously not an easy task to undertake. It takes some time and also a great deal of courage. And yet, if you are tired to the bone of experiencing life through your 3D identification with all its suffering and irritation, letting it go can be done. And, in fact, it's easier now to make the shift than ever before, because the denseness of the Third Dimension is disappearing and fifth-dimensional light is shining through more clearly every day. The control of the off-world beings is continuing to lessen and fall away. The Veil is lifting.

This is especially so if you have already had experiences of yourself as a Higher Self or a Soul. Perhaps you've really related to the insight that you are a Soul or Spirit that's "having a human experience". Or maybe you can relate to the teaching that who you really are is *what always remains*, while emotions, thoughts, events and relationships constantly come and go. You realize that you are that essential awareness of being that transcends and continues on, after all phenomena have ceased to flow through you.

And maybe you have had increasing experiences of what feels like your true inner Essence or 5D Self. In fact, as time goes on, you are probably clearly experiencing 5D consciousness more frequently. There are increasing opportunities to slip into fifth-dimensional consciousness now, and it can feel very fluid as we travel through the Fourth Dimension.

At the same time, if you are still fully identified with your 3D self, it can initially be difficult to see that self objectively, because it is so familiar to you. Like most people living in this controlled third-dimensional reality, you've probably been trained your whole life to believe yourself to be a somewhat flawed body/mind entity known as a human being – and that's it.

It is therefore all too easy to slip out of the 5D experiences and realizations you're having because your identification with your 3D self is so ingrained in you. Therefore, in order to recognize some typical ways you may be identified with your 3D self, let's look at some usual ways this manifests. Most of the ways you get identified with your 3D self are probably pretty obvious. But it's helpful to be clear about them so you can more easily recognize the 3D trance when you're experiencing it, so you can wake yourself up out of it.

3D Emotions and Beliefs

One of the most obvious signs that you are identified with 3D consciousness is when you're gripped with fear, or feelings of abandonment, anxiety, depression, shame, betrayal, or guilt. When experiencing any of these types of emotions, you are also probably feeling disempowered, unsafe and helpless – and maybe believing you are essentially alone and only have yourself to rely on.

These emotions often accompany a belief in lack, that there's not enough of what you need and want to go around. And this belief, in turn, can engender such feelings as survival anxiety, competition, self-pity and helplessness, as well as a movement into blame and complaining. All of this can then turn into hatred, envy, greed, resentment, judgment and control. It's actually quite impressive to see how far into insecurity and hopelessness the 3D belief in lack can take you.

It's quite possible in 3D consciousness to get caught in a space where you're completely unaware that you have any real power over what you're experiencing. You feel as if you have no control over stopping your reactions of fear. And you have a strong tendency to get identified with your pain. You begin believing that your pain is who you are – forgetting that it's merely something you *have*, something you can relate to, something you can learn to calm down.

All this is obviously 3D. In general, when you're in any kind of emotional suffering, you are identifying with 3D consciousness.

Feeling Disconnected from Source

Another indication that you are identified with your 3D self is when you somehow forget that you have a Higher Self, and you're not aware of your connection to Source. As a result, you feel somewhat vulnerable and alone, and you also feel separate from other people and untrusting of them. The world feels unsafe.

And, due to this feeling of separation, the reality of Source may revert back to a concept in your mind of a separate entity outside of you called "God" – perhaps even a heavenly, glorified father-figure who needs to be somehow petitioned or pleaded with in order for you to receive the help you need. When this becomes your concept of Source, feelings of unworthiness, shame, guilt, abandonment and self-hatred can easily arise.

3D Relationships

3D identification can also become obvious when looking at the dynamics you get involved in when in relationship with others. When you're identified with your 3D self, because of an inherent sense of separation you feel from other people, you tend to automatically develop patterns of anxiety and unworthiness in your relationships. You are prone to feeling disappointment, grief, anger, blame and hurt with those you know when they do things that feel hurtful to you. And, in general, you likely mistake a feeling of need, desire or lust to be love.

In 3D consciousness, you probably also have the belief that the purpose of relationships with family, spouses, partners and good friends is to give you an essential sense that you are lovable, valuable and important. You believe that your loved ones are there to fill these emotional needs; this is their job and responsibility to you. And you're there to fill their needs.

You don't realize that the belief that others are responsible for filling your needs has created power struggles steeped in feelings of hurt, betrayal and guilt. Having given the responsibility to others for your happiness and sense of value, you therefore have no real power to create these feelings for yourself and you will blame them for its absence in your life.

Believing You are What you Do

It's common when you're in 3D consciousness to believe that who you are is what you do, how you act, and how you interface with other people. There's a "story" you have about yourself in regard to the world and what you accomplish in life, either in your work or in regard to the roles you play with other people.

This story of who you are may feel really positive. Perhaps you feel successful at your work and what you're able to accomplish, despite challenges you constantly encounter. Or maybe you believe you mediate well between people in conflict, and pride yourself on your interpersonal skills. Or that you're an accomplished speaker, musician, artist or salesperson. For the most part, you're not aware of the deeper Essence of who you are, beyond the story you've made up of your personality characteristics and accomplishments.

And, of course, if the story you believe about yourself is negative, you're not only missing who you really are – you are making yourself miserable, as well. You're feeling you are a failure, that you're inadequate, or maybe even that you're a "loser" in some way.

3D Belief about Happiness

When you identify with 3D consciousness, you have very little understanding about the nature of happiness or how to achieve it. When you do manage to feel happy at some point, you generally believe this is due to some outside circumstance, event or relationship. There's a sense that you are always at the effect of external forces.

And yet, when you're identified with your 3D self, your whole game plan is to try and ensure lasting happiness in your life. You keep trying to convince yourself (usually quite successfully) that your 3D game plan for happiness will work: All you have to do is simply follow your desires. First you become aware of all your desires, and then you do everything you can to fulfill them. You run after and cling to things that you believe bring you pleasure and run from or resist those things that bring you pain.

This is familiar, right? It should be, as it's precisely what just about everyone in the world is doing: seeking happiness through attempting to fulfill desires. Unfortunately, most people don't realize that this 3D strategy simply doesn't work. If you're honest, you'll realize that, no matter how many desires you've fulfilled in your life, none of them has ever brought you true, lasting happiness. Any results from following desires have always been temporary and brief. There are always more desires to fulfill; they are, in fact, endless.

As valiantly as you may try to accomplish your goal for happiness, you are totally unequipped to do so. As your 3D self, you don't understand that. This is because you do not understand that the cause of your suffering is actually your belief that you are this 3D identity, rather than your true Self. I will go into this unsuccessful game plan in more detail in a later chapter; but for now, just be aware of this illusion you are operating under when identified with your 3D self. When in 3D consciousness, you really can't know how to create true happiness.

Now, this doesn't mean you need to immediately let go of all your desires to create a freer and happier life. Not at all. In fact, an intermediate, fourth-dimensional step in this process is to realize and develop the power you have within you to create circumstances in your life that will bring you greater fulfillment. You do have this innate ability; and, as a step toward realizing the power you inherently have as a multi-dimensional Being, it is important to discover and develop this ability.

What I'm pointing to here is a step beyond discovering your power to "create your own reality". It is to realize you are a Being for whom there is no more need to try to create and manifest things and situations in your life. The wonder of it is that when you are fully identified with your 5D Self, all that you need and desire comes to you automatically, without any effort. And usually quite quickly – sometimes even before you realize you need or want it.

In 5D consciousness, you *can* focus on creating things or circumstances in your life, and you do that naturally and easily when inwardly directed to. But there is no fear or concern that your basic needs or desires will not be met. There is never a feeling that you will ever lack what you need for feeling happy, fulfilled, and peaceful. There's a trust it will all come to you in the right way, in the right timing. It's simply what naturally happens when you are functioning in 5D consciousness.

Another way to see it is, when identified with your 3D self, there's no true understanding that you have access to a happiness that resides inside of yourself – that you can actually *choose* to be happy, no matter what's happening. In your 3D self, there's always a sense of waiting for happiness to happen in the future, a belief that something has to first change before you can be happy. So you're never quite satisfied with what is happening in the moment. Even when circumstances are really okay, there's always a niggling sense of dissatisfaction. And, because of this, you may be drawn at times to some kind of substance abuse or other type of addiction to fill the emptiness you feel inside of you.

The Cause of Suffering

I emphasize here that the most important thing to understand about the 3D self is that the sole cause of your emotional and mental suffering is your identification with that very self. No matter how calm or happy you can sometimes become when identified with it, if you're honest, you'll realize that you are also, on a subconscious level, always experiencing at least some small sense of anxiety, unease, attachment or need. And, of course, when something upsetting happens, you lose your sense of calm and happiness, anyway.

In contrast, when identified with your 5D Self, you realize you exist in unchanging peace and freedom, no matter what is happening, either within or outside yourself. As this Self, you are aware that you have no birth or death, no beginning or end. You are beyond feeling stuck in experiences of insecurity or struggle. Truly knowing yourself to be the 5D Self therefore essentially eliminates all psychological suffering.

Now, this doesn't mean that negative thoughts or emotions don't arise when you're in 5D consciousness; these things just seem to be part of the human experience. But you don't experience them in a way that causes distress or suffering. You simply note these energies are with you and you allow them to be. And then, with equanimity and a positive sense of empowerment, you do whatever you can to change the situation you're in, or you easily let go of what is not working and focus on finding a solution. You feel in charge of what is occurring within you and trust that all truly is well, even though it may not seem like it at the moment.

The contrast between the two selves in this process of dealing with negative events, emotions and thoughts, is quite clear. It takes some time to make the shift into such a higher frequency, so give yourself a break and restrain from self-judgment. You will likely see that, as you begin to shift into 5D, there will be parts of you that continue to remain in 3D consciousness longer than other parts. If you do become aware of this, know it is to be expected.

Something you can learn is to simply watch your 3D self as it continues to struggle, based on its belief that it is a separate, disconnected being, subject to the whims of the universe and fate (or God). And since you know more and more that this is not who you are, this aspect of yourself clinging to 3D beliefs will not overly trouble you. You can simply watch it with increasing detachment and compassion, as it doggedly but futilely continues with its strategies to create a sense of security and happiness. You can remain untouched by the struggle and watch it naturally dissipate with time.

3D Self-Help Practices

Once you become aware of your identification with your 3D self and the trouble it brings, you may begin shifting into a mode of trying to heal and "fix" yourself. At first, this healing journey is very important; it's a fourth-dimensional process that helps to move the big stuff out of the way so you can see more clearly what's been holding you down and preventing you from loving yourself. It can also eventually help you realize that all the woundings and traumas are just stuff you've picked up along your journey through lifetimes in the controlled reality of the Third Dimension, things that have become stuck to your sense of identity. They aren't actually a part of YOU – they're things you *have*.

But after a while, continuing on and on with not enough seeming to change despite all your attempts to heal yourself can be very discouraging. This is because continuing to change and fix your 3D self is endless. This self is naturally flawed and imperfect. So, in the end, this repetitious effort at self-improvement will not produce your identification with your true Inner Essence.

If you have already been through years of healing and self-improvement, you might consider abandoning the ingrained "self-improvement urge", at least for awhile. Try instead to simply relax and let go. Let yourself be, just the way you are. Learn to love everything about yourself – even all the irritating and unpleasant aspects that give you grief. And then focus on gently surrendering all of your attachment to your identity, along with its 3D thoughts, emotions and body sensations, and see what is left.

And, very importantly, remember that the cause of your suffering has been a case of misidentification: believing yourself to be the 3D self. Begin waking up from this 3D trance and focus on discovering your true identity.

In the next chapter, we will look more closely at the 5D Self and then explore ways in which you can experience it more fully and begin to shift your sense of identification to it.

Chapter 5

Understanding the 5D Self

You may wonder why I am not fully addressing the subject of a 4D self. I have described this self at length in previous books, so I will not be doing so here. But, in a nutshell, 4D consciousness is a state of being that is somewhere in between 3D and 5D consciousness; and, when functioning from within it, you're generally slipping back and forth between these two states of being.

For this reason, as I've indicated, trying to navigate life while in 4D consciousness can be very confusing and disorienting. Your vibration is higher than when you're fully identified with 3D consciousness, so in certain ways, you are not so reactive emotionally and you're more spiritually aware. However, you're essentially still identified with your body, mind and emotions and still believing you are someone who needs to heal and fix yourself in order to "grow" and "heal". At times, you may experience periods in which you feel very empty, like "no one's home".

5D consciousness is a big leap up from this. And yet, you may realize you are sometimes identified with 5D consciousness more often than you've thought. Let's explore some of the main characteristics of this identification to give you a clearer idea of what it is.

What is the 5D Self?

As with many spiritual concepts, it is extremely difficult to describe in words what the 5D Self is. The experience of this ethereal Self is so far beyond what the rational mind can comprehend that words cannot truly express its true nature. Yet words can sometimes *point* to the experience and ignite the recognition of it in other deeper aspects of the human psyche. Hopefully, the following description will help do this for you.

Your 5D Self is something that has very little to do with what you do, feel or think. It's something that you simply *are*. Indeed, it is so natural, so familiar, that it can be easy to miss. It is closer to you than your breath, closer than your thoughts. It is that most subtle Essence that animates your body, gives it life. It is the awareness inside you that has never changed, no matter how much older your body has gotten or how mature your personality has become; it was the same when you were a child, a young adult, and all other ages throughout your life. It has never been born; it will not die. It is changeless, permanent Beingness.

Your 5D Self is the Stillness deep inside you – clear, pristine, untouched. It is quiet, serene Silence. It is the presence of fathomless love, profound joy, boundless freedom. It has no boundaries, no limitations – you can fall endlessly into its blissful depths. This Self is the true YOU.

At times, you might experience yourself as an expansive field of consciousness – perhaps as a field of pure light. Or maybe a field of pure love, or simply pure awareness. As this energetic field, you're aware of how emotions, thoughts and fluctuating identities all flow around inside of you; they come and they go. You may also be aware of how large you are – that your body is actually inside of YOU.

At other times, you may realize that you are vast, formless intelligence, a pure consciousness that permeates all of reality. You have no particular form or shape or size – you exist everywhere in everything. There is nothing that is not YOU. Everything in life, from the most dense level of matter to the most subtle level of energy, exists within you. You are the very life force itself.

You could call the 5D Self the "Soul", or your "Higher Self", or your "I-Am Presence". In a way, it is a combination of all these aspects, but the terms are not very helpful because they have been so over-used and are usually only understood on a mental level. It could perhaps be better called your *True Nature* – or maybe your *Primal Essence.* Or the *Infinity Spark* within you. If you can feel into less-familiar terms like these, it can be easier to move past the words altogether. Ultimately, it's a profound experience, beyond any words, of what you simply *are*.

Whatever term you give it, your 5D Self is not a static identity; it is extremely fluid – ever-changing, ever-evolving in every moment. Yet, paradoxically, there is a constant, eternal quality that is changeless.

When you tap into this Self, you immediately recognize it. Although in one way, it's brand new, in another, it's deeply familiar. You may even recognize it as something you once knew yourself to be in the long-ago past but have been out of touch with, perhaps for eons of time while you've lived in 3D. And yet, as deeply familiar as it is, the initial experience of it can be so powerful, it can stun you.

You have likely on many occasions tuned into this higher-dimensional Self that you are. Perhaps you've been aware of it and have had profound experiences that have left a deep impression on you. Or maybe you are just beginning to experience it lately since Ascension has begun. Either way, you may have the knowing that you are closer than ever to merging with this primal Essence of who you are and long for it with a deep ache in your being.

Full Embodiment of 5D Consciousness

When you are fully embodied in 5D consciousness, your identification is constantly as the clear, eternal Essence of Source. You're totally aware that you *are* this Essence of Source. This is not just an intellectual understanding; it's an ongoing experience of it, the full knowing and living of it.

There's an understanding that, as this Essence, you have extended part of yourself into lower, denser dimensions to have an experience in human form on earth – but that the human form is just one small part of you. Because you experience yourself as a multidimensional Being, you're aware of living in a number of different dimensions. You realize there are other higher-dimensional selves that have always been with you – identities you've not been consciously in touch with for a long, long time.

As a part of you, these selves have been dwelling in higher dimensions, even those higher than the Fifth Dimension, and have been guiding you all along. In third or fourth dimensional consciousness, you may have been referring to them simply as your "Higher Self", not realizing that they are actual multiple aspects of yourself living in different dimensions. Or perhaps you've assumed they were your "guides", but you realize now they've actually been a part of you.

There's a profound knowing of your oneness with all people, with all of existence. You feel no sense of separation or duality; you're one with all of creation. You may experience yourself at times as a point of awareness in the Ocean of pure Consciousness. And, with this, there's an expansive sense of freedom, a knowing of the vastness of yourself, a huge spaciousness. And, other times, you may experience yourself as an individual spark of Source, housed in the denser form of a physical body – but free and in charge of it.

As your 5D Self, you experience a sense of great power and force; you know yourself to be a completely sovereign Being. Your presence is commanding, yet gracious and respectful. You easily speak your truth at all times. You can sometimes experience yourself as a very large presence of energy that can fill an entire room.

5D Mood and Emotions

When identified with 5D consciousness, you experience a freedom from all emotional suffering, all lack, and all limitation. There is a sense of natural well-being you feel, no matter what is occurring; there is no anxious need to feel or think or act in a way that is not natural for you.

You have a knowing that emotions and thoughts are like the weather – they come and go. When they arise, you feel them – and you may express them – but they generally just pass through you. There's no need to follow them, attach to them, or create a story around them. At times, you might experience a period of intense bliss, joy, love, or gratitude; but generally, your mood is likely to be peaceful, happy, balanced, and optimistic. There's often a sense of quiet bliss.

This state of being is not dependent on any outer circumstances, events or relationships. It's just there as a natural, basic default mood. The chattering monkey mind is gone, leaving you with a feeling of clear spaciousness in your mind. And, because of this, there's a sense of exhilarating inner freedom.

There's an easy acceptance of what-is – no longing, no desires for anything to be different from how it is. The constant annoying dissatisfaction that has always been present in your 3D/4D consciousness, usually on a subconscious level, is completely gone. Whatever is happening in your life is just fine. And there's a curiosity about whatever may be next – even an anticipation, knowing it will be interesting and engaging.

In 5D, you have a total trust in the benevolence of the Universe. No more concern about survival or any of your needs not being taken care of. You know with certainty that all you need will be given to you. Manifestation, when needed, becomes natural and very rapid.

Your Expanded and Open Heart

At the core of 5D consciousness, there is an expansion and openness of the Heart, an outpouring of love from your whole being. There's a feeling of compassion, emotional receptivity, and a flowing of love toward all you encounter and for all of life, including yourself. There's an absence of judgment or separation. The love you feel for people has no attachment with it. It's a clear, more detached type of love, with no strings attached, no expectations or demands.

You are also very aware that your inner guidance emanates from your Heart. It is no longer your rational mind that guides you in all your decisions and actions – it's your Heart.

5D Relationships

In 5D consciousness, you feel no need to receive approval, love or connection from other people. If they offer you these things, it's a bonus, an overflow that is much appreciated and valued; but you have no need to receive these things from anyone in order to feel lovable, valuable and important. You have no expectations or demands on people to meet your needs in this way. Rather, all your emotional needs are met by your own self-love and your knowing of your inherent value.

And, very importantly, your love for others springs solely from your true caring and compassion for them – not from a need that they provide you with something in return. No longer is your love for others conditional on some sort of "bargain"; it is unconditional, free of demands or expectations that a person act in a certain way or be something different from who they are.

Your relationships therefore tend to be harmonious, peaceful and loving, with effective communication. People who function in a low vibration may be drawn to you in order to receive energy that will be helpful to them, but you don't generally attract them to you.

Openness to the "Impossible" Happening

When identified with your 3D self, because of your experiences from the past, you can often feel caught in the limitations of what your rational mind thinks it knows. The limitations you believe you see can seem formidable, and there is little or no belief that you can get around them.

When functioning from within 5D consciousness, you understand that what might sound impossible to your lower-dimensional awareness is actually quite possible. You understand that there are actually no limitations on what you can create or bring to yourself. You know that, if necessary, the "impossible" will occur and it will feel natural to you.

5D Focus

In fact, when you're living in 5D consciousness, your focus is often on exploring and creating new experiences and adventures. You also find you love learning and expanding your awareness. Even with the smallest things you discover or experience, you feel a sense of wonder and excitement.

You're totally enjoying your life that's filled with joy, peace, freedom, and a sense of fulfillment. This, of course, is very different from your experience in 3D consciousness. Gone is any irritating dissatisfaction with your life; there's no more waiting for something better to happen.

In general, when living in 5D, there's a buoyant optimism about life, a feeling of being totally alive and aware. You are confident that whatever is ahead for you is going to be wonderful, intriguing and delightful as that's simply the way life is for you.

* * *

If you can relate to these descriptions of 5D consciousness, you can probably also relate to how frustrating it can be to have had these experiences and felt the elation of the inherent freedom and joy in them, but somehow not be able to hold onto them. You don't know why, but somehow your everyday life tends to pull you back into 3D/4D consciousness.

In the following chapters, I will present ways to first of all help you to better recognize 5D consciousness when it appears and how to prolong the glimpses you have of it. Then I will discuss how to more fully let go of aspects of your 3D identification to help you to eventually begin living your life more fully as your 5D Self.

Chapter 6

Experiencing your 5D Self

Experiences of tuning into 5D consciousness could be called "glimpses" of your truer Self. These glimpses can happen in countless ways. They can occur with your eyes open or closed. Perhaps you have had them at times in meditation or during a spiritual awakening experience.

When they've happened, you may have suddenly had a clear knowing of yourself as an eternal Being, as the essence of pure Beingness. Perhaps you've had an expansive, blissful experience of knowing yourself to be one with all of creation. Or you've had profound realizations that your true nature is pure Love. Maybe it's been clear that you are essentially a field of clear Light. Or that you are simply abundant joy and aliveness, incarnate.

At their most subtle, these glimpses can bring joy and peace into your life; at their deepest, a sense of rapture and ecstasy that can alter your life in the most profound way. Because the rapturous and ecstatic glimpses are the easiest to describe, they are the most obvious and also naturally the kind that people long to have.

One description of a profound glimpse of the 5D Self could be that it's like an experience of suddenly waking up from a long, unpleasant dream that has seemed very real. Upon awakening, you realize you've just been dreaming, and the world into which you have awakened is what is actually real. An enormous sense of relief comes with this realization, and a profound joy. You are remembering, after a very long time of being unconscious, who you truly are and what life is really about.

With this kind of awakening, there can be an exquisite feeling of timelessness, a sense of stepping out of ordinary consciousness into a broader view of life, a seeing of the big picture – which brings about a peace and serenity that is profound beyond words. All worries and concerns about life are amazingly absent. A deep sense of well-being pervades your entire being. An exhilaration lifts your heart.

Some 5D awakenings focus specifically on the Heart and you feel immersed in profound energies of Love. You can suddenly feel overwhelmed with a Love beyond any type of love you've ever experienced in your 3D life, An overwhelming sense of compassion, joy, connection and passion can suddenly flood your entire being. It may even bring you to your knees in overwhelm and gratitude.

Tears may suddenly appear as this profound experience of your eternal 5D Self washes through your entire being. And yet, because it may have been a very long time since you've experienced yourself in this most profound way, there may also at first be a sense of grief running through the joy.

Glimpses You Can Miss

But there are other experiences of your true eternal nature that you may have during your everyday life, experiences that you might fail to acknowledge or dismiss entirely because they seem so faint or fleeting. It can be a true loss to let these go by, because there are ways to allow these faint glimpses to deepen into more profound ones. And there are ways to help prolong them, as well.

It's important, of course, to recognize these more fleeting glimpses when they do appear. You might, for example, experience a glimpse of Reality out in Nature. In the out-of-doors, your mind tends to be a lot more at rest, and you are more open to the pure and silent way in which your 5D Self manifests itself. You may find that the trees, the sky, the mountains, and all bodies of water – along with all the animal and plant life living in them – have a clear and unobstructed way of reminding you of simply *being*. Within this environment, you likely find it easier to feel more at peace with yourself and slip into a higher frequency.

But there may be moments in Nature when a sudden deepening of this peace occurs, when a stillness pervades your being. Perhaps you experience a shift in perception about your life for a moment; your worries about your future recede. In view of the timeless reality in which all of Nature resides, your concerns about life seem dim and unimportant. The experience deepens for a moment – or perhaps for a number of moments – but then it begins fading as thoughts tumble into your mind again, and you follow them into the more familiar 3D reality. But you're aware that when this shift happened, an immediate sense of freedom and joy arose within you. A smile suddenly lit up your face.

You may experience similar moments when you are particularly moved by a piece of music or work of art. Perhaps you have experienced this when you suddenly feel a lifting of the heart, an expanding of your awareness...or a flooding of love. Your breath is taken away. Or perhaps this has happened when you've watched a beautiful sunrise or sunset. The vastness of the universe pervades your being; your spirit rises. You are awestruck. Again, this feeling can last a moment or may persist for a while. But eventually, it generally fades – usually when thoughts, emotions, or body sensations once again claim your attention.

There may be times when you become aware of your 5D Self while you're walking along somewhere and you suddenly experience yourself as a clear energetic body that your physical body fits inside of. The sensation is that your physical body is somehow walking *with* you, not *as* you. You're experiencing yourself as an individual form; but with just a slight change of focus, you realize you also extend out into everything else around you. There can be a surprising sense of relief that your physical body feels when you are identifying with this more energetic body, rather than with your denser one. It's as if your identification with your physical body has always tended to weigh you down.

Other fifth-dimensional experiences can come at those times when a disaster of some sort has struck. Ironically, at the very time when you would expect to be overwhelmed by emotions of fear, anguish and heartbreak, a quiet, still peace will slowly enter your body and mind. A surprising sense of well-being begins to pervade your consciousness, a knowing that, despite the tragedy that is obviously taking place, everything really is okay.

As in the other examples, this feeling begins to recede, either slowly or abruptly, when thoughts again invade your awareness. It is as if you've been visited by an angel for a spell and then are left again on your own. You might simply attribute the experience to a strange side-effect of shock. And in one way, it is. Shock often stops all thought for a period of time; the mind goes numb. In this rare absence of thought, your higher-dimensional Self has the opportunity to make itself known to you.

You may have had other experiences of your 5D Self due to an empty mind, moments in your everyday life when your mind just naturally becomes still. You may be staring out the window, daydreaming for a while, when a simple, clear stillness becomes present inside you. For a change, there are no thoughts, just a clarity of awareness. A subtle feeling may be drawing you inward to a deeper state.

Perhaps you've even had profound experiences of this 5D consciousness in your body – such as a sudden, deeply-pleasurable expansion in your chest, or a lighting up of the third-eye area in your head, a powerful tingling of energy in your crown chakra, or a sensation of energies running up and down your body.

These types of moments described here are usually brief – often fleeting. But it is important to not dismiss them – no matter how faint or subtle they may be. This is because these are times when, if you only knew what to do (or not do), you are standing at the doorway of what could become a profound and rapturous glimpse.

Prolonging the Glimpse

Indeed, when you first become aware you are experiencing a glimpse of your 5D Self – no matter how faint or fleeting it may be – it's helpful to pay immediate attention to it. If you can, stop everything you are doing. Become still and meet this visitation of your eternal Self with instant acceptance, welcome and love. Your warm receptivity to the glimpse will greatly enhance the clarity and intensity of it.

Then gradually and gently open to the experience. Allow it to slowly deepen in whatever way it might. Remain quietly receptive, as if a butterfly has just landed on your shoulder: be as relaxed as possible, while delicately focusing your attention on it.

Then move slowly into surrender to it. Allow it simply to have you – all of you – with complete abandonment. Hold nothing back. This is your Beloved come to call. Lovingly, give yourself to its ardent embrace. Fall deeply into its tender care. Be willing to die in its arms if this is what's called for. Allow yourself to be swallowed by it until there is no more you.

At the same time, take care not to be clutching. Make no attempts to possess the experience. It cannot be captured or controlled. It will do with you as it will for as long as it wishes. All you can do is openly trust and embrace it while it is present.

Do your best to linger in this place of openness and surrender as long as you can. At some point – probably much to your dismay – thoughts, emotions, and bodily sensations will reappear and try to claim you. Stay alert to these. Even thoughts about what is happening to you at the moment can unwittingly bring your mind back into play and dissipate the power of the glimpse. Therefore, do not follow the thoughts, but do not try to get rid of them either. Simply let them be, without giving them any energy. The object is to focus as fully and intently – yet gently – as you can on the experience of the glimpse, allowing it to take you where it will for as long as possible

When you finally feel it receding, do not fret. Simply continue to be still. Allow the fragrance of the experience to linger as long as possible. Do not try to get up or move too soon afterwards. To do so will cause you to immediately lose some of the afterglow. Be careful not to try to speak right away. Stay centered within. At some point later, you might find it useful to write down the details of your experience. Often, as the ordinary concerns of your world finally flood back into your awareness, the glimpse and experience of your 5D Self will begin to dim. In other words, do everything you can to prolong the afterglow.

Once the Glimpse has Passed

Although certainly not inevitable, once the glimpse of 5D you've experienced has passed, a period of depression may occur. You may feel an enormous sense of loss. You might even believe you have somehow done something "wrong" to have lost that incredible experience. Know that you haven't. Most likely, you were just not familiar with the nature of glimpses into 5D reality and may have had inaccurate assumptions and expectations about them.

Something else that may happen during a glimpse is that Truth may stand out for you with profound clarity. It seems impossible to think you could ever lose this clarity. There might be a feeling that, having now entered into this new awakened state, you will never again return to "ordinary 3D consciousness."

Unfortunately, almost without exception, this illusion eventually bursts. Everyday concerns start slipping back into your awareness as the mind begins to "return". Unbelievably, the crystal clear knowing of 5D Reality and the profound feelings of joy and peace begin to fade.

This may be especially dismaying if your glimpse has extended for weeks or even months. You may feel as if you had transcended your 3D consciousness once and for all and have become the higher 5D form of yourself living in a whole new reality, one you hoped would continue forever. If you have no reference points as to what has happened to you nor any support or guidance for it, you may be nonplussed and filled with grief when you eventually feel the experience beginning to fade and your old 3D consciousness is starting to return.

This is a common reaction if you are not aware that the eventual fading of a glimpse is natural and to be expected. What needs to be understood is that these rapturous highs, filled with clarity, understanding, and bliss are *states of mind*. And the truth about states of mind is that they come – and they go. That is the nature of the mind. They are not permanent. *The important thing to realize, however, is that, although the states of mind do not last, the Truth that is revealed in the glimpse does. It is permanent.*

Something else that can follow a powerful glimpse of 5D reality, especially if it is your first, is an unhappy dissatisfaction about your life. You might actually experience your whole life has been turned upside down by the glimpse, and you can't seem to "right" it in any of the old ways.

You might become irritable and disgruntled at everything and everyone around you.

The feeling is that something inside you that has been numbed for years has suddenly thawed – and there's now a deep yearning that is demanding to be fulfilled. You can no longer go about your life in the numbed way, trying to satisfy superficial, mediocre desires. Your priorities have abruptly rearranged themselves. You are being thrust forward on your Ascension path, and, in certain ways, nothing will ever be the same again.

Indeed, your life will undoubtedly go through major upsets and changes after a powerful 5D glimpse – necessarily so. This is all part of the Ascension path. It demands an entirely new experience of your whole sense of identity, and much has to change. But what is important to remember – even while experiencing disappointment, depression, and upset about the turmoil in your life – is the gift of the 5D experience that has been given to you. Gratitude for this gift will go a long way to help assuage the upsetting feelings.

Realize that, with this glimpse of 5D, you have been granted the clarity to see what at some point will be your ongoing and permanent experience in life. You have been kissed by your 5D Self; you have been given a foretaste of the Fifth Dimension and are now being beckoned Home. You can finally understand the essential purpose of your life in this embodiment: to fully and permanently wake up to the Truth of who you are.

Once this realization has been given to you, it is up to you to begin living your everyday life more in accordance with what you have realized. You now have the opportunity to set different priorities, make important changes in your life if necessary, and live with greater integrity because of what you now know to be true. You really have no other choice. But, if you can simply stop resisting the changes and allow them to take place naturally, it is an effortless choice.

What is perhaps most important following the passing of a 5D glimpse is to be alert to what it is that has not left you, even though all the blissful sensations have receded. Something very precious always remains – the whole point, in fact, to these glimpses of 5D. And that is the *realization of Truth* of who you are.

You just need to ask yourself what has *not left*. What knowing still remains, even after the high has totally dissipated? What is it that can never be taken away? This realization is the true treasure – not the glorious high. The rapturous glimpse was simply the exquisitely beautiful wrapping in which the treasure of realization was brought to you.

Attracting 5D Glimpses into your Life

Actually, it probably won't be difficult to keep focused on these fifth-dimensional experiences once you've begun having them, because once you have, you will likely find yourself preoccupied, even obsessed, with how to have more of them. This is a tricky area, because it's important to realize that we have no actual control over *causing* them to happen. Somehow, Grace bestows them on us – sometimes at the most unlikely and surprising times.

However, you can discover ways in which to "cultivate" your inner environment so as to open yourself for more and more of these experiences. The first thing to do is to look for them, everywhere, expecting them to happen at any time. Your 5D Self truly is everywhere, in everything – in a certain way, it is ALL that exists. The opportunities to see and experience it are therefore countless, available in every moment. So the point is to focus your attention on potential glimpses in every way you can, as often as possible throughout your everyday life. You can actively invite these visitations into your life through a prayerful openness of attention.

Another suggestion is to remember that every glimpse of your 5D Self is unique. Be careful not to expect the same experience to happen twice. Every glimpse, although possessing certain similar qualities, happens each time in a new and fresh way. This is where you may get tripped up. Once you've had an incredible glimpse, you may want a repeat performance; you may want the same feelings, the same sensations, the same insights. This can greatly hinder the next glimpse from appearing in its own unique and new way.

And yet, there are certain things you can do to invite the visit of a 5D glimpse. As mentioned earlier, going out in Nature is one of these. Listening to music or visiting an art gallery or museum are others. You can also read inspiring books, or go to spiritual gatherings (online, if that is the only choice). Spending time with others who are on a similar quest is also very helpful. Talking about 5D and spiritual experiences can be uplifting and can also greatly enhance your own experiences.

Do try to avoid spending time with people whose company brings you down in some way. You might want to be careful as well about which videos or TV shows you choose to watch and which books or newscasts you choose to read or listen to. In other words, be responsible for creating your own inner environment, one that will be as conducive as possible to visitations from your 5D Self.

Who Am I?

One of the most effective tools I know for inviting glimpses is asking yourself, "Who am I?"– and then focusing inwardly and directly looking to see who is actually there inside you. The object is not to come up with an intellectual answer to this question, but to wait quietly for an experiential response.

You may make the awesome discovery each time you ask this that no one is there. Indeed, nothing of any substance is there – except Consciousness – pure Awareness that never changes. There may be a flavor of love that is present in this field of Consciousness – or peace – or wisdom – or perhaps all of them. But be especially aware of the clarity and light that are there. Your thoughts and emotions and body sensations actually pass through this clear and empty Space that is YOU – but they are not really a part of YOU. They are temporary energy forms that pass through this space.

There are variations on this technique. If you are upset about a particular issue, you can ask yourself, "Who is upset?". Again, at this point, investigate directly – look within. See what is actually present. Other variations might be, "Who is thinking?" or "Who is feeling anger (joy, love fear, etc.)?". All these questions lead back to the primal Essence within you having the experience, rather than to some idea that exists in your mind. This is what is so unusual and powerful about these questions: they can liberate you from a false bondage to some limiting "Who" you imagine yourself to be.

Centering Your Awareness in your Pineal Gland

Another powerful technique that can lead you to the awareness of your primal Essence is discovering the location of your pineal gland and focusing your attention there. The way to discover this is to first of all bring your awareness to the center of your head, right behind your eyes. You may think that is always where your awareness is centered, but it probably is not. Your mental and emotional bodies extend outside of your physical body, and often people's focus of awareness is somewhere outside in front of this body.

When you bring your attention to that place just in back of your eyes, you realize you are looking out at the world through your eyes from inside your head. When you first do this, you may feel a sudden sensation of being centered and grounded, with a feeling of greater control and power present. A relaxation comes with this.

Then, from this place, raise your awareness up inside your head a couple of inches or so, and you will be looking out at the world from your pineal gland – and the sensation of power and presence will suddenly deepen. You will be aware of the field of expansive Light that extends all around you that you realize is YOU. A sensation of expansion and profound peace may wash through you.

At first, staying focused on this awareness can be difficult. Thoughts and emotions begin taking hold of you again and it slips away. But, as with all these ways of discovering – or remembering – who you are, your task is to focus on them more and more often, until you discover you are suddenly and quite naturally there, without having given any thought or effort to the goal of arriving in the awareness of this essential YOU.

Meditation

Most spiritual teachings tell us of the importance of practicing some kind of meditation on a daily basis. With all that is occurring in today's world that can cause upset and fear, this practice may be more important than ever. If you have been meditating daily for a number of years, you may realize how the years of meditating have helped your mind to remain relatively clear and calm most of the time. And you have likely experienced a number of 5D glimpses, as well.

However, if you still find it difficult to calm your mind and relax, and you have not yet experienced glimpses of your 5D Self as deeply as you would like, adopting a daily meditation practice may be very useful. Meditation habituates the mind to moving consistently inward toward relaxation and clarity – even during mundane or demanding tasks or normally-upsetting experiences.

If you're not used to meditating often, it may be that such a practice takes time, discipline and patience. You might feel you should be successful at it immediately, simply because you want to be, but be aware that it's not that easy. Generally, the mind, the emotions, and the body are not habituated to being still for any length of time while we are awake. Quieting the mind, pacifying the emotions and relaxing the body are very positive benefits of cultivating the habit of meditation.

It is therefore helpful to practice daily meditation beginning with short periods of time and then gradually increasing the time. Even ten minutes a day can be productive at first – any amount of time spent entirely and fully on promoting an inner environment conducive to experiencing your deeper inner Self has its rewards. Little by little, the time can be increased, as is comfortable.

You may discover that finding a particular time of the day in which to meditate is also helpful, as well as finding a particular place in your home for it. In doing this, you begin creating a certain energy during that time and in that place that will eventually actively serve to draw you in. Making sure you will be comfortable (not too hot or cold, too full or hungry) will further ensure success in your practice.

You may also have difficulty meditating because you think you should just sit and try to still your mind. This rarely works at first; it's difficult to achieve it right off the bat. The mind simply rebels and tends to bring in as many thoughts as it can. Frustration and a sense of failure are sure to result.

You might initially try different things to help still your mind – anything that will gently encourage it to relax and begin focusing inwardly, past your thoughts. Focusing on watching your breath is a simple and effective way to begin. Listening to guided meditations or certain pieces of relaxing music can be helpful, as well. Different forms of yoga, t'ai ch'i or qi gong can be extremely beneficial. You might even find it helpful to start out by journaling, allowing your "higher self" to write something. All these activities can serve as a way to eventually enter into more serious and demanding forms of meditation.

It can also be helpful to find a meditation teacher who will teach you a particular form of meditation that feels right for you. Do be aware, however, that a certain form of meditation that once worked for you may be less effective after a while. It may be time to begin trying new forms. Sometimes we can "outgrow" a particular spiritual practice (or teacher) and need to look for what is "next" on our spiritual path.

At any rate, developing a daily spiritual practice of some kind – at least at first – is generally important in a quest for attracting glimpses of the 5D Self. The aim is to learn how to still the mind as much as possible. As a wise teacher once said, "When the mind is still, Reality rushes in." It's as if your 5D Self is just standing there, waiting patiently for you to put aside the habitual, sometimes compulsive thoughts – even just for a moment – so it can then rush in to greet you.

Shifting your Identity from your 3D Self

In summary, to eventually make the complete shift from 3D to 5D consciousness, it's helpful first of all to recognize 5D glimpses when you've had them and to realize what they are. They are signs of the birthing of 5D consciousness within you. Focusing on them is especially important during these times when it is so easy to move into fear, because so much has become unfamiliar. There's a knowing that we will never be going back to "normal" again and that we've entered into the totally uncharted territory of the Fourth Dimension.

And yet, there are things you can do to assist in the shedding of different aspects of your 3D identity so that you begin living more and more in 5D consciousness. I will describe these in the ensuing chapters.

Detachment

In doing so, I will sometimes be using the word "detachment" – how it is important to detach from certain aspects of your 3D identity. I wish to make it clear that, with this word, I am not referring to a type of dissociation or denial. In particular, when I suggest you detach from your emotions, I am not suggesting you enter into a dissociated state in which you are not in touch with them. Or if I suggest detaching from your body, I am not suggesting a denial of your body.

What I am referring to with the term "detachment" is creating a distance in your awareness from your emotions, body and mind so that you become more of a witness to them. It's about becoming an observer of yourself, one who is not so embroiled in the drama or so attached to the outcome of events and circumstances.

As such, far from putting you out of touch with your thoughts, emotions and bodily sensations (as in the experiences of dissociation and denial), detachment can actually help you to be *more* aware of them. You are training yourself to carefully observe what is happening within you. Ironically, the process of detachment can actually assist you to participate more fully, with greater interest and caring, in the activities of all these aspects of your life – precisely because you are not so attached and lost in the miasma of emotions and sensations that are going on.

Spiritual Polarization

Another misunderstanding that might occur as you begin the process of detaching from the identification with your 3D self is what is known as "spiritual polarization". This can happen if you begin to make your 5D Self "good" and your 3D self "bad" – and then attempt a program of "getting rid" of this 3D thing that's kept you from lasting happiness. This approach is based on a false understanding of the truth – and furthermore it simply doesn't work. This kind of polarization simply indicates that one part of your 3D self is trying to get rid of another part of that self that it doesn't like.

The 3D self is not inherently bad. It just is what it is. The problem is you have simply given it too much power; you have imagined it to be who you are. So the answer is not to attempt to be rid of it. It is simply to see it clearly for what it is, see its inherent illusory nature. In doing this, you can experience your identification with it begin to dissipate and disappear – and your sense of identity shift more and more into 5D Consciousness.

The Next Step

As you can see, the step described in this chapter – having direct experiences of your 5D Self – is important. If you can directly experience this true Self and become familiar with it, you will be able to more easily trust and eventually surrender to it.

Although this process is easier to undertake if you've had at least one true glimpse of the 5D Self, having such a glimpse is not at all mandatory for starting the process of detaching your identity from your 3D self. Much can be learned and experienced by simply understanding more clearly what the 3D self is and how you can get caught into believing that that is who you are.

In fact, it may even be possible that this kind of initial understanding about your 3D self can help prepare the way for a first experience of your 5D Self. The following chapters will be helpful in guiding you to become as aware as possible of your habits of identifying with different aspects of your 3D self – and how you can let go of these identifications. In doing this, you will be making room for experiences of 5D consciousness to take firmer residence within you.

Letting Go of 3D Identification

Chapter 7

Shifting Your Identification from the Roles You Play

The first type of misidentification with the 3D self we will focus on is with the roles we play in life. Identifying with roles we play is an important part of 3D identification and a good place to start. It is also perhaps the most obvious and therefore the easiest aspect of misidentification to see and understand.

Of course, in everyday life, roles are unavoidable. They develop organically in relationship to other people. From the very beginning, each one of us was born as someone's child and perhaps as someone's sibling or grandchild. We were likely the patient of a doctor or midwife, as well. Later, we became somebody's friend, and eventually somebody's student, and on and on throughout life. As adults, we also take on roles within the work we do. Roles are simply an integral part of human life as we know it.

There is nothing inherently wrong with roles and playing them. Where the difficulty can arise is in how we become attached to these roles and in how much we identify with them. This is where we can create a great deal of unnecessary suffering for ourselves.

Rules and Expectations in Roles

First, it's important to understand that, when you're in 3D consciousness, expectations and "rules" seem to naturally go along with any role you play – both your own and those of other people around you. For example, if you are playing the role of someone's wife, your husband may have a number of expectations of you – both spoken and unspoken. Some of these expectations may be so important and believed in so strongly that he inwardly sees them as "rules" that someone in that role should obey.

For instance, even though you work a full-time job, he may expect you to be responsible for all the housework. Or he may assume that you'll act as the primary parent to your children. He may expect you to be loyal, supportive, and responsive to his needs. Or he may expect that he will make certain decisions for the two of you. These kinds of expectations, of course, can go on and on. Many of them are assumed and unexpressed between spouses, and this so often causes difficulties in a relationship.

On the other hand, what can cause just as much distress inside you are your own expectations and rules about yourself in your role as a wife. Your husband may, in fact, have very few expectations or demands on you as his wife; but for whatever reason, you may have many expectations of yourself. If you take this role very seriously and use it as your primary identity, for instance, you might have very stringent (and ultimately unachievable) expectations of yourself – like maybe believing you should always be supportive of him, always have the housework done, always pay the bills on time, never feel attracted to another man, or whatever. This is what "wife" might mean to you.

It is clearly important to be aware of the expectations you are living with as you play a role in order to avoid unrealistic or conflicting notions about what you "should" be doing. However, the important thing to understand, beyond your expectations within the roles you play, is the question of whether you are identified with them. If you are, you are likely to be distressed every time you don't live up to the rules and expectations that you believe go along with the role you are playing. Your sense of worthiness, even your whole sense of "self", can be greatly disturbed by your judgment. In fact, the degree to which you hold a role important and identify with it is precisely the degree to which you make yourself vulnerable to discomfort in the role.

I once had a client I'll call Diane who took her role as the mother of her five-year-old son Randy very seriously. It was clear she felt herself first and foremost to be a mother in life; more than anything, this was her identity. In some ways, of course, this was wonderful. Randy had a mother who deeply cared about him, and the two of them had a very close relationship.

On the other hand, I could also see that her seriousness in her role involved a great deal of attachment to it and therefore could lead to much distress for her. Sure enough, this began happening almost as soon as Randy entered school. Because of hyperactive tendencies, he was soon identified as a "problem child". Many notes from the teacher, the counselor, and the principal began to arrive home about Randy's learning problems and misbehavior. Because he also seemed incapable of making friends, he soon began resisting going to school every morning. Diane was devastated.

Of course this kind of situation can be distressing for any parent. But because Diane was so heavily and solely identified as Randy's mother, she was particularly vulnerable to this distress. Even the smallest problem with him at school threw her into deep anxiety and depression. Each time she received a new note or complaint, her entire sense of self and worthiness were profoundly threatened. Wondering how she had failed as a mother, she constantly asked what she was doing wrong. Being told that hyperactivity was a biochemical problem seemed to have no effect on her. Her attachment to being the "perfect mother" was so blinding that she could not absorb this information.

Diane probably wasn't that unusual. I think we all at times become overly attached to certain roles in our lives. They seem important and necessary for us to play, and we naturally become very involved and identified with them. And since we can't always play the roles perfectly as we think we should, we too often end up suffering.

Remembering that Roles Aren't Who You Are

So how to solve this dilemma? How can you play the roles that are necessary in life without causing this type of distress? The answer, of course, is to remember that these are roles you're playing, not who you really are. This idea is probably not new for you. Perhaps you've even found help in dealing with problems in a certain role by using this understanding. But if you are still suffering within that role, even just occasionally, perhaps your understanding is simply intellectual and not a deep enough or direct experience of knowing it.

The best way to truly *realize* that you're not the role is through fully experiencing your true identity as a higher-dimensional Self that exists beyond the role. It's to learn how to play the role without fear or anxiety, so that your sense of self and worthiness remain intact, no matter how well you play it. It's to experience that your performance of the role has no power to threaten the core of your identity, the essence of who you are. The point, in effect, is to learn how you can be *free* while playing a role, undisturbed by it or anything you associate with it.

Detaching from your Roles

So how can you achieve this kind of freedom? Very simply, you begin detaching your identity from the roles you play in your life. To be clear, this is not just a mental exercise, in which you understand that you are not the roles you play solely on the intellectual level. What I'm referring to is something that involves a whole shift in your experience of identity.

The first step in achieving this shift is perhaps fairly obvious: to realize that you are not the role being played but the human being who is playing the role. You are, in fact, a person who plays many roles in life. And each time, after a role has been played, you can drop the costume and script that went along with that role and resume just being the person you are behind all the roles you play. You can feel free to be your "natural self".

This was brought home quite poignantly to a client of mine, a young man I'll call Josh. He had been an associate attorney in a large law firm for about a year. Like many people – and perhaps mainly men – he took his profession quite seriously, and his sense of self-worth was deeply hooked into his performance in this role.

Unfortunately, he was having a lot of difficulty at his job. He struggled constantly with feelings of not being as good at his work as other associate attorneys in the firm. He felt he wasn't being given any of the most coveted assignments and also that he was being judged unfairly by one of the partners in the firm. Because his work was so important to his sense of identity, he was suffering greatly on an ongoing basis.

After listening to his long tale of woe about this situation, I asked him, "So what else do you do in your life?". He seemed a bit taken aback by this question. I suppose he was expecting me to begin delving into the work drama he'd just spent so long describing. He paused a few moments after my question, but then he answered, "Well, not much. I sail sometimes on the weekends with friends. And I play racquet ball. Sometimes I go to concerts or plays with people."

"And when you're doing these things with friends, are you playing the attorney?"

"Well, no. I'm just having fun, relaxing."

"And what else do you do with your time outside of work?"

"Well, I spend time on some weekends with my 3-year-old daughter, Sarah." His eyes softened as he said this, and he smiled.

"And do you play attorney when you're around her?"

He laughed and said, "No. I play father – and friend. We have a lot of fun together." He became somewhat quiet.

"And how about when you're alone? What kinds of things do you do?"

"I don't know. I guess I read or watch TV. Sometimes I just sit and look out the window. I like watching the birds."

"And I don't imagine you're playing attorney at those times."

"No," he said quietly "I'm just me...I'm just someone watching birds." He began smiling. "I'm just a human being. Playing attorney – as you so quaintly put it – is just something I do for a job. It's not who I am." A sense of relief and then a deep peace settled into his face, as what he said registered within him.

This was such a simple realization for Josh and yet so powerful. He told me later that from that point on, his experience at work shifted dramatically. Just coming to the realization that behind his role of attorney he had an identity as an interesting and complex human being brought in an unprecedented sense of calm for him at work. His sense of worth in his role as attorney rose; and somehow, "coincidentally," the partners began giving him more desirable cases to work on. As obvious an insight as it had been, he had received it on such a deep experiential level that an important and actual shift happened in his life.

Most therapeutic and self-help strategies would tend to leave the matter here, figuring this is the best that can be done. (And, at the time, it was where I left it. Both Josh and I seemed satisfied that if he could accomplish just this much. If he could feel relatively free as he played the roles in this life, it was the most that could be expected.) And certainly, this kind of insight is a step above being caught in the 3D belief that your identity rests in a role.

Needing to be a "Good" Person

But if you think about it, you may realize that this approach doesn't really solve the problem, because there is still a catch involved: Even if you now believe yourself to be a human being behind all the roles you play, there's still potential suffering in this – because, usually, to feel good about yourself, you need to feel like a "good" human being. Probably much of the time you do feel you are one; you're generally kind, loving, and considerate of others – or whatever your belief system dictates you need to be in order to be considered "good" or "valuable". But what about the times you're not? What about the times your laziness or greed or selfishness or arrogance slip in? What happens then? What happens in your gut?

If you're like a lot of people, probably a deep, automatic, subtle (or maybe not so subtle) sense of distress occurs. It's generally not comfortable to feel "bad" or "unspiritual" in some way. And so you're still trapped. You are still subject to suffering, even while knowing yourself to be a human being behind the roles you play, because there are expectations – your own and those of others – about being a certain way as a human being, in order to be a "worthwhile" and "good" one. And, as we all know, it's impossible to live up to these expectations all the time.

The usual advice offered at this point is to simply let go of these kinds of expectations. You might tell yourself it's okay to make mistakes, you're only human. You can't be perfect. Or you simply need to learn how to forgive yourself. All this can be helpful, up to a point. But does this kind of self-talk ever really do it? If you're like most spiritually-oriented people, the urge toward perfection can be too insistent, too ingrained to let you "off the hook". And since perfection on this level is inherently unachievable, the suffering remains. You're stuck in 3D consciousness.

Going the Step Beyond

What is necessary is to go a step beyond trying to fix and change expectations and judgments – to a place where *there simply are no rules, expectations, or beliefs* to begin with. It's to find a place within you where you do not fall subject to disappointment, regret, unworthiness, anger, or any of the other 3D experiences that seem to go with believing yourself to be simply a human being.

This can happen when you truly realize that who you are in reality is not anything so limited as a human being. In fact, "human being" is just one more role you are playing; it's one more costume and script you've taken on. It is not who you truly are.

Becoming the Observer

A powerful way you can begin to directly experience who you are beyond the role of human beingness is to step outside yourself in your awareness and begin observing yourself in your life. As you begin to play a role, sit back in your mind and watch yourself as you go through all the activities in the role.

Then tune into a more subtle level: Begin watching the expectations you have of yourself in the role and also your response to the expectations of others. Watch the judgments that appear, the anxiety. There is no need to react to any of these feelings; just observe them. When feelings of unworthiness about the role arise, observe those. When feelings of pleasure or success arise, observe those. Observe it all.

In other words, become the audience as well as the actor or actress in this drama you call your life. Watch the whole thing: everything going on outside on the stage and everything inside the hero or heroine. Then see yourself changing into another role. Observe the new set of feelings and experience that come with this new role. Watch the entire drama that goes on in the life of this human being up there on the stage.

If you do this exercise for a while, you will soon begin to feel the relief and freedom that naturally come with being simply the observer of a play. Then, at some point, you can take it further: Try stepping back one more step and observe the observer. And ask yourself, "Who is it that is observing the observer?"

A number of years back I tried this technique as an experiment. I had made what I felt was a very serious mistake as a young psychotherapist with a client who had just begun therapy with me a short time before. Sandy had come to me originally with profound wounding around trust and abandonment issues. I was aware of this and had been attempting to keep this in mind in all my interactions with her, both in and out of session.

But one day, I had a lot of my own personal issues on my mind concerning my marriage; and inadvertently, I scheduled another client for the time when Sandy was due to come in. To make matters worse, when I first discovered this, I forgot to call Sandy or the other person ahead of time in order to reschedule one of them. Then, unbelievably, I was also unavoidably late to the appointment I'd made with both of them. When I arrived at my office, they were both sitting in my waiting room, feeling anxious and confused.

A bad situation to start with, it got even worse as I somehow managed to treat Sandy in a way that came across as uncaring. I knew I was making a mess of things, but I somehow couldn't help it. I was still in the process of dealing with my own difficult emotions on that day, and it was all I could do at times to keep on breathing. So I'm sure it was clear to Sandy that her feelings were not uppermost in my mind; and understandably, as she left my office, she felt rejected, abandoned, and hurt by me.

Feeling guilty and angry with myself – and unworthy as a therapist – I fell into deep distress about all this. Being fairly new at the profession, I was taking my role very seriously and had quite deeply attached my sense of worth and self-esteem to how well I performed in the role. Although I attempted to apologize to her later on the phone, I realized I had messed up too badly with her; she had been too fragile to be handled the way I'd treated her and she had decided to find another therapist.

Although I told myself that all therapists make mistakes, that I couldn't have known the depth of her fragility, and that I'd done the best I could under the circumstances – none of this helped. My stomach wrenched in the agony of having not only failed a client but of actually doing her more harm than good. I was feeling that, through my irresponsibility and my self-centeredness, I had failed as a therapist and even as a decent human being.

I sat at home that evening, going through the scenario in my head over and over again, attempting somehow to fix the situation. It was to no avail. Finally, in great pain, I decided to sit back and simply become the observer of this drama that was going on in my head. Somewhere I'd heard about this observer technique, and although it seemed somewhat simplistic, there appeared to be nothing else I could do at this point. I could not dislodge the knot in my stomach. I took a deep breath and inwardly created some distance from the poor woman who was agonizing over her failure, the "me" who was currently berating herself. I saw her up on a stage, writhing about in emotional pain.

I smiled as I realized that the name of this drama I was watching was called "The Great Therapeutic Fuck-Up". Becoming more and more still and detached, I watched as this woman (who was such a good actress!) continued to agonize in inner turmoil. Such guilt and shame she was feeling! My heart went out to her with compassion – and yet *I* was somehow no longer suffering. I knew this to be simply a play; it wasn't real. *I* was the one who was real, sitting here in the audience watching her. I knew at some point the play would be over (she'd either resolve her turmoil or not), and I'd simply get up and go home. As I sat there becoming more and more detached about this drama, I became extremely relaxed and calm for the first time that day.

Then suddenly I became aware that I was now in back of the one in the audience who was watching the woman on stage. Startled, I asked myself: "What's this? Who am I now?" And I realized that I was no one in particular – nobody. Simply pure Awareness – something without thoughts, without emotions. I was just there as this Awareness, watching. As this realization deepened, an incredible serenity swept through me. The woman on the stage finally became very small, insignificant, altogether unreal. The suffering about the situation was utterly gone.

But the real test came the next day, once the blissful experience had faded. Upon awakening, and on a number of occasions thereafter, I questioned how I felt about my therapeutic error with the client. To my great astonishment, I felt a clear absence of guilt and shame. Of course, what I'd done wasn't something I felt good about; I experienced a lot of compassion for Sandy. But I no longer felt bad about myself. There was just a clear knowing that I'd learned some important lessons, nothing more. I was just going to go on with my life.

I realized that the observer exercise I'd experimented with had given me great rewards indeed. More and more deeply, from that point on, I knew that I was not a therapist; this was simply a role I was playing. And I further knew on a deep experiential level that I wasn't even a person playing the role – or even someone watching the role. I was pure and simple Consciousness that was totally untouched by my drama as a therapist. Today, I would call this a glimpse of 5D consciousness. Back then, I just knew I'd tapped into something profound, something I couldn't name.

I have since shared the technique with a number of people. I've seen that it can work in any number of situations. And from my experience, if you can sincerely and persistently become the observer throughout the day, you will begin to directly experience what it is that is simply watching it all – the true essence of who you are: pure Awareness. This is a major aspect of your 5D Self. It is that which never changes, that which is never touched by anything that is going on, that which never suffers. And as this Awareness, you simply observe the drama dispassionately – and yet utterly compassionately at the same time. This is an experience of your true nature – your 5D Self – free, loving, and at peace.

***

It's therefore clear that roles in themselves are not inherently problematic. They can even be a lot of fun to play. You can be very present and involved in these roles; and at the same time, you can sit and watch the show and really enjoy yourself. You just have to stay alert to the fact that you are not the roles you are playing. Nor are you the human being who is playing the roles; this is just another role. What you are is pure Consciousness, pure Light/Love, temporarily taking on all these roles.

Chapter 8

Shifting Your Identification from Your Body

Perhaps the next most obvious identification you can attach yourself to when in 3D consciousness is that with your physical body. However, before diving into how to shift your sense of identification from your body, it is important first to realize the extremely important value of this body – as, of course, without it, you would not be able to be living in physical form on Earth at this time.

The Body Elemental

Even aside from that, it's important to realize your body is not just a lump of physical flesh; it actually has an individual consciousness of its own. And, as part of you, it evolves over time through experience. Indeed, your physical body is what has been called a "Body Elemental", a specific form of consciousness created precisely as a "vehicle" for the human Consciousness to embody in, in order for consciousness to experience form. And your specific Body Elemental is the particular one you chose to be with during this incarnation, perhaps because you have been with it in other lifetimes as well.

Therefore, creating a close relationship with your body is, of course, important – as is learning to understand how, by listening to your thoughts and emotions, your body tends to follow your lead. Although your body was definitely born with certain genetic tendencies and physical characteristics that seem outside your control, you *can* learn how your positive thoughts, beliefs and emotions tend to create a healthy body, and your negative ones quite often create illness, weakness and early aging.

Another reason to stay in close touch with your body is that, during this time of Ascension – and Descension – the energies of your 5D Self are now increasingly weaving into the energies of your physical form. An integration process is in full swing. Your body is shifting into 5D along with you.

You are Not Your Body

But it is a complicated dance. Because, at the same time, it's essential to understand that your body is not YOU – it is *with* you, it's something you *have*. This may seem obvious; but if you're honest, you'll probably realize that much of the time, especially if you are in physical or emotional distress due to how your body feels or looks, you are feeling identified with your body.

Detaching your identity from your physical body can be harder than detaching it from the roles you play in life. In fact, just bringing up the subject of detaching from the body might even cause nervousness or resistance. If you have a strong identification with your body, this idea can be threatening. Or you might feel this idea is not a good one, because you have experienced your body as a vehicle toward greater spiritual awareness. Perhaps you have spent time practicing certain types of yoga or other body-based practices; and, believing the term "detaching" to mean a denial of your body or a lack of importance of it, you are wary when encountering this term.

Again, when I speak about "detaching from the body", or when I state that "you are not the body", I am not referring to dissociating from your body or denying it in any way. As anyone who has experienced these states will attest, dissociation and denial offer very limited relief from suffering, if any at all.

When I use the term "detaching from the body", it does not refer to detaching from your awareness of the body or to seeing the body as "bad", or in any way ignoring it. Indeed, true detachment can actually enhance your awareness of your body, as well as your love for it; it can even help you to take better care of it. More importantly, what detaching from the body does is help you to detach from the emotional and mental *suffering* that identification with the body can cause.

Even without direct experience of your 5D Self, it can be understood that the body is not who you are, that it is only one very small, limited part of you. But because the identification with the physical body is so strong for most people, I generally speak in extreme terms about it not being who we are.

So, with this preamble, in hopes of easing any resistance to the notion of detaching from your body, let's now take a look at what this detaching process actually entails.

Attaining a state of detachment from the body is usually difficult because most of us have deeply-embedded conditioning that this physical form is who we are. From an early age, we've been taught that we were born, we get bigger, we get old, and then we die. As a result when asked how we are, we often report how our body is: "I'm sick", "I have a cold", "I've lost weight".

Many religions, perhaps inadvertently, also teach that we are bodies. They tell us that we *have* a soul – not that we *are* a soul. So, believing this, people go around feeling that they, as their body, have to somehow be careful and "take care of" their soul. This is all part of the 3D paradigm under which most of the world is struggling, based on the illusion that each one of us is the particular physical form we inhabit.

As becomes only too apparent, this belief that we are the body creates much suffering. This is because inherently – like all form – the body is imperfect, is subject to disease and aging, and eventually dies. And if we believe that this is who we are, then this is what we believe is happening to *us*. Our sense of well-being and our feelings of self-worth are all attached to how our body happens to look, what it is capable of doing, how healthy it happens to be, and what others may think about it.

Certainly this identification causes more distress to some than to others. Some people are fortunate enough to have been born with relatively healthy, strong and attractive bodies. But even the most fortunate have to face, from time to time, an illness in the body, injuries to it, and its eventual aging and death. So, although there are degrees of suffering involved in the identification with the body, there is always suffering of some kind, simply because the body is vulnerable to all the same laws of the universe that all other 3D forms are: injury, disease, aging and death.

Ways in Which We Suffer Due to Body Identification

There are three important ways in which identification with the body commonly causes people emotional and mental suffering: a) when their body experiences either illness or injury; b) when they don't happen to like the way their body looks; and c) when thoughts or feelings about dying arise.

Like most people, you may tend to numb yourself as best you can to distress imposed on you by your belief that you are your body. Feeling somehow that this distress is inevitable and that nothing can be done about it, you may do whatever you can to push it out of your conscious mind. But, if you're aware, you'll find that the distress is nonetheless there, always nibbling away at your awareness in some way or another, and often affecting many of your actions and attitudes in life.

You have probably discovered that there are times when you can no longer avoid suffering around your physical body, and you seek relief from it through medical services, alternative healing practices or self-help approaches. These approaches tend to include either changing the body itself in some way, changing the beliefs about the body, or accepting the body the way it is. All these approaches can provide some relief. However, you may have found that such results are all ultimately limited.

Altering the Body Itself

For example, the first approach – altering the body itself – can have certain favorable results. Certainly when you're ill and you find a cure, there can be considerable relief in experiencing better health – at least for a while, until the next illness or injury occurs.

And, if you manage to successfully alter your body by changing it in some way to look more to your liking, this can also help you feel better about yourself. After you've dieted and exercised to lose weight or if, by chance, you've had some sort of plastic surgery, you probably feel happier, at least for a time.

But you've probably discovered that this relief is often sorely limited. Even if you have managed to greatly alter your body, if you're like most people, you have likely continued judging what you look like; you have probably found you are never quite satisfied with what has changed. You can never quite reach the perfection you want and are keeping track of what more can be done. It can be a painful process.

I once knew a woman like this who had nine different plastic surgery procedures done to her poor body. I personally did not find her body all that unattractive to begin with, but she certainly did. And, over and over again, after each surgery, she would come home feeling pleased with herself. With each procedure, she felt she was coming closer to "perfection". But she could never reach the perfect state. Even after nine procedures, she still felt a sense of dissatisfaction with how she looked.

She finally had to cease the operations because doctors told her they were seriously threatening her health. Unfortunately, she never saw the meaninglessness of what she'd been doing. She was left believing that, had she been able to continue altering her body's appearance, she would have finally achieved true happiness.

This isn't to say that you should never seek to change your body in any way. Of course not – dieting, exercising and even plastic surgery can often produce a sense of well-being and increased self-esteem. The point is that if you hope these kinds of changes will end the suffering around how you feel about your body, you will be sorely disappointed. This is because physically changing your body does not strike at the root of the suffering. It only touches the symptom.

Changing your Beliefs about your Body

The second approach, changing your beliefs, may be another healing method you have attempted. It is a typical healing approach that has especially become popular since humanity entered the Fourth Dimension. If so, you've likely felt some relief with this method as well. For example, if you were unhappy about how your body looked, you might have attempted to develop new beliefs about what makes a body "attractive", so that your body might eventually look more appealing to you. Or, realizing you've been misjudging how you look, you might have tried to develop more accurate beliefs about what your body actually does look like.

If you are suffering from ill health, this belief-changing approach might encourage you to develop new beliefs about how to create a healthy body. New age literature abounds with these methods, teaching basically that we create our physical health through our mental beliefs and our emotions.

This approach is perhaps more effective for many problems than the first approach of changing the body itself. It can bring significant relief by helping to turn a negative outlook on the body into a more positive one. It can even create better health. But the important contribution of these belief-changing teachings is the positive and therefore happier attitude you can adopt while your body is handling a serious disease.

However, as effective as this belief-changing method can be for relieving suffering, you may have found that it, too, is ultimately quite limited in its success rate. This may be partially due to the fact that you have tried to make these changes too late in life. Your beliefs (many of them unconscious, to boot) are simply too deeply ingrained. The work involved can therefore be discouragingly gargantuan and apparently endless.

But your low success rate may also be due to the fact that all you are doing with this approach is replacing one belief for another. Unfortunately, beliefs are only that – something you *believe* in – not something you *know*. They are not a true, direct understanding of Truth. So long as you simply believe something to be so, you will likely never experience the continuous serenity or the lack of fear you long for in life.

This is because beliefs, no matter how close to the Truth they may be, are constantly challenged by other beliefs you have, by beliefs other people have, and by your experiences in life that seem to contradict them. Simply replacing them with other beliefs is therefore ultimately ineffective in bringing lasting relief from suffering. Only true knowing of who you are can give you this.

Accepting your Body as it Is

The third common approach to relieve emotional and mental suffering around issues with the body – learning to accept the body just as it is – is perhaps the most effective for some people. This is especially true if they are facing a serious illness or the approach of death. But this is only so if true acceptance of the body, rather than a passive, depressed resignation to fate, is adopted as a wise and realistic approach to life.

Unfortunately, I have encountered this resignation all too often in people who have been deeply inculcated with a certain religious belief that implies that we humans are on this planet to suffer – it is what life is about. We must accept our fate or karma and have faith that some day, if we have been "good", we will experience an afterlife in which there will be no more suffering. Not only is this type of teaching frightfully depressing, it doesn't remove the suffering; all it does is attempt to explain it.

A very depressed woman, Barbara, came to see me for a healing a few years back, telling me that whenever she would just barely begin to achieve some semblance of happiness in her life, an automatic sense of fear and doubt would immediately take over. In exploring this with her, we discovered that, as an ex-Catholic, she was dealing with a deeply-rooted belief that the nature of life was suffering. In fact, she realized that, in her ingrained subconscious belief system, suffering was actually seen as a good thing; the more you suffered, the better a person you were and the more likely you were to go to Heaven after death. Her fear was that if she were to stop suffering, she would somehow cease to be a "good person" and might ruin her chances for Heaven.

I think we all probably know "recovering" Catholics who suffer from this unfortunate delusion. Of course, Catholicism doesn't have a patent on this belief system or its ensuing suffering. Other religions can lay claim to it as well.

Clearly, a passive, resigned acceptance of suffering does not give us relief from it. But even the most realistic and uplifting acceptance of what-is can ultimately be ineffective as well. If we still experience ourselves primarily as the body, then unavoidable suffering can still occur, simply because the body is imperfect and impermanent.

I think few people can truly be at peace with the body's inherent imperfections and impermanence if they believe that this body is essentially who they are. They somehow need to experience, beyond belief, beyond doubt, that they are that which is untouched by any illness or by death. This need seems to be natural; it may arise from the deep intuitive knowing we all have that, in truth, we *are* that which is beyond the touch of mortality.

So how can this intuitive knowing be reached? And how can the seemingly inevitable suffering due to identification with the body truly be resolved? As you've probably surmised by now, the answer is in somehow detaching from sole identification with your body. It's in realizing that your body is a manifestation of form you created to give you the ability to be part of the material world in 3D reality. And, although it is important to fully embody yourself in it, it is *temporary*. You are the eternal space, the field of luminous Light, your body fits into.

If you can truly know that who you are is this Light – something that is totally untouched by how your body looks, feels, acts, or survives – only then can emotional and mental suffering about the body truly cease.

In the next three chapters, we will look more closely at the basic ways in which you may tend to cause suffering for yourself due to your identification with your body, and then specifically at how you can begin dissolving this common 3D identification.

Chapter 9

Living Free with Health Issues

For some of us, the Ascension process seems to demand, at least for a while, that we experience a great amount of discomfort in our physical bodies. The reasons may vary, but it seems as if this experience is necessary for a full awakening into 5D consciousness. Sometimes, it is just a matter of a completing either the personal or ancestral karma we've brought in from the past. Other times, an illness or injury may serve to awaken us to the greater reality of who we are – and, in particular, to the experience that we are not the physical body.

If you are dealing with either a serious disease or an injury, you have undoubtedly experienced some form of fear, anger, or depression. This is only natural. But what you can realize is that these emotional reactions can be all the more severe, if you have your identity deeply attached to your body.

In some ways, these reactions to serious illness and injury to the body are caused by certain values that seem profoundly embedded in society. As the dozens of websites and magazines on health and fitness published today attest to, our culture seems to worship the healthy body. Allopathic medicine – perhaps still the most highly-revered "god" in Western society, despite the egregious flaws so many are now seeing about this institution – promotes this worship. Its main goal appears to be keeping the body alive and as healthy as it can for as long as possible – as if this alone assures the quality of life everyone wants.

There also seems to be an extraordinary emphasis on strength and fitness. Of course, making this important in life can be helpful; it feels good to have a strong and fit body. It enables us to enjoy life in many ways. But so often, the preoccupation with fitness seems overdone. In fact, the extreme emphasis on both health and fitness can at times do much damage.

The worst problem may be that it ignores, and actually denies, the fact that bodies are not designed to be perfect. They're part of the 3D material world, subject to illness, injury and eventual death. And some bodies are genetically more vulnerable to disease than others. No one can successfully avoid these realities. And yet, living amidst the tremendous emphasis in our culture on health and fitness, it's hard not to feel pressure to keep our body constantly healthy and fit at all costs. If we don't manage this, it is often assumed that something is flawed or deficient about us.

To make matters worse, new age literature on healing has unfortunately added even more pressure on people. Although teachings on how we create illness through our thoughts, beliefs and emotions can be helpful, they can also cause a sense of guilt and shame in someone whose body becomes ill or injured.

Furthermore, what is usually forgotten in this common interpretation of the "mind-body connection" is that it works the other way around as well: the body also appears to have some control over what is happening in the mind. This is supported by the number of mental and emotional illnesses that seem to disappear almost magically when people start taking antidepressants, hormones, lithium, or thyroid medication, all of which alter the body's chemistry.

Something else seems to be missing in much of the new age literature concerning healing the body through the mind. It is the fact that many, many people, who ardently and assiduously apply the principles involved, simply do not succeed in healing their bodies, and they often end up feeling they have "failed" in healing their bodies. It's assumed that somehow they just aren't "spiritual" enough to make the principles work. If you have experienced this, you likely know how painful this can be.

It seems clear that something else is definitely at play here. It can be argued that the people who fail to heal their bodies just haven't used the metaphysical principles well enough or long enough. But it does seem somehow that a force is at work, overriding anything the mind may set out to do.

Some might explain that it's just karma and the suffering must be endured. Another explanation sometimes offered is that the person who has been unsuccessful in healing their body through metaphysical principles is suffering because this is what Spirit has deemed to be best to help bring about a spiritual awakening. This idea can seem to have some merit, because people who have undergone serious injuries and illness do sometimes make considerable positive changes in their lives. Their relationships with loved ones are sometimes healed. And, at times, remarkable spiritual awakening may even occur.

However, if you keep in mind the information discussed in Chapter 2 about the beings often referred to as the Archons and their devious control over humanity, you must question any religious or new age teaching that essentially states that suffering has a positive purpose. Remember about the primary implant containing AI technology that creates guilt and shame – and how these beings actually feed off of human suffering.

And then, of course, there is also the ever-increasing evidence that the so-called covid "vaccines" are actually creating disease and even causing death in people who have taken it, and all this is still being denied by the majority of doctors who continue to insist the vaccine will prevent covid. Add this whole mess to the mix, and all metaphysical principles probably cannot be relied upon.

If anything, people who are able to make positive changes in their lives and in their relationships, despite the physical and emotional suffering they are experiencing, are a testament to the magnificence of the human spirit. They express the spiritual power that is inherent in this species of beings we call humanity. I know it can be difficult to let go of spiritual teachings you've trusted for so long and accept this possible explanation. If it is, then for now simply put this information "on the table for further evidence".

Whatever the reasons may be for the illnesses or injuries people experience, and whatever the reasons are for why they can't recover from them no matter what they do, the fact remains that physical bodies do get sick and can be injured. It's a natural phenomenon while living in 3D. It's important to see the emotional suffering we can experience by ignoring this fact and accepting the pressure society seems to put on us about the inherent superiority of healthy, fit bodies.

Freeing Yourself from Identification with your Body

Even more important, however, is to understand what lies beneath the extreme emphasis on health and fitness: a belief system based in fear – fear that an ill or injured body means an ill or injured identity, a deficient or flawed self. If you have undergone serious physical illness or injury and you relate to any of this, what is important is to focus on how you can let go of this belief system so that, no matter what state of health or fitness your body happens to be in, you are free simply to be as you are and feel good about yourself.

Before discussing how to do this, however, I'd like to make clear what I mean when I speak of "suffering" in terms of the physical body. I am *not* referring to physical pain. Physical pain seems to be a fact of life while we're in 3D bodies. There seems little way to get around it (although even this pain, as I will describe later, can become much more manageable if the psychological suffering is not added to it). What I mean by "suffering" is the psychological suffering – both emotional and mental – that we commonly add to the physical pain. This is something you can definitely eliminate from your life. You can discover, in fact, that it is utterly unnecessary.

So, with this distinction made, let's turn now to how this suffering can be alleviated. It is, of course, through learning how to detach your identity from your body.

Surrendering to the Pain

Much research has been done on bodily pain and how people can increase and/or decrease it. The results of this research show quite consistently that the more people resist and fight the pain, the worse it becomes. And conversely, the more they accept and relax into it, the weaker the pain becomes.

A good friend of mine can personally attest to this. Over a number of years, she had experienced bouts of intensely painful colitis with which no health practitioner or doctor had ever been totally successful in helping her. For years, especially after she learned that her father was dying of colon cancer, she would enter into fear and anger whenever she would begin to experience intestinal pain. As she entered more and more deeply into her fearful and angry thoughts about what might happen to her, the pain would continue to deepen. The worst was when she'd begin projecting into the future about it. What if she never got over it? What if she ended up in the hospital? Sometimes she'd go into guilt, regret or shame about it: How did she cause it? If only she'd done something about it earlier, and on and on.

One afternoon, as she lay in bed in great pain, thinking these thoughts, she finally began seeing the craziness she was creating in her mind – all stemming from fear and from resistance to simply what was. She decided that rather than fighting the pain, for a change, she would just accept it. Somehow, she realized that this whole experience was something that her Ascension path was demanding at the time, that there was something to learn and hopefully release. Much to her relief, the pain immediately began to recede.

Some time later, when she was experiencing another bout of the same pain, she decided to try to go even further with the act of acceptance. Rather than simply allowing the pain to be and refraining from thinking about the possible dire scenarios concerning her condition, she decided to actually *surrender* to the pain – just give herself to it completely. She not only stopped resisting it, fighting it, and attempting to change it – she focused on taking a deep breath and fully relaxing into it.

What an incredible experience that was! Not only did she experience less pain and a much needed sense of relaxation, an unexpected peace and bliss also began washing through her as well. As she lay in bed, still very aware of the pain in her abdomen, she was soon floating in a cloud of gentle and detached awareness, serenely watching herself. Although the pain continued, she was actually luxuriating in a total state of surrender.

She was no longer emotionally suffering because of the pain; it was simply something vaguely present within her awareness that she could focus on if she chose to – or not. She said that this experience lasted for almost an hour – at which point, totally at peace with the fact that she was once again undergoing the dreaded intestinal pain she had suffered from for so many years, she finally fell asleep.

Since that experience, she has actually learned to *embrace* pain in her body when it appears. The discovery she has made is that her resistance to pain not only increases the pain itself, it also keeps her attached to her sense of identity with her body. And acceptance of her pain and illness, surrendering to it and actually embracing it, help her to detach from this identification.

At times, she still experiences mild symptoms of colitis, but much more seldom. She is clear that her whole experience with the disease was brought to her as part of her Ascension journey, a learning situation, and is grateful for it. And she's come to experience a great deal more compassion for her body whenever it is experiencing pain.

Having Compassion for Your Body

This brings us to another method that can assist you in detaching your identification from your body when you find yourself ill or suffering from an injury: to focus on developing a strong compassion for your body in its pain. You can become aware that this poor entity, your body, is struggling valiantly to heal itself from some terrible insult that's been thrust on it. What it most needs from you at these times – besides help from appropriate outer sources – is love, support and compassion.

Although understanding this intellectually, it can be hard to actually experience compassion for your body when it is in pain. Your fear and anger at the suffering it is causing you can be too powerful. But there is something that can enormously facilitate your moving into compassion. This, again, involves taking the time to mentally step outside your body and see it objectively.

I was once suffering from a severe headache I'd had for several days. No matter what I did or what I took to clear the headache, it kept getting worse;

it would not let go. I found myself getting more and more irritated and fearful that maybe something might really be wrong with me.

After a spell of tearful frustration, I finally let go for a moment and gave up in despair. Suddenly, I found myself standing outside myself in my awareness, looking at my body. My poor head! I could see it was throbbing in agony. My response to it at this point was one I might have in seeing a puppy in pain. My heart immediately reached out to it and enfolded it in love. I felt so bad about how I'd been treating my head, adding all my negative emotions to the pain it was already feeling. I sat there in my mind's eye, holding and stroking my head, just pouring love into it.

Giving my head this soft, gentle healing energy instead of anger and fear, of course, helped it to finally relax and eventually let go of the headache. It was obvious to me afterwards that my callous treatment of my headache had only made it worse. Compassion for my body as a living being in pain made all the difference.

But what really struck me was how the experience of standing outside my body had made this realization so clear. It had served to remind me that I wasn't my headache or even my head. Who I truly was, my real Self, was untouched by the headache. It was as if the headache were actually happening to someone else. It had nothing to do with me and so could not affect my sense of myself or my well-being. I was therefore free to give true comfort and healing energy to it.

Dealing with Severe or Chronic Illness and Pain

I realize that the techniques I have described here – surrendering to the pain and having compassion for your body – may seem helpful for minor illnesses or pain; but, you may be asking, "What about when you are confronted with truly severe pain or an ongoing illness?". In these cases, the feat of fully detaching your identification from the body can seem insurmountable. Pain does seem to anchor us into the body. But detaching from it *is* possible; and, in the end, severe or chronic pain can actually be seen as our ally in this process.

I had a friend who had been suffering from chronic fatigue syndrome for over eight years. If you have ever known anyone with this disease – or others like it – you know just how debilitating it can be. It not only causes great ongoing distress in the body, it also interferes with a person's entire life. Often someone with the disease cannot even work. And, of course, any social life or pleasurable activities they once enjoyed eventually disappear from their lives. They have no energy to do much of anything but sleep or lie exhausted in bed. I heard about one person who actually decided after five years of this kind of life that it wasn't worth living – and she committed suicide.

My friend Karen certainly had come close to doing just that on a number of occasions. Throughout some of the years she had the disease, she had been able to keep a therapy practice going, but just barely. It was about all she could do. Frequently, much to the irritation of her clients, she had to cancel appointments – sometimes at the last moment. Eventually, she was unable to work at all.

Throughout the years, Karen had sought help from every source she heard about. Help from the medical profession gave out quickly. She then turned to every sort of alternative healing source she could find. At times, it looked hopeful; she would find some relief and feel that she had finally found something that would help her to heal. But always, after a time, it would become apparent that the healing was only temporary – or illusory. She wasn't really getting any better.

For the first six years or so of this dreadful experience, Karen's attitude toward her illness was filled with frustration, fear and depression. It was also laced with great self-doubt and despair. She wondered what terrible thing had she done to "deserve" this. Why had God abandoned or punished her? The many years she'd spent on a spiritual path seemed to offer her nothing that could give her any real solace.

Then there came a time when she was rather seriously considering suicide; she was feeling the most depressed and desperate she'd ever felt. As often happens at such times, a "miracle" occurred; she came across a book about the spiritual teachings of surrender. With great joy, she latched onto something in this book that she now sees as the life raft that has kept her afloat on the planet to this day. The teachings were about how surrender can assist in the discovery of the true Self.

Since then, she has also become involved in teachings about the Fifth Dimension and realizes she is now slipping in and out of 5D consciousness more and more as time goes on. She increasingly knows on an experiential level that she is not her physical body. And this has given her the opportunity to be all the more compassionate with her body and with her emotional self.

Life, of course, can still be very challenging for her. She has days that are still difficult for her to stay in the light of 5D consciousness. But she is much more at peace with what occurs. And she now has endless love and compassion for others in pain. As she says, she has given her life into the hands of the Beloved, trusting that whatever is happening to her is in her best interests. I have never known her to be so at peace with herself.

Karen, to me, is a living testament to the power of surrender in one's life. Her body may never recover from chronic fatigue – or it may. What is important is that it no longer really matters to her. All she lives for now is the joy she experiences in the process of surrendering her will to that of her 5D Self.

Thus it seems that even chronic and severe illness need not stand in the way of detaching our identity from our body and from the psychological suffering this misidentification can produce. In fact, the impetus and motivation of severe difficulties with our physical bodies can actually assist us in shifting into 5D consciousness. Surrender and trust in the Ascension process seem to be the key.

Chapter 10

When You don't Like your Body Image

A second way in which body-identification can bring great distress is if you don't happen to like how your body looks. This can happen in early childhood when you discover that people prefer physically-attractive features you don't happen to possess, and it can also happen when you discover your body is showing signs of aging. And, of course, at any other time in between when you feel uncomfortable with how your body is looking.

You may be fortunate enough to like the way your body looks and not experience much of this kind of distress. But most people seem to have at least some reservations about their body's appearance and suffer as a result of their judgments.

Most cultures these days not only worship the healthy and fit body, but also the beautiful and youthful one. There exists enormous pressure to have as beautiful and youthful a body as possible – especially if you are a woman. Even those who have what are considered "beautiful" bodies may experience displeasure with or criticism of their body's appearance because even these people must eventually experience the process of aging.

In fact, it is sometimes even harder for people who had a beautiful body in their youth to undergo the inevitable process of aging. Often, having deeply invested their sense of identity and their feeling of self-worth in their body, when the aging process becomes apparent, they are particularly vulnerable to deep distress. We are all familiar with the stereotype of the pathetic aging starlet who feels her life is over now that her body is no longer considered beautiful. Plastic surgery can only do so much.

The process of aging in the culture of America and other first-world countries in particular is even more difficult than it is in many others across the world. There is no automatic respect given to someone of advanced age as there often is in other cultures. At best, a sort of patronizing pity is bestowed upon elderly individuals in our society; at worst, a dismissal, an ignoring, or even an abusive attitude. Underlying all this, there seems to exist an attitude that the aging body is something undesirable and repulsive. Revealing this attitude are the many jokes about women with aging bodies.

These attitudes and the inevitable distress they cause would not be so prevalent – or indeed, might not even exist – if so many people were not so completely identified with their bodies. Their sense of self-worth and identity would not be dependent on what their bodies happened to look like. But as it is, most people, especially in our culture, do see themselves as bodies, and so this suffering continues.

You may know well that you are not your body; you know yourself to be a Soul or Spirit inside your body. But how often do you forget this – especially when you have a bad hair day or note that you've gained weight again and can't get into your favorite jeans? Body identification can be extremely ingrained.

If you are still distressed from time to time due to how your body happens to look, this probably indicates that your "knowing" that you are not the body is still simply intellectual. Knowing something with your mind is an important start, but for the identification with the 5D Self to truly occur, a more direct and deeply experiential understanding must take place.

Releasing Judgments about Your Body Image

One of the things that can keep you hooked into believing yourself to be your body is your judgments about it. Negativity about anything always serves to keep us in bondage to the very thing we are negative about. So a first step toward freedom from body-identity is to do what you can to release whatever negative judgments you may have about your body. The following is a technique you can use to do this.

Exercise: *Releasing Negative Judgments about Your Body*

1. **Write out your judgments.** Write down all the judgments you have about your body. Include all negative thoughts and feelings and also any negative messages about your body you can remember that were given to you by others during your life, including those in childhood or adolescence.

2. **Draw your body.** On a large piece of paper, draw a picture of your body (preferably undressed). With words written directly on the drawing, write down the negative thoughts, feelings and judgments you have about

the different parts of your body. Include all aches, pains, and injuries your body is currently handling. Also write what your body is saying about itself.

3. **Feel the pain of judgment.** Sit and look at your drawing, allowing this representation of your negative attitudes toward your body to sink in. Feel the pain that your judgments cause you. Feel your body's sorrow in response to them. Become aware of something obvious but usually forgotten: your body is doing the very best it can. All it knows is how to be the way it naturally is. Heaping judgment and shame onto it for how it looks or feels accomplishes nothing but suffering. Realize the pointlessness of your judgments of your body.

At this point, I offer a caution: As you become aware of the suffering you have been causing yourself through your judgments, be careful not to progress further into guilt and shame about these judgments. This is another aspect of what I call "New-Age Neurosis": feeling guilty about feeling guilty or ashamed of feeling ashamed. Simply mentally note the feelings and insights and let them be.

4. **Burn your drawing.** If there is a way at this point to safely light a fire and put your drawing into it, do this. Rituals of this sort can be very helpful for releasing feelings, thoughts, and judgments. Watch the drawing disappear into the flames and feel all your judgments, negative thoughts, feelings, and memories disappear along with it. If building a fire is not safe, tearing the drawing up into tiny pieces and throwing them into the trash can also work.

5. **Relax and love your body.** Now close your eyes and become aware of what your body is feeling. If there are parts of your body that are not relaxed, gently focus your attention there and coax them into relaxation. Tune into your love for your body. Become aware of all it has done for you, all that it has survived – often without your help. Feel gratitude about this.

6. **Write a love letter.** Finally, write a love letter to your body. Include your gratitude to it for keeping going at all costs during your life. Tell your body all the things you do like and love about it. Give it positive love messages. Thank it for all the pleasures it has given you. Let it know that you are going to try to be more accepting of it and allow it to be simply the way it is.

After you have written this letter, sit with it and allow what you have said and your commitments to sink in. Allow yourself a sense of trust about your body, accepting that perhaps you have the body that is perfect for you at this time.

Detaching from Identifying with your Body

The next step, then, is to become truly aware that your body is not who you are. Although it is important to fully embody it during this time of Ascension, see if you can remember that it is simply a vehicle you are using in order to experience the material 3D world. There is no reason to feel ashamed or proud of how it looks or functions, no reason to feel anything about the process of aging that is taking place. This is just a natural process of all 3D form. You are not "to blame" in any way. It means nothing about YOU.

Completing an exercise such as the one outlined above can be helpful in releasing the distress caused through judgments and negative feelings and thoughts about your body. It may even be a necessary first step in releasing the suffering since negativity toward something tends to keep you attached to it.

However, these kinds of exercises are sometimes not enough. The 3D conditioning that we humans are our bodies is usually so powerful and ingrained that a further step must be taken. Once again, this involves doing whatever you can to truly experience a sense of detachment from your identification with your body. The following two exercises may be useful in doing this.

Exercise: *Observing Your Body*

The first is an exercise you can actually have some fun with. It involves, once again, standing outside your physical form in your awareness and watching yourself in everything you do.

In your mind, stand or sit right next to your body during all of its activities and observe it. Become aware of everything this fascinating thing – your body – is doing. Watch your hands (such amazing instruments!) in all their various activities. Watch your legs, your feet, your stomach – all the different parts of the body you can see. Then, in your mind's eye, watch your head and your face. Become aware of what a complex, fascinating vehicle and tool your body actually is.

Now become aware simultaneously about what is going on inside of this body on the physical level. Blood runs through every part of it, all on its own. Food digests automatically. Your lungs breathe without any help from you. So much is happening inside this form; it's totally mind-boggling! Absorb the mystery of all this. Your body is wondrous, indeed.

Once all this has been experienced, begin to be aware of what is going on in the mind inside this body. Watch the thoughts and feelings as they pass through. Also observe your body's reactions to these thoughts and feelings. Be aware of all the passing sensations that are occurring within this marvelous machine.

Although it is obviously easier at certain times more than others, this exercise can be done at almost any time, during any activity or non-activity. The times when your body is engaged in interesting activities, such as eating or moving in some way, can be the most fun, but it can be equally interesting when you are performing mundane everyday rituals, such as showering or driving a car. You may be struck with wonder: How does your body know how to do all this?

During this process of observing everything your body is involved in from the outside, from time to time, also reflect on who *you* are – the consciousness watching all this. Although you may have the sensation of being outside your body, you will still have the awareness of being inside your body as well. This can help you to realize that who you are has no specific location; you are both inside and outside your body. In fact, if you really check, you may experience that you have no boundaries at all, that there is no outline where you end and the air begins.

After doing this exercise for a while, a greater and greater appreciation for your body may begin forming in you. Seeing it so objectively can assist you in releasing both judgments about your body and your identification with it. It becomes a wondrous form you are simply playing with as you explore the world of 3D physicality.

Exercise: *All Bodies are an Expression of the One Self*

Another focus you can have as you step outside your body is to look around at all the other bodies around you. Take in the infinite variety of them. Experience the marvel of how Consciousness can appear in so many different shapes and forms. See the unique beauty of each one. Observe them as if you were someone from another universe. Then look back at your own body and see that this is just one of many forms – one with its own unique attributes. Suspend all judgment about any of the attributes – just observe them.

Now realize that, in one way, every one of these bodies is an aspect of YOU. As pure Consciousness, who you are includes *all* bodies. You are also the space within which they all appear. You are all that exists; everything is YOU. You are the Source of all these forms.

I once knew a man who was anxiously intent on keeping his body in shape, mainly through running. Jonathan felt that, in order to keep the body image with which he was happy, he needed to run. He was in his mid-forties and beginning to put on weight, and this was unacceptable to him. So, almost religiously, he made it a priority to take time to run every day.

One day, I happened to pass him on the street as he was coming to the end of his running for the day. I was amazed at the elation on his face. His whole being seemed to emanate an ecstatic joy, and I was curious about what was going on with him. I knew that running can produce a kind of high for people, but what I saw on his face seemed quite beyond an endorphin high.

After he caught his breath, he told me what he had just experienced. He said that running had started out that day pretty much as usual: He ran along the same streets and pathways, seeing much the same scenery as he always did. He maintained his usual inner sense about his breathing, his pulse, and his leg muscles.

Suddenly, out of the blue, he felt a strange sensation. He surprisingly found his awareness outside of his body. He explained that this was not like astral travel in which you find yourself completely separated from your physical body; he was simply outside his body in his awareness. He was aware of his body from the outside of it, not just the inside. He could see his legs moving, one after the other. He could see one shoe and then the other. His arms were also alternating, moving forward and backward. He could also somehow see his breath. All this, understandably, considerably changed his experience of running. He was not only the runner; he was also the observer of the runner.

Then, he explained, something else began occurring. He found himself looking around at all the other bodies he was passing. Some of them were also running, some were walking; others were standing or sitting. Although every body had similar characteristics – arms, legs, head – they were all so different. He found himself marveling at the variety of these things we call "bodies".

At some point, he said, he "dropped into a whole different dimension". No longer was he seeing all of the bodies as different from each other – they all became obviously one and the same thing. All bodies, including his own, were made of the same ineffable essence. And, the truly amazing thing, he said, was that he realized that this essence was, in reality, himself. There was nothing else that existed. There was only the One Essence of Life. Indescribable joy rushed through him with this realization.

He told me he floated along in this ecstasy for the full half-hour that was left of his run. He continued to be aware of his body as it moved, but it was like watching it from a distance. He was no longer confined to feeling his awareness inside his body. He could be present in that experience if he wanted – at times, of course, it could be totally pleasurable – but he was no longer limited to that one experience. He could be inside all bodies at once – or outside of them – or nowhere in particular. It didn't matter. He was free to simply be conscious awareness.

He told me some time later that his experience of running after that – and indeed, of doing almost anything – had totally altered. He had come to know on a profound, experiential level that he was not his body. I believe he continued to run as much as before – but his anxiety about his body image had greatly diminished. "My body's getting a little flabby," he said. "So what. That's what bodies do." It seemed that, because he'd experienced on a direct level that this was not who he really was, he'd come to accept the inevitable aging of his 3D human form.

Chapter 11

Facing the Fear of Death

Even prior to the advent of the covid pandemic in 2020, the fear of death had been plaguing humanity for millennia. But, with this new reality of death hitting the planet, the fear of it has naturally entered into the collective consciousness more strongly than ever.

Indeed, since most people are not very aware, if at all, of who they really are – their identification with the body is the norm. And since physical bodies can die, there is a natural fear that death will mean the end of their entire existence. For this reason, people have generally attempted to alleviate this fear in a number of ways.

Dealing with Death through Denial

Perhaps the most common way people tend to deal with their fear of death is through denial – denial that death even exists. Although things have certainly changed in the last two years, it's probably safe to assume this is still true. By and large, death is still something that is not much spoken about. It is neatly hidden away in back wards of hospitals and retirement homes. It is carefully pushed out of sight so that people can avoid experiencing it in their everyday lives. In fact, people who do dwell on death at all or who want to talk about it are often considered "unstable" or unduly "morbid".

Of course, no matter how much denial is practiced about the reality of death, or how many methods we might seek out to help us deal with our fears about it, sooner or later we all have to face it. We have to face the fact that our physical form was born and is going to die; and, as a matter of fact, it started dying as soon as it was born. This is the nature of 3D matter. At least, this is true at this time; once ascending into higher dimensions, this will not be the case. But until that time, we are all still faced with the seeming inevitability of eventual physical death.

The good news is that, if we choose, we all have the opportunity to face death before it actually happens. And, if we are so blessed, we may even discover what it is that does NOT die when the death of the physical body occurs. If we are smart enough to take this opportunity whenever it presents itself, we can go through the rest of our lives never fearing death again.

Turning to Religion

Another way people generally deal with their fear of death is to turn to religion. Evidently, since 2020, many have done this. It's understandable, when so much in our lives is falling apart. Especially when faced with either the death of loved ones or the specter of personal death, religion for many has provided some spiritual support.

Most religions strive to address the fear of death by telling us that we have a soul that lives on after the death of the body. This information is probably helpful for some people. But unfortunately, even those who very badly want to believe this can still suffer from uncertainty. This belief requires faith that a soul and an afterlife exist, and some people just are not convinced of this. They want proof; they want to know beyond a doubt. As noted before, faith and belief are not true knowing.

Furthermore, many religions add an important adjunct to this teaching that counteracts much of the solace they could bring. First, they generally tell us that we *have* a soul – not that we *are* one. And then they often add that our soul will only go to a better place if we're "good"; otherwise, it might go to some penitential abode state like purgatory or, even worse, an eternity of punishment in hell.

You likely know ex-Catholics who grew up being taught about heaven and hell but have eventually been able to drop this belief. Some of these are successful in freeing themselves in this way. But many find at some point later in life that, underneath their intellectual overlay of disbelief in such things, the fear about death and hell is still in their subconscious minds, sometimes quite active and alive. Even those who grow up practicing Eastern religions often do not feel good about what death might mean for them. Although more compassionate, these religions also teach that we are imperfect and have to reincarnate over and over again, until we learn our "lessons" and balance our karma.

New Age Teachings about Death

Those of us who have studied new age teachings have been fortunate in certain ways, in that these doctrines tend to be much more positive and embracing of our true spiritual identity. However, as described earlier, although we may generally learn from them that we are divine Beings, there is usually still a subtle message in many of them that there is something inherently wrong with us. We have to keep incarnating over and over again to improve ourselves.

In addition, many of the teachings speak about the death space as a wonderful place where Souls are received in great love and given much needed comfort; they don't truly understand it to be a space very cleverly created and run by the Archons in order to keep humans captive to the Karmic Wheel. Nor are they up to date about the fact that, during these times of Ascension in the Fourth Dimension, this whole space in which afterlife has previously taken place is currently collapsing.

Even aside from this, when it comes down to it, until someone is actually dying, they really never know how firm their belief is about any ongoing existence after the death of the body. Only at that point can they discover how much of their supposed "knowing" has simply been belief and hope. I have been surprised in this regard by a couple of friends who were in the process of dying. Both of them had been long-time spiritual seekers who firmly believed they would not experience fear when they knew they were dying. And yet, when it came down to it, fear arose in both of them at the end. It was very dismaying to see this.

Reincarnation

Perhaps you may still feel you are someone who knows for sure that you've had past lives and will live again after death. Maybe you even remember some of these lives, and this gives you confidence that who you are will not die. You know that death is only a temporary, in-between state and that you will live again.

You may even be aware that the death space in the Fourth Dimension is now collapsing and that humanity is in the process of being liberated from all hostile control – and that sometime soon, reincarnation on Earth will be voluntary. In the future, the whole experience of death will be very different. This is incredible news; it is all part of the Ascension process occurring on the planet at this point. In understanding this, it can bring great joy and a sense of freedom from the fear of death.

And yet – it's important to understand that your physical body does not likely know all this yet. It has not yet ascended out of the Third Dimension. So do your best to be aware that, even with everything you may intellectually know about the reality of death, there is probably still a sense of fear within you about it. Just knowing that death of your body isn't the death of YOU does not usually free your body from its fears about its own demise.

Resolving the Fear

As we've seen with other fears about the body, the only truly successful way to deal with them is through directly experiencing who you are beyond the body. In dealing with the fear of death, it is the same: The point is to get to know, on a direct experiential level, that that which dies is not YOU. It's having the experience that who you are is eternal, that you have never been born and therefore can never die. It's realizing that you are that which exists beyond these polarities of birth and death.

Of course, those who have near-death experiences and return have direct knowledge of the reality of life beyond death of the physical body. And those who have clear out-of-body experiences also have that advantage. But most people have never had these experiences, so it's necessary to find other ways to create the deep knowing of the eternal Self that never dies.

The exercise in the previous chapter involving stepping outside the body can be helpful in creating this direct experience of the eternal nature of yourself. But for many, this is not enough. The fear of death is simply too profound and powerful. If this is true for you, something more may be necessary.

Exercise: Plunging into the Fear

One way to experience the reality of who you are beyond death is through an inner journeying process, which can have dramatic and surprising results. The process involves directly facing a fear in the moment it arises. Rather than attempting to push the fear down, or distract yourself with other thoughts or activity, you instead find the courage to immediately focus on the fear itself and plunge directly into the core of it. You investigate what is actually there. This can be an a life-altering discovery.

The process can be a fairly quick exercise, or it can take some time, depending on the depth or complexity of the fear. I have done it myself on numerous occasions with various fears and have assisted others in doing it as well. If done with courage and sincerity, I have found it can release the fear entirely.

I once assisted a woman with the process. She had come to me with enormous fear about her own death and described how she experienced this fear as a frightening black hole inside her gut. Jane was terrified when

I first suggested the inner process to her: "You mean, just jump in there, into the middle of the black hole?" That idea had never occurred to her; she had come to me, hoping I could give her some sort of convincing philosophy about life after death. I told her I didn't think my philosophy could solve her fears. She needed to explore and directly investigate death herself. She hesitated for a few minutes, but then decided she might as well give it a try.

At first, as I tried guiding her in her imagination down into the "black hole" of fear she sensed inside her gut, she managed to dance all around the outside of it. Accustomed to dealing with her fears through her mind, she began talking once more about her thoughts and feelings about her fear of death, rather than diving into it directly. This, of course, was her mind's ploy to procrastinate. Persistently, I kept encouraging her to leave her mind behind, to stop following any thought whatsoever, and simply "jump" inside of the fear.

At last, she made the plunge. Barely breathing, she reported, "It's so dark in here. Pitch black. I'm so alone – I'm really scared. Ooh, there are bodies in here, dead bodies – yukky stuff, body parts lying around...it's awful!"

I could feel her understandable revulsion to what she was inwardly seeing and her immediate desire to retreat back from that frightening place, but I said, "That sounds really awful...I know it must be hard to want to stay in there. But see if you can just keep going. Who you are is much bigger, much more powerful than all that stuff you're seeing. Just keep dropping deeper and deeper into it – go right to the core of it."

I heard her gasp, and then immediately she nervously began analyzing her fear. Unconvinced by what I'd told her, she had somehow managed to scramble to the top of the hole and was once again engaging her mind. And once again, gently, I coaxed her to let go of her mind and dive back into the hole. After some deliberation, she finally did.

This time she told me it was just "blank" – nothing there. All gray. And that she was suddenly feeling very depressed. I reflected this back to her and then encouraged her to drop down even more deeply, this time into the core of the depression. Soon she was reporting a sense of despair. "There's just nothing here, nothing at all. I'm all alone. This is like my life – just dead grayness. I hate it. It's awful." I could feel her attempting to find her way out of this miserable despair and encouraged her to instead continue dropping further down into it. "Go to the very core of the despair and see what you find there."

A few moments later, she exclaimed "Wow, I see a wild woman screaming. She's enraged – totally enraged! God, is she wild – she's just raving. (pause) Hey, it's me! This wild woman is me! She's all my anger, all my rage about..." Before she could get caught up into the story of her rage, I reflected that she had found rage at the core of despair, and then encouraged her to keep dropping even further, now into the core of the rage.

She finally seemed to be involved deeply in the process. Her mind and its fumbling attempts to prevent her from facing her fear had been left behind. She now began reporting different things: "I'm really falling now – like down this long, dark, narrow chute. But I'm seeing these little windows – gorgeous scenery and neat little scenes with people. I see my dog and my mother...Oh! I can stop myself from falling by just holding onto the window sills..."

If we had been doing another kind of process, one that simply explores the various and often delightful recesses of the psyche, I would have encouraged her at this point to take a better look at these little scenes she was passing to see where they would take her. But I knew this would probably be a diversion – simply another way her mind had found to distract her. So I instead coaxed her to keep dropping further down the chute. Although reluctant, she finally followed my instructions. She had finally found some relief from the despair and rage she had been experiencing and wanted to stop there. But I sensed there was much more to discover.

Sure enough, within a few moments, after bypassing the delectable scenes through the windows she was passing, she found herself suddenly at the bottom of the chute. "I've landed! I'm not falling anymore...."

"So, what's happening now?"

"Oh," she moaned, as a sweet delight washed across her features. "There's this incredible light coming toward me." I let her experience this for a few moments, then asked again, "What's happening now?". I saw a tear appear in her eye and then run down her cheek. "Such beauty, such incredible beauty...someone's here with me...they're doing something to me...I don't know what, but it feels so good. (pause) There are these beings here, like angels. I think I'm being anointed or something..."

A radiance began shining from her face. I decided to allow her to linger there for perhaps another minute or two to see what would happen. Tears began running down both her cheeks. I could only guess at what she was now experiencing; she was unable to explain anything further. But I sensed that she still had not reached as far as she could go in this experience, and I once again encouraged her to go even more deeply into this experience to see what might appear.

Again, she let out a startled gasp. "Oh my God," she cried, as tears now flooded her eyes. "I'm expanding...I'm getting so big, so vast..." I could see on her face a remarkable glow beginning to form. And I could feel a warmth flowing from her. "I'm so vast, I'm everywhere...everywhere!" she whispered in awe. "I no longer have a body or anything – I'm just clear space. I'm nothing. I'm no thing at all...I'm totally free! Oh my God...oh my God...."

She could no longer speak, and I no longer wanted to interrupt this glimpse she was having into eternity and into the source of her true identity. We sat in silence for almost twenty minutes before she finally opened her eyes. She was radiant and profoundly serene. She spoke from deep within the silence in her. She said very simply, "I know who I am...I know who I am...."

I smiled and nodded. Then she exclaimed, "God, there's really nothing to be afraid of, is there?" She laughed a delightfully spontaneous and free laugh.

I laughed too, overjoyed. "Strange what you can can find in the core of your darkest fear, isn't it?" She nodded, then shook her head unbelievingly. Who would have imagined? Who would have thought this kind of bliss could be waiting for her in the very core of her fear of death? She knew then that this tremendous fear she'd found haunting her for so long was simply her eternal Self calling her Home.

I saw Jane again two weeks later. "I had a dream!" she exclaimed excitedly, as she sat down. "The same dream I've had so many times since I was a kid. Except that this time it ended differently."

"Tell me about it," I said with great interest.

"Well, it started out like it always use to: I'm in my house alone at night. I'm just sitting reading or watching TV or something, when I suddenly become aware that there's someone – or something – out on my front porch, trying to get in. It's always really scary. I'm sitting there not knowing whether my door is locked or not, but I'm too scared and frozen in my chair to get up and check. I just sit there, not being able to breathe, as I hear this thing turning the knob. Usually I wake up at this point, and it's really awful. I'm always too afraid to go back to sleep.

"But this time, it was weird. In my dream, as I was sitting there, I was scared, but then I got up and went to the door. For some reason, this time I was able to do it. My heart was racing and I was really frightened, but I stood there, without moving. Then the door started opening slowly. Then more and more. Soon it was all the way open – and I saw there was nothing there! Nothing at all.

"But the weirdest thing was I looked outside and realized it was daytime. The sun was really shining, and I knew it had been night time just a few minutes before. And then, the strangest thing of all – I looked across the street and saw the ocean! And I thought, 'Gee, I didn't know I was living so close to the ocean!' And I felt so happy. I started to walk out to the beach there, and then I woke up!"

She was beaming by the time she finished telling me the dream. Then she said, "We don't have to process the dream to figure it out – I already have. That thing I was so scared of was death – and it turned out to be nothing. And the sunshine and the ocean – all the joy I've been feeling since I was here last. It's just amazing, you know? I've been realizing, really realizing I'm just not scared about death anymore. I can't believe it!"

As is clear, fully facing a fear head-on as she did can be a powerful approach to not only dissolve the fear you're feeling, but also to discover the deeper reality of who you essentially are. You can experience yourself as something so much larger, so much more powerful than you can imagine yourself to be, something so much greater than the fear you felt.

Exercise: *Body Expansion*

Another exercise to assist you in detaching from your identification with the body, and thereby letting go of fear about death, is a form of meditation in which you can experience yourself as vast, uninterrupted spaciousness – rather than something enclosed in a body. It can be easier to have someone else guide you through the steps, so that you can completely relax into your experience. But you can also read the steps beforehand to get the general gist of the process, and then close your eyes and do it.

1. **Take deep breaths:** Begin by sitting comfortably and closing your eyes. Take a few deep breaths and let them out, and then start breathing naturally. Begin watching your breath as it flows in and out.

2. **Be aware of your body:** Become aware of how your body is feeling. Focus first on your head, then move down to your throat and neck, then your shoulders and arms, and all the way down to your toes. As your awareness moves into each part of your body, gently bring relaxation into that area.

3. **Be aware of the chair you're in:** Now become aware of the chair you are sitting on. Feel your body sinking down into it. Sense how friendly it is, how receptive it is to your body.

4. **Feel the air:** Next feel the air around you. Feel it on your face, your arms, your legs. Be aware of how your body fits into this air, in this space all around you.

5. **Feel your cells floating apart:** Now focus on the space that feels like the "center" of your body. Feel it beginning to slowly expand, and feel the cells of your body in that area beginning to gently float apart from one another.

6. **Feel the atoms floating apart:** Then become aware of the atoms in these cells; feel them floating apart, as well. Sense the air completely filling the spaces in between them. All the atoms of your body are floating more and more freely now, as the spaces between them get larger and larger.

7. **Feel your body becoming larger:** Feel this sensation extending into your chest. The cells and atoms that make up your heart and lungs are beginning to float gently apart, as air flows freely into the spaces in between them. Your body is becoming larger and larger, lighter and lighter, as your cells allow more and more space to surround them.

8. **Feel your physical boundaries blurring:** Feel the contours of your body now beginning to blur, disappearing into the very air around you. Feel how little distinction there is between your body and the space around you. You are becoming pure energy extending into space. Now realize that even the energy is disappearing into the clear, vast space. You have become the space itself.

9. **See where your breathing takes place:** Take a long inhale and then a long exhale. Be aware of how this breathing happens inside of the vast space you now experience as YOU.

10. **Be aware of yourself as pure Awareness:** Know that you are Awareness itself, pure and simple Awareness. All objects exist inside of YOU. You are the space around and through everything. Indeed, the whole universe exists inside of you.

11. **Experience how your body is *inside* of you:** Experience all this for as long as you wish. When you finally open your eyes, look down at your hands and see that they are inside of the

spaciousness that is YOU. Then see this with your feet and legs. This form you know as your body is something *inside* of you, not the other way around. Yet you flow all through it, as well. There is nowhere that you are not.

Doing this exercise can assist you in directly experiencing the illusory nature of your body and the reality of your true identity as the primal Essence that exists beyond the realm of form. Once you've done it several times as a meditation, you can then begin to do it with your eyes open while engaged in different activities. As you begin to know yourself to be that which has no form, you may find your experience of doing these activities greatly altering. Observing your body doing things without your personal involvement becomes a reliably curious adventure.

These exercises may or may not work to relieve your fears around death. You may have to find what will work for you. The key to remember, however, is that simply approaching your fear intellectually or philosophically probably will not work. You need to directly face your fear head-on and to find a way to experience who you are beyond the body. Otherwise, the deeply ingrained body-identification will remain – along with the psychological suffering and the fear that goes along with it.

A Complex Task

It's important to remember that learning to detach your identity from your body is a process that takes some time. Of course, experiencing profound glimpses of your 5D Self assists tremendously in the process. But so does a constant and sincere effort to detach your awareness from the limited form of your body.

But it is a complex task. As I've mentioned, while you are detaching your identity from your body, you need to also stay very much in touch with it. In a certain way, you are anchoring ever more deeply down into it, as the high-frequency Ascension energies upgrade your vibration. Remember too that your body is an individual consciousness, a Body Elemental, in the process of evolving, just as you are. It's important to get to know this Being as well as possible: treat it as a friend who is making this journey through life with you, in partnership with you.

Your body, just like you, is going through challenging changes: attempting to integrate the new energies into an old 3D structure, to activate long-dormant DNA strands, and to let go of all energies within the cells that are not vibrating at the higher level you now are. Have compassion and understanding for this intimate friend of yours – while, at the same time, continuing to detach your identification from it.

The experience that your identity is not confined to your body can become tremendously joyful and exciting. You can still enjoy your body and the pleasures it gives you – perhaps even more so. But you need not be caught in the fears and suffering that identifying with it can bring. You can just become the curious investigator, exploring this delightfully wondrous planet, as you drive around in partnership with your beloved Body Elemental.

Chapter 12

Shifting Your Identification from Your Emotions

Now that we've explored how you can keep yourself from being trapped in your 3D self's suffering due to identifying with either the roles you play in life or with your body, let us now turn to your emotions. How can emotions keep you entangled in the knot of 3D suffering?

Once again, it will become apparent that your suffering is caused by your attachment to your emotions and by your belief that your emotions are part of who you are. And that, once again, the way out of this suffering is, of course, to detach your sense of identity from them.

As always, by "detachment", I am not talking about not feeling emotions or denying them. And I'm certainly not talking about getting rid of them – if this could even be done. There is nothing at all wrong with emotions. There is no reason not to feel them. Indeed, emotions bring color and juice into our lives in a way nothing else can. What I am speaking of is detaching your sense of identity from them – truly realizing that emotions, with all their unreliable, ever-changing impermanence, are not who you are. They are energies that are simply *with* you – and they come and go.

The process of detaching from emotions can generally seem harder for women than it is for men. Many women are, in fact, rather entrenched in their emotional identity; emotions for them are very real and of utmost importance. It's hard to tell if this is so because women have generally been socialized to become emotional beings, or whether they are inherently more emotional than men. Probably a bit of both. Either way, it seems that women are generally more in touch with their emotions and tend to base their sense of identity on them more than men do.

Paradoxically, I believe this is probably to their advantage in getting free from emotional suffering, because we must first be aware of what emotions we are feeling before being able to free ourselves from identifying with them. I have known many men who have tried to bypass the process of getting in touch with their emotions through attempting to move directly into the "spiritual realms". Only too often, it is finally brought home to them that avoiding or suppressing emotions does not make them go away. Being out of touch with our emotions can, in fact, increase their power over us and complicate our lives by having them pop out in distorted and inappropriate ways.

To men's credit, however, I must say that I've noticed more and more of them now turning to the wisdom of attuning to their emotions. Perhaps the appearance of many men's groups over the years is responsible, at least in part, for this welcome change. Or it's the divine feminine energy in the 5D frequencies that is now permeating the planet. Either way, this growing awareness among men, I believe, has greatly assisted the communication between the sexes. More than ever before, emotional exchanges tend to be much better understood by both men and women.

The Worship of Emotions

Unfortunately, however, it seems that the same forces that have produced a greater awareness about emotions have also now managed to create in some people a kind of cult out of them; emotions have become a god. This is especially true of people who have been involved in intensive therapy or self-help programs, in which it has been emphasized that most problems are caused by suppressed emotions, and it is therefore necessary, beyond all else, to get in touch with them and experience them fully.

Up to a point, this is, of course, very helpful. However, sometimes people are encouraged to deeply experience the wounding they have undergone in their lives over and over again, and to continue re-experiencing and analyzing their wounding in all its aspects. As a result, they end up feeling stuck in the trauma.

People who espouse such an approach, much to the discomfort of their families and friends, also prod their loved ones to adopt the same philosophy. I have heard women, in particular, complain at length about the men in their lives who have not "acknowledged their own emotional wounding". There is certainly some truth to the notion that if we are not in touch with our feelings, they will get in our way in creating healthy relationships. However, the examination of emotions can be overdone and become a barrier to true 5D freedom.

I have found that the cult of emotion-worshipping can entice people into misidentification for many, many years. I realized this several years back when I received a phone call from an old friend, June, to whom I hadn't spoken in over twenty years. We had spent most of our time together back in our youth sharing emotional dramas in which we were each currently involved. It was something we did with most of our friends in those days; it was what life and friendship were all about. We were all intimately involved in each other's stories – wanting to hear the latest episodes, giving our advice about the situations, and offering our support to each other in our suffering.

Talking with June brought this all back to me. I remembered the warmth and love we had felt for each other and the depth of emotional sharing we had experienced. It also brought the realization that I was no longer relating to people in that way. I had come to see that dramas of suffering could get rather boring after a while, especially if the same story kept happening over and over again. In effect, the subject of emotional suffering no longer had its old appeal to me.

I soon realized that June had not made this same transition. After our initial catch-up exchanges about what we were now doing and where we were living, she launched immediately into the emotional drama currently unfolding in her life. As I sat listening to her on the phone, I was incredulous. It was as if no time at all had passed. All the same drama of suffering she had been experiencing fifteen years before was still occurring; the prime players around her had simply changed faces and names. What was really startling was that she appeared to be still reveling in her role as the martyred-victim heroine and still analyzing and attempting to deeply experience and understand it.

I was especially amazed, because I knew June was not only a very bright woman, but also very spiritually-oriented. I couldn't quite believe that she was still putting so much energy into her emotional suffering and the analysis of all the intricate reasons for it. I realized that she had truly become a victim of the emotional cult so prevalent in our subculture, and that sometime in the years since, I had had the good fortune to escape its seductive clutches.

Focusing on Negative Emotions

It can be difficult to escape from the cult of emotions in the new age culture, in part because of the thriving smorgasbord of therapies and self-help programs designed to assist people caught in such emotional turmoil. Although certainly serving an important need, I have found that some of these processes end up doing more harm than good. They not only glorify emotions in general, they glorify negative emotions, in particular – and end up repeatedly creating wounded-victim heroes and heroines like my friend, June.

Back in the earlier years of my practice as a therapist, I was guilty of leading certain clients down this unfortunate path. Aware that my clients were suffering from suppressed emotions, I began using the approach known as "insight therapy", which involved guiding them into the internal pathways that would reveal to them their unconscious emotions and traumas they'd experienced. Quite often, this would initially produce immense relief and joy; finally allowing negative emotions to come to the surface can be greatly rewarding.

But a problem would always arise when we began "recycling" the client's emotions. Believing that talking about these negative emotions would eventually get rid of them, my clients and I would process and reprocess, analyze and reanalyze them – where they came from, who was responsible for them, etc., ad nauseum. Far from bringing relief, after a while, this process increased the suffering. The client became the emotionally wounded victim whose whole identity was caught up in this role.

It took me a while to realize that becoming aware of negative emotions was only the beginning of the road. Insight into how to release or heal the emotions did not automatically occur in most cases. Even when I saw this, and I suggested ways a client could release and heal these emotions, I found that many of them were resistant to doing this. They were getting too much out of the role of the wounded victim. Their sense of self-esteem was being fed by the feeling of specialness created by the understanding of how incredibly wounded they were.

I remember in my early days as a therapist a client by the name of Melanie, a very sincere woman, who was suffering terribly from depression and low self-esteem. She had been to doctors and been given a number of different anti-depressants, none of which had ever done much to give her any relief. In our initial sessions together, as I led her through the labyrinthine corridors of her past, exploring together her childhood wounding and all the negative emotions she'd managed to suppress, she would be somewhat worn out by the end of our session – but she'd also be elated. Exploring all these issues was both fascinating and relieving for her.

However, as we plowed on in this work for months and as we covered the same ground over and over again, her hopefulness understandably turned once again into depression. Nothing new was happening; her old problems in life dragged on.

I finally realized that insight therapy wasn't working for her. It wasn't producing the intended automatic knowledge of how to change her life. So I brought in new approaches: behavioral therapy and cognitive therapy, processes based on making changes through new behaviors and new beliefs. The novelty of these approaches lifted her spirits for a while, and it seemed as if perhaps some positive changes might be happening. But ultimately, it became clear that these approaches weren't going to help, either. We were still covering all the same ground; we were still focusing on her wounding and what to do about it.

I then started bringing in the more experiential, transpersonal processes I was learning: past-life regression, Gestalt, dreamwork, inner child work, visualization, body-centered therapy, chakra-balancing, spirit releasement – you name it. As I introduced these new forms of therapy, I began reframing the work we were doing, referring to it as "transformational work". We were now focusing seriously on "healing" her wounding.

Again, initially, these new processes brought hope for a while. But ultimately, since we were still focused on her wounding, her old depression reappeared, this time laced with profound feelings of failure. After all her hard work, she still wasn't "healed" of her depression.

She was soon feeling anger – and much of it was directed at me. So we dealt with that for a while. Although she was able to work through the anger and feel good about working with me again, we were still back to where we had started. She was still feeling depressed and experiencing a lack of self-worth. The only difference was that she was now very informed as to why she was feeling this way – and she was also very established in the role of the victim.

It wasn't that Melanie didn't want to change. She did, quite desperately so. She took all we processed very seriously. She'd dutifully come in each week having done all the homework I'd prescribed. In many ways she was the "ideal" therapy client. It was just that we had focused for so long on what was "wrong" with her and how she had to be "fixed" that she had become stuck in the victim role. Neither one of us at that point knew how to help her out of it.

I knew I wasn't the only therapist producing these self-glorified victims; many clients came to me from other therapists already well-established in this role. I was to find that it took quite a bit of time and energy to lead someone out of this kind of distorted identity once they were already deeply entrenched in it.

Focusing on Positive Emotions

One path I eventually took with such clients was helping them focus on positive emotions instead of negative ones. Although limited in its own way, this approach did at least begin to turn the glorified victim into a happier and more empowered human being. I found that numerous self-help approaches and metaphysical, positive-thinking teachings can help transform negative emotions into positive ones. Often for the first time, people can begin to enjoy life and feel empowered to create their own happiness. This was a good shift in my practice of therapy, as I was to find later on that this is a way to help someone to begin turning toward 5D consciousness.

For a number of years, I used this focus on positive emotions as my basic approach with clients. I taught them about affirmations and visualization, how to communicate with their spirit guides and angels, how to manifest what they wanted, and how generally to keep focused on everything positive in their lives. Although much more successful in helping people toward happiness and empowerment, this approach, I was to find, also had its limitations.

I discovered that trying to experience more positive emotions in our lives actually isn't the answer to ending emotional suffering. Eventually, we realize that we simply can't focus on positive emotions all the time, no matter how disciplined we are. Try as we may to keep negative emotions away, they keep arising.

In fact, even while we are experiencing positive emotions, there is always the awareness (although often subconscious) that they will eventually be gone, and that compromises our happiness even at the best of times. I've even known people who actually fear feeling good at all, because they know the good feeling will eventually leave, and they'd therefore rather not feel the positive emotion to begin with.

Another problem is that if we focus exclusively on positive emotions, making them "right" or "good" and negative emotions "wrong" or "bad", we are likely to begin suppressing the negative ones that do arise, and then we have to deal with the unfortunate consequences of this action. We also may miss how we have automatically assumed that feeling "bad" emotions automatically means that *we* are bad – and this can then cause a sense of shame to add to the mix. Suppressing emotions doesn't make them go away; it just gives them more power. So, that would take us back to square one in this whole process of striving for emotional happiness.

Remembering about the Inner-Critic Implant

Even aside from realizing all that, something that is extremely important to remember when you feel yourself getting caught in negative emotions is the information presented in Chapter 2 about the Inner Critic implant. This is the AI structure that has been spliced into the DNA of your brain and is programmed to constantly give you messages of fear, self-doubt, shame, guilt, and self-judgment. If you can remember to keep this in mind whenever you fall into these emotions that weaken you and cause you suffering, you can be reminded that these are programmed messages; they are not telling you the truth about yourself.

It can take a while before you can begin to catch these insidious messages coming from this implant and realize what they're designed to do. You may initially only become aware of something uncomfortable happening when you begin feeling the emotions and hearing the self-defeating messages running through your mind. Because this dynamic is so familiar to you, you will probably continue for a while to believe the messages to be true – that there is something wrong with you and you should feel ashamed, guilty or that you don't deserve to be happy.

But then, when you can become aware of what is really going on, you can begin to realize the truth of what's going on: you are being given messages designed to weaken you. There is really nothing wrong with you; you are simply experiencing negative emotions caused by an AI system – and you don't have to listen to it. Your awareness of this will give you a sense of power and sovereignty, and you'll see that the programmed messages about you begin to fade away.

So this awareness can be helpful – as can remembering to move away from a focus on negative emotions and focusing instead on positive ones. These approaches can produce great relief in the moment and are certainly a step toward 5D consciousness. However, even these approaches do not produce true and lasting happiness or emotional freedom. A further step must be taken.

Chapter 13

Experiencing Emotional Freedom

If you are at a point in your life where you are truly tired of being buffeted about by emotions and are not satisfied with being just somewhat happy some of the time, you are probably finally ready to move out of the knot of emotional suffering altogether and take the next step toward experiencing the freedom of living from within your 5D Self. This next step is not necessarily an easy one. But it is an essential one – and can ultimately produce the emotional freedom you're looking for.

I wish to emphasize, as always, that letting go of your identity with your emotions does not mean letting go of the experience of them, or in any way denying them. It instead entails allowing feelings to simply be – without judgment, and without attachment. It means not dwelling on them, not indulging them, not analyzing them. And it also means not running from them, not fighting them, not avoiding them. No clinging and no resisting. It means just letting them be.

Except for severely painful emotions (which we will explore in in future chapters), the following is a description of steps that can be helpful in finding a path toward emotional freedom.

Freeing Yourself from Emotional Attachment

1. See Emotions for What They Are

The first step is to become aware of what emotions actually are: simply energy – free-flowing energy. They arise within your body and into your awareness. And, if you experience them briefly and allow them to simply be, without either attaching to them or resisting them in some way, they can bring a great deal of juice and flavor to life. Other than that, they are nothing to be much thought about. What you can discover is that the emotions you experience aren't even inherently "your" emotions. They belong to nobody. They are just a specific kind of energy that happens to be floating through your awareness and body at that time.

There's no reason, therefore, to grab onto them and make them your important possessions – or allow them to become lodged as stuck energy somewhere in your body. You can just let them float on through – enjoy them if you wish – and then let them go without allowing them to stick to you in any way.

2. Begin Observing your Emotions

As you learn to simply allow emotions to float through your awareness, the next step is to begin observing them in a relaxed and neutral way. As they appear, just note them, acknowledge their presence and observe what they feel like. Of course, you will also be experiencing the emotions as you do this; feeling them does not stop. But you can observe and feel them at the same time.

You can start this practice by closing your eyes, relaxing and taking a few deep breaths. Then become aware of emotions as they appear in your awareness. They often appear on the tail of certain thoughts. If you think a positive thought, wait a moment and you'll likely see that a positive emotion will come in its wake. Think a negative thought, and watch for the emotion that follows that one. Play with this process for a while.

Emotions come in differently for each person, but they generally appear as a sensation somewhere in your body – usually in your gut or chest area. But they may also appear with visual images or colors, or in some other way. Become familiar with what occurs for you.

At the same time, be careful not to get caught up in analyzing the emotions or in giving them any other kind of energy. Simply watch them in a relaxed and detached way, without interfering with or interpreting them. Allow them to do whatever they want or go where they want. Most importantly, do not follow any thoughts about them. Don't go off into the familiar stories from the past or possible futures based on the feelings. Simply stay relaxed, watching the emotions themselves.

For example, let's say you have your eyes closed and are watching what is floating through your mind. Thoughts and images begin passing through. Perhaps there is the thought about how your partner left the week before after an argument you had, and then there's the image of him, angry with you, as he was going out the door. Watch to see what emerges in your body with these thoughts and images. Is there a tightness, a fear, a sense of anger arising in your body? Rather than either falling into the emotion or trying to suppress it, do your best to simply watch with curiosity what is happening.

You may, for example, become aware of a sensation of loneliness also making its appearance. As you begin to watch this new emotion as it settles in with the fear and anger in your gut, you might realize this combination of emotions has a particular form and color – perhaps it is a gray, amorphous mass that generally seems to settle in the pit of your stomach.

Your tendency at this point might be to automatically begin thinking about how sad your life is. With that thought there usually comes the emotion of self-pity. It will settle down familiarly with the other emotions already clustered there in your body. This may then bring in memories of times when you've quarreled with other lovers in the past and all that you suffered after those episodes. Do your best to avoid following these thoughts; instead stay completely still, simply observing the whole process.

Now become aware of what has has just happened: Thoughts initially began floating through your mind. In their wake, certain forms of energy entered into the force-field of your body and have now settled into a place where they have probably habitually settled in all the past times they've ever visited this body. You are not the emotions or the body in which the emotions have settled. Nor are you your mind and the thoughts that may be forming during this process. You are the *observer* of all of this. Gently and quietly keep focused on this realization.

You'll find that this process will at first take some concentration and practice. The habit of attaching to an emotion as it enters your consciousness and then going for the ride it wants to take you on is usually so ingrained that it can happen in a split second before you know what is happening. If this happens, and you find yourself trailing off after your thoughts about the emotion, simply let go of your focus on it and once again sit back and begin watching what is going on in your body.

It takes some time to develop a new response to emotions; but after a while, it won't even be necessary to stop and close your eyes to observe every emotion that arises. It will become a natural way to respond to them throughout your daily life. You'll be happy to learn that simply observing a mass of energy floating through your awareness is really much less exhausting than being dragged around by it.

You can even begin to get playful with the tough emotions, such as addressing them with love and gentle humor as they settle down within your body, saying something like: "Hi there! So you're here for a visit, are you? That's okay. Make yourself comfortable." And then turn your attention to something else. You're not judging or resisting the emotion, but you're not giving it much attention either. You'll find it needs your attention and energy in order to survive in you.

3. Accept All Emotions Equally

As you simply observe emotions as they float through your awareness and refrain from grabbing onto them, you will likely next become aware of an automatic tendency to want to cling to the positive emotions as they appear and to resist the negative ones. This is to be expected; naturally, you want to hold onto what feels good and pleasant and get rid of what doesn't.

This is all part of the 3D self's plan for achieving happiness – grasping at what's pleasant and resisting what's unpleasant – and it is ultimately unsuccessful. We can't get rid of negative feelings, while holding onto positive feelings. Positive and negative emotions come together in the same package; and, because of that, we can't discard some emotions without losing the others. Thus, we must somehow let go of this urge to either resist or cling to emotions. We simply need to accept all of them equally, without judgment or preference.

One way to begin doing this is to stop discriminating between what you deem to be "positive" and "negative" emotions, and attempt to see them all as simply emotions, period. This can be difficult if you have any notions about certain emotions being either "spiritual" or "unspiritual". If you do, you will likely try to avoid feeling any emotions you see as "unspiritual"; and this, of course, leads to denying these emotions – which does nothing to get rid of them. The whole notion of spiritual and unspiritual emotions is fallacious to begin with. Emotions themselves have nothing to with spirituality; they're just energies that are part of the human experience.

Whether you give emotions spiritual qualities or not, discriminating between positive and negative emotions in any way can hinder your becoming free of the suffering they can bring. This 3D habit of discriminating is deeply ingrained, and initially it may take a great deal of vigilance and discipline to break and lose that automatic tendency. But it is ultimately essential. To be truly free emotionally, the propensity to resist and cling to emotions must be abandoned. All emotions need to be responded to equally, with detachment – and ultimately without even a preference.

How can this deeply-ingrained habit be broken? Let's look more closely in the next two steps at how we tend to react automatically to emotions when they appear in our awareness and what can be done to begin dissolving this reflexive habit.

4. Allow Negative Emotions Simply to Be

Simply allowing negative emotions to flow in without reacting to them is perhaps more challenging than not reacting to positive ones. Because they can be so painful, we naturally react to negative emotions in a way that we hope will get rid of the pain they appear to be causing. But these habitual reactions do not get rid of the pain – and they do, in fact, keep us recycling back into it. These reactions usually fall into three categories: resistance to an emotion, indulgence in it, and attempts to fix it.

a. Resistance to the Emotion: Resisting a negative emotion can take many different forms: pushing it away, ignoring it, denying it, judging it, distracting yourself from it, fighting it, getting angry with it. All these maneuvers, far from dissolving the pain of the negative emotion, actually create even more pain. Just as we saw earlier how resistance to physical pain can increase the pain, so resistance to emotional pain can compound it in a similar way.

First of all, if you look clearly at what happens to the emotions you've attempted to resist in one way or another, you'll see these emotions do not go away. They may go underground for a while and give you some respite, but they do not disappear. And they usually seep out at some later time in a displaced and inappropriate way.

Besides being ineffective in getting rid of a negative emotion, fighting it can compound the pain. It requires a great deal of energy to resist something, and it causes much tension in both your psyche and your body. If resisting unpleasant emotions has become deeply habitual for you, you might not be aware of the price such persistent resistance is costing you. But if, when a negative emotion appears, you take the time to gently stop your automatic resistance to it, you will be able to experience the beautiful release of a tension you may not have even known was there.

Joseph was an engineer in his late forties who came to me with a massive amount of pent-up tension in his body. He told me that people saw him as "uptight" and "rigid", a man of whom they were often afraid. They intuitively sensed the intense anger he had stored inside him; and, for fear he might "blow" at any time, they were hesitant to be around him. He was aware of the amount of rage he was carrying but did not know what to do with it. The times in the past when he'd stopped resisting his anger and let it simply explode had been disastrous for him. People had been completely alienated from him; he had actually even lost his job a couple of times.

I asked him what he did to keep his anger in check. He told me he just kept a very tight rein on it. He did his best not to express it at all. If ignoring it didn't work, he'd try to tell himself how "evil" it was to get angry. If this didn't work, he'd often start eating voluminous amounts of junk food to try and stuff it down. Or he'd try turning on the TV to try to deaden it.

"Wow," I said. "It must take so much energy out of you, just to keep the anger from exploding."

"Yeah, it does," he replied with a pained sigh. "I get so exhausted."

I then suggested that he might perhaps stop resisting his anger. He immediately became very fearful. "Oh, I couldn't do that! I have to keep it in check. It's catastrophic when I don't!" He was only seeing two options: either he could resist his anger and hold it in, or he could let it explode. I explained that there was a third option: he could simply allow the anger to be, without resisting or expressing it. He might try to accept the feeling of anger as it appeared in him, not making it wrong or bad; and, at the same time, he could avoid expressing it in an explosive way.

This was a novel idea to Joseph, and it didn't seem possible to him. How could he just accept the anger, without having it explode? The more I suggested this was indeed possible, the more defensive he became. As I persisted, his anger began to rise. I decided at this point that I might as well help create a situation while we were together in which I could perhaps demonstrate what I was talking about, so I continued to push him further to increase his anger.

Finally I said, "You're pretty angry right now, aren't you?"

Rather loudly, he exclaimed, "You bet I am! You're a therapist – you're not supposed to be making me mad like this!"

"Why don't you take this opportunity right now to test what I've been talking about?" I knew I was taking a chance with this, because his anger at me was probably producing even more resistance to my suggestion. So I added gently, "This kind of anger feels pretty awful, doesn't it?"

"Yeah," he muttered, somewhat mollified. "I hate it. I hate it. I just want to kill people!"

"I can really see that, just looking at you. You know, I'm not suggesting that you kill people."

Despite himself, he smiled a small smile. "Well, what are you suggesting then? I don't get it."

With this opening, I began to speak again about simply allowing his feeling of anger to be – without doing anything at all with it. I suggested he close his eyes and relax his body as best he could. He did this and took a couple of deep breaths. As I guided him through the process of identifying and locating the anger in his body he found that it was a massive, throbbing, red "fire-monster" that had his entire body in its clutches. Even doing this beginning exercise had an effect on his body. I could see certain muscles in his face and his shoulders begin to relax.

He finally began simply to observe the anger as it grabbed and squeezed at different parts of his body. And as he learned to keep focused on the anger itself, rather than the mental stories around it, he found that the monster began losing its vividness and strength. Eventually, after about fifteen minutes of keeping on track with this process, he finally reported to me that it had disappeared. I saw that he now sat on the couch before me ten times more relaxed than I had ever seen him before. When he opened his eyes, relief shone in them. He couldn't quite believe what had happened.

Of course, this was not the end to all of Joseph's anger. As could be expected, it was to appear over and over again. But, as he began working with it in this new way, he found there was no longer any reason for him to be fearful of his anger. His new approach of not resisting it – either through fighting it, attempting to contain it, or distracting himself from it – began to lessen the clutches of this monster on his life. He experienced that who he really was in the depths of his being was so much more powerful than this form of energy called "anger"; simply accepting it and letting it be was changing his whole life.

After that session, he became visibly more relaxed. He eventually reported that people weren't so afraid of being around him anymore. And for the first time he could remember, he wasn't letting anger – or fear of his anger – run his life. Very importantly, he was finally able to see what had been underneath the anger all along – feelings of hurt, rejection and self pity – new emotions he could then begin to explore and learn to free himself from.

No matter what you stop resisting, you can have the same kind of results. Take depression, for example. You may be someone who has suffered from this debilitating emotion for most your life. Perhaps you're asking, "You mean I should just let the depression stay when it comes in? It'll take over, if I do – I know, I've let this happen in the past. I can't afford to let it ruin my life again like that!"

If this is what you're thinking, then, like Joseph with regard to his anger, you are assuming that there are only two options with depression: either you resist it in some manner or you let it take over your life. What I am indicating when I say, "Let it be" is not falling into it; that is a form of indulging in it (which I will address shortly). I am not encouraging you to give in to the depression, nor am I suggesting you give up responsibility for how you're feeling. I am speaking only of stopping the reaction of resistance toward it – and simply allowing it to be, without reacting to it at all – except perhaps feeling compassion for yourself.

I am also not suggesting that stopping habitual patterns of resistance is easy or that it can be done overnight. Obviously, as in changing any ingrained habit pattern, it takes patience and time. But it can be done. Even if you can just begin the process, you will experience quickly the wonderful result of greater relaxation in your body. It can be such a relief to let go and stop resisting.

b. Indulgence in the Emotion: The second type of 3D habitual reaction to negative emotions is to give in to them and indulge them. One common and obvious way to indulge an emotion is to project it into action. If the feeling is anger, for instance, as in Joseph's case, the tendency may be to blow off steam at someone or something, in hopes the pain from the anger will diminish or go away with this action.

We can sometimes get an immediate sense of relief in expressing anger like this. At times, if no one has been hurt by this expression of anger, and we are able to simply let it go after we've expressed it, this can be okay. No great harm is done and it may provide temporary relief. But few people can actually do this with anger. More often, the same anger about the same thing shows up again later on, sometimes over and over again. Thus, acting out our anger in this way obviously does not resolve it.

Similarly, acting out other negative emotions can also end up strengthening them. The reaction of bursting into tears over upsetting events is a good example. Again, like the brief expression of anger that is quickly released and forgotten, a burst of tears now and then can be harmless, and probably even helpful – simply as a release of pent-up energy. But so often, this reaction can become habitual and completely non-productive; far from resolving the hurt, it can actually start a spiral of depression and despair.

A sensitive, fragile young woman came to see me a few years back. Theresa had been struggling with deep depression for many years, along with a sense of helplessness and anger toward many people in her life. Often she would report to me how, after something had happened, she just "bawled her eyes out," or that she had spent the entire night crying. When I finally asked her one time if this crying had ever given her any relief, she answered, "No – not at all. I always feel worse. But I just can't help myself."

Somewhere along the line, Theresa had developed the habit of acting out her hurt, depression, or anger through bursting into tears. As so often happens with the habits we form, it wasn't doing her any good – but she just didn't know what else to do. The habit had taken over. I began talking to her about adopting a new response to hurtful situations. I suggested that instead of falling automatically into her torrent of tears, she instead become still and simply watch the hurt as it floated through her awareness and into her body. At the time, she looked at me very doubtfully. She nodded her head, but I knew that, like Joseph, she didn't believe this could do her any good.

Fortunately, during our session a few weeks later, I had an opportunity to help her try out this new approach in handling hurt. As she talked to me about a situation during the previous week at work in which she had felt threatened and helpless, she began crying. Immediately, I suggested, "Rather than going into this old reaction to your pain, perhaps you can simply close your eyes right now and become still." Rather reluctantly, she finally complied. She stopped crying and closed her eyes.

I said, "Just relax and watch your breathing for a few moments." Presently, I said, "Now scan your awareness and look for your hurt – it's probably settled somewhere in your body."

"Yes, it's in my belly. I see it. It's kind of a grayish-pink." Suddenly I heard a catch in her voice, as she started to cry. I said, "No need to react to this hurt; just observe it. Tell me, how else can you describe it?"

"Well, it's soft and fragile. It's kind of like a cloud, a grayish-pink cloud." She paused and then said, "I always feel this kind of hurt whenever anybody threatens me or tries to intimidate me…"

I gently stopped her in this thought process. I said, "No need to follow that story about your hurt. You've gone over and over that one. You understand it well, how and why it happens. This has never resolved the pain. What I'm suggesting is that you simply stay still and watch this energy form as it sits in your belly – and just see what happens."

She frowned but began concentrating in this way. Soon she said, "It really hurts. It's tight and it squeezes the muscles in my belly."

"That's an important observation. This emotion called 'hurt' constricts your belly and causes it pain. Don't go off into anything else about this now; just keep observing. Tell me what else is happening."

"I just keep thinking about all the times I've felt this hurt…."

"See if you can move out of that thought right now – just let go of it. It'll just take you for a ride. Come back to observing. What is happening to the grayish-pink mass of energy in your belly now?"

She was silent for a while. Then she said, somewhat surprised, "It was there, really permanent feeling for a while, but now it isn't there anymore."

"Is it somewhere else?"

"I don't think so. It just kind of disappeared…."

"How is your belly feeling?"

"Well, it's kind of relaxed now. It's fine." She opened her eyes and smiled a tentative smile. "That's really weird! It just disappeared. I'm not feeling it anymore." She was puzzled but very relieved. She had discovered, through direct experience, that simply observing an emotion, rather than indulging it, could have an amazing result. When we give it no energy, it simply fades and disappears.

This is because all that emotions want is to be noticed, allowed to express, and accepted without judgment. They also want to be experienced – but just a few moments of the experience can be enough. When you can do this with any reaction, it can be amazing how it will simply begin to fade and float out of you, just as it floated in.

This isn't to say that handling an emotion this way once will get rid of it forever; undoubtedly, it will be back. If it has been a welcome guest in your consciousness and has been given lots of attention for many years, it will continue to return, as if attempting to recapture this pampered-guest status with you. But by persistently refraining from giving it the kind of energy on which it thrives, you will find that it eventually fades and has less and less pull on you. You will finally be able to just note the appearance of this guest on your doorstep, smile at it graciously, and then go on about your business, completely undisturbed by it.

Another way to indulge a negative emotion, besides projecting it into action, is to do what Theresa started to do several times during our process: move into the "story" of it and begin analyzing it. We often react this way to a chronic emotion, with the hope that if we can just analyze it enough, we will eventually discover how to release ourselves from the pain of it.

But instead, we find ourselves stumbling down memory lane, remembering all the times we've experienced the emotion before and the drama that's surrounded it. Obsessively, we attempt to analyze how it all happened and what we could or should have done to prevent it. We then, in despair, often indulge in self-pity, self-doubt, and self-hate for how we've failed, thanks to the Inner Critic Implant described in Chapter 2.

To pile on the pain, we may also fearfully project into the future about it, as well. We fear the next thing that's going to happen and wonder if we'll ever be free of it. It all becomes a horror story by the time we're done (if we ever are). And all this, simply because a negative emotion happened to appear in our consciousness!

Indulging negative emotions like this is ultimately responsible for the negative thought patterns and belief systems we develop in life. Because we have fed and nourished these emotions with so much energy, they get stronger and stronger and eventually become habitual. It is therefore really important to watch and release any tendencies, habits or compulsions to automatically move into stories about our emotions.

c. Attempting to Fix Emotions: The third type of habitual response people tend to have to negative emotions is to try to fix or change them in some way, in order to make them more positive. If you have spent time learning how to transform and heal negative emotions, this reaction may now be habitual for you. Trying to do this with an emotion might seem more "spiritual" than the other two reactions of resisting or indulging them. It may have a more pleasant and loving sense about it.

Attempting to heal an emotional pattern can be seen as a more fourth-dimensional form of responding to negative emotions. This is initially helpful, and it's certainly better than other more 3D types of responses. But it is ultimately as much a rejection of negative emotions as the other two approaches are. Its purpose is to change them, rather than simply allowing them to be.

It is true that many techniques people use to heal negative emotions do seem to work – at least for a while. For many years, I worked with numerous processes to help transform and heal clients' negative emotions. During these processes, and for a time afterwards, they usually experienced a great high. They'd forgive themselves and others, and they'd reach into some really clear and loving spaces inside themselves. Feeling free and clear at the time, they'd consider themselves "healed" of the emotions.

There always seemed to come a time, however, when they got honest with themselves about this process. One woman I worked with had been working long and hard with many healers and therapists before she came to me. She reported that when she finally became really honest with herself and delved into some of those places where the negative feelings "used to be" – much to her dismay, she began finding that those old emotions were still there. Anger at her mother for things that had happened forty years before were still in her, biding its time. Despair about her whole life was still alive and well; the unbearable loneliness from her childhood was still pushing at the door. What had happened to all the "healing" she'd done on these emotions?

She realized that the feelings certainly weren't as powerful as they'd previously been, and they no longer seemed to be running her life; but they were still in there. And it felt as if they probably always would be. She realized that they were still emerging any time her defenses were down. It seemed that all the transformational work she'd done on them hadn't, in the end, really achieved what she had thought it had.

I had discovered this myself years before with my own transformational work. It had initially really changed my life; I felt generally happier than before I'd started it. But, when I was really honest with myself, I would realize that the negative emotions were still inside me, nestled within my subconscious – and probably lodged within my body. I was to find out later when I studied quantum healing that these emotions, and the belief systems that related to them, had become energetic patterns that had actually attached to my DNA.

At the time before learning this, however, I wondered if I were alone in this predicament. I began an informal survey of friends who had also done a considerable amount of work over the years on healing their emotions. Not surprisingly, most of them admitted (although somewhat reluctantly) that the same was true for them.

One of them who had been a healer for many years, revealed that she had been somewhat alarmed by this fact for quite a while. She had not only been working the principles of emotional healing for many years on herself, she'd also been been working them with many clients. And just as she was seeing her own "healed" emotions still causing her pain, she was also seeing this same occurrence with the clients she'd worked with for some time.

It was indeed a disturbing phenomenon, bringing serious doubt into her whole paradigm of life and how the universe worked; it also threatened her source of income. I knew that I was in a similar position. I completely understood her alarm. Becoming honest about my experiences of "healing" was shaking my universe. What did it all mean for me?

What I finally saw was that a new paradigm about life, emotions, and healing was necessary – one that could encompass and integrate the revelations of my honest inquiry inside myself. It had to include the realization that although methods of healing do often bring relief to people, they do not necessarily resolve the challenging experience of negative emotions. They certainly don't get rid of them. Nor do they completely defuse their ability to trip us up somewhere down the line when we are again triggered.

Perhaps the most important realization I had was that trying to "heal" an emotion was simply a polite way of rejecting it. And I wondered if perhaps it was the act of rejecting the emotions that kept them unresolved. Maybe what needed to be done was simply to accept them, just as they were. In fact, maybe the answer was to no longer even care what emotions were floating around inside us at all.

I'd like to make a note here, however, that I am not suggesting that techniques for healing emotions are completely useless. In fact, for very deep emotional wounding, I believe they can be extremely helpful to reduce the suffering involved. Most people probably need to do a good amount of this work initially before attempting this method I am suggesting.

But when someone has already been through a period of time of sincere emotional healing and learned how they've dealt with emotions throughout their lives, I've found they have realized that healing techniques are limited. And that they are ready for this new approach which can help them begin to finally free themselves from the suffering that is being caused by their misidentification with their emotions.

When I finally began working with these clients in this new way, I discovered they began experiencing an enormous relief. They started realizing that there is nothing inherently wrong with negative emotions, that they are essentially no different from the emotions they had deemed "positive," except that they found them unpleasant. Negative and positive emotions are simply different forms of the same energy.

After working successfully for some time with certain clients, it eventually became clear to me that we really need do nothing at all to change negative emotions. We truly can just observe them objectively and let them be. If they have been well-fed by us in the past, they will probably return for a while. But if we can stay neutral and non-reactive, they will eventually let up and move on out of our awareness. It can be such a relief to experience this!

I once had a very aware client who had been coming to me for several reasons: depression, relationship problems, and career issues. Jennifer had spent years before coming to me, working on herself through therapy, twelve-step programs, and the Course in Miracles processes. She knew herself well and had made good use of the information she'd learned throughout the years. She was certainly a much happier and more empowered person than she'd been ten years earlier. She just felt at this point somewhat stuck in certain areas of her life.

In our initial months together, Jennifer and I worked on how she could create a happier life for herself. Very enthusiastically, she'd go home after our weekly sessions and assiduously work on fixing and changing her life situations and her emotional responses so as to become a happier person. Then, at some point, I realized that enough was enough. She could do this forever. She had fixed and changed and fixed and changed so many things in her life; and although she had become a happier person, she was finding that there was always more to fix and change. It was endless.

At this point, I started a new therapy with her that I called "So What? Therapy". Each week when she'd come in describing a new emotional issue (or generally, it was an old one dressed in new clothing), I would inevitably say to her, "So what?" Or "Who cares if that's still happening? What difference does it make? It's not who you are."

The first time I did this, she was surprised by this new tack I was taking and somewhat perturbed. Her emotional issues were important to her, and she took pride in all the work she'd done in fixing and healing them. But then she began to smile. She had had important glimpses of her true Self and knew what I meant when I'd say she wasn't her emotions. But she, like anyone else who has worked for years on healing their emotions, kept forgetting. She kept falling back into believing she was her emotions, and if her emotions weren't positive or "spiritual" ones, she then felt she needed to change them.

This process continued for several weeks, until Jennifer would catch herself before I did, and she'd smile and say, "So what?". Such relief would flood her at these times, she'd laugh a beautiful liberated laugh. She was realizing she could finally put down the burden of having to constantly fix herself in order to be "spiritual" or happy – she could just be as she was. The 3D self that she kept trying to fix was ultimately imperfect, and more importantly, it was not who she was.

She became one of most most delightful clients after that. We'd barely get seated across from each other, and she'd be beaming at me, knowing she really no longer had any problems to solve. Her only problem all along had been one of misidentification. Needless to say, she didn't need to come to see me for much longer.

The three habitual reactions to negative emotions that I have described – resistance, indulgence, and attempting to fix – are often unconscious and automatic. It is therefore important to bring them into your conscious awareness, so that you can begin to let them go and start creating a new response of simply allowing them to be. As always, this requires some practice.

To avoid any misunderstanding, note that allowing an emotion simply to be does not rule out the possibility of also taking appropriate action concerning a situation that helped trigger the emotion in you. For example, upon noticing hurt in yourself due to a misunderstanding you've had with someone, you might decide to speak to the person in hopes of resolving it. Or, in the case of feeling anger because of having been taken advantage of, you might take action to make sure you are not taken advantage of again in that same way.

These are examples of appropriate *responses* to negative emotions (as opposed to the *reactions* I have been describing), that can work quite effectively to help relieve the suffering caused by the emotions. You can easily do them while you are also engaged in the observation process inside yourself.

5. Allow Positive Emotions Simply to Be

It can sometimes be just as difficult to allow positive emotions simply to be, without reacting to them, as it is to allow negative ones to be. The automatic tendency is to grab onto them and cling to them as long as possible. When these positive emotions eventually leave, suffering is again experienced due to the attachment you have formed toward them.

It is just as necessary to be as neutral and non-reactive with positive emotions when they appear as with negative ones. As you learn to do this, an incredible sense of freedom can arise. You'll find that being neutral and non-reactive towards positive emotions doesn't in any way detract from the good feeling such emotions bring; it actually increases it. You'll no longer clutch at the emotions out of fear they might leave. You know they *will* eventually leave, so there's no point in trying to hang on to them. You simply enjoy them while they're around, and then willingly let them go, when they go. You're free and flowing, no matter what's happening.

6. Take Time to Practice

If you come up against a negative emotion you have given much energy to in the past, it will naturally take more practice and time to let go of it. But I have found it can be done. Certain emotions that have caused you tremendous suffering in the past will eventually appear in a very anemic form and then will hardly come around at all anymore. What is important is that, even if they do come back, you will no longer be upset by them. You can note their presence, and even feel them if you want to, but you will not enter into the familiar suffering about them.

7. Stop Identifying with Emotions

This brings us to the last step in this process toward liberation from emotional suffering, which is to stop identifying with the emotions that come into your awareness. If you have become proficient in simply watching them objectively and allowing them to be, this is relatively easy to do. You've begun to see, through direct experience, that you are something beyond the emotions that float through your consciousness. It is obvious how these flimsy, impermanent, and ever-changing things called emotions cannot possibly be who you are. The YOU that has been watching them all along has stayed constant and unchanging, no matter what emotions might be visiting you at the moment.

If you can shift deeply into this Observer, the eternal Witness of all that goes on in your life, you will discover the YOU that you have been seeking all your life. And emotions will never again cause you the kind of suffering they previously had. You will then be well on your way to ceasing your identification with the emotional aspect of your 3D self.

In 5D consciousness, there is no longer the struggle or need to do anything with negative emotions. If they do arise, they just flow through you; you have no need to respond to them. In addition, there is a quality about them – as there is about positive emotions, as well – that is somewhat different from what you generally experience while in third/fourth consciousness. There's a lightness to them; they float through you almost as part of the air you breathe.

But meanwhile, as I've explained, you first need to begin experiencing the emotional freedom that exists in the higher Fourth Dimension where negative emotions can still have a heavy impact on you. It's necessary to learn how to simply allow all emotions to be and not identify with them.

However, dealing with certain chronic and deeply embedded negative emotions may be another matter; simply observing them as described above may not work so well. I will therefore devote the next chapter to ways of dealing more intensively with these more challenging emotions.

Become aware that, as you are embracing yourself, you are also embracing your pain – both physical and emotional. Make sure you are including all of it; reject nothing that you are feeling. It is all part of what-is at this moment, and all must be allowed, accepted, and embraced.

3. Quiet Your Insistent Mind.

In the midst of doing all this, you may find your mind urgently barging in, over and over again, with its stories about incidents and people who have caused your pain or about what you should do to set things straight. This is when you really need to take charge and not allow yourself to be carried away by this familiar reaction of the mind. It's very important at this point to stay centered and focused on your body and on giving yourself nurturing.

If your mind is insistent, you can tell it, "Later! We will go through all that later. Right now, I'm bringing a calm, loving stillness to myself." Then bring your focus back to your body and to giving yourself love and understanding. There's no need to get angry with your mind for its interruptions; it's only doing what it's been conditioned to do. In fact, as you embrace yourself, be sure to include your mind in your embrace. Embrace ALL of you, just as you are.

This can be a very powerful exercise if you have felt overwhelmed by emotions and pummeled by your judgments toward yourself. You can realize that beating yourself up with judgments does nothing to release the hurt, anger, and pain; indeed, it simply serves to pile more pain and guilt on top of them. Again, remember that these judgments are caused by an implant that is not a natural part of YOU.

4. Don't Stop Here – Reflect Further.

At this point, you will probably be experiencing a sense of relief and relaxation. It can feel so good finally to stop resisting the pain and to accept and embrace it! So, this is where you might be inclined to stop – and either go to sleep or find a distraction of some kind.

That can be a big mistake, since the core of the problem has not yet been addressed. You have only put a salve on the symptoms. The problem is *misidentification* – you are mistaking yourself to be a small and separate 3D entity that can be overwhelmed by energy forms known as "emotions". Unless you go to the root of this problem, the same suffering is going to continue to come up every time the same emotion is triggered.

Therefore, once you are somewhat still and relaxed, take the time to look more deeply into the reaction you had to the emotions when they first appeared. This will require thought, but not in an analyzing way. It's more of a gentle reflecting and inquiring process inside yourself. See if you can become aware of any resistance to the emotions you were experiencing. As we saw in the last chapter, resistance will cause greater pain. If you were in so much pain that you were overwhelmed, some resistance was bound to be involved, some attitude of rejection or pushing the emotions away. See if you can identify what types of resistance were involved. Examples might be pushing away, ignoring, denying, judging, distracting yourself, being angry at them.

It is important to identify these reactions of resistance to negative emotions, because it is not the emotions themselves that generally put you into overwhelm – it's the resistance to them. When emotions are experienced purely, without any resistance or mental stories added to them, they can usually be tolerated – and eventually released. This becomes clear if you can remember, for instance, times when you have simply experienced sadness, with nothing added to it. When sadness is truly pure, there can almost be a sweetness about it. It's only when judgments or stories are added in that it becomes intolerable and eventually evolves into depression.

Sometimes you have to observe yourself very closely. Resistance to emotions can disguise itself very well. Let's say, for instance, that when you went into emotional overwhelm, you had been experiencing deep hatred toward a particular person in your life. When an incident between you and this person triggered this hatred, you suddenly found yourself "over the edge". Your hatred was raging; you wanted to kill the person.

What you might find, in looking clearly at this later, is that you intellectually accepted the emotion of hatred; philosophically, you believed that it's okay to feel hatred. You knew that you're human and everyone feels it from time to time. But underneath this intellectual overlay, perhaps you were not truly accepting the emotion. It felt wrong and "unspiritual", so you were very subtly resisting or denying it. Whatever you've done, just take note of it.

As you continue this process, check to see what other reactions you may have had toward your hatred. As we saw in the last chapter, another habitual reaction is indulging an emotion. This indulgence – the attempt to release the pain through action or entering into the mind to analyze it – is a form of rejection. You are not simply allowing it to be as it is. Going into the mind and telling the story about the emotion is a strong habit for many people. Take note if this is what you were doing when you were hit by overwhelm.

5. *Catch Your Automatic Attempts to Fix or Change Yourself.*

Next, check for the third form of resistance to an emotion, which can flow very naturally out of analyzing the story: immediately attempting to fix or change the emotion in some way. If you were also doing this, note this as well. There is no need to judge yourself for using any of these forms of resistance; simply observe that this is the way you have been conditioned to react to certain emotions.

Once you have discovered which of these habitual reactions of resistance you used to help create your experience of overwhelm, you can then learn how to catch them *before* an experience of overwhelm is created. Before the emotions begin drowning you, you can begin to detach from them. Awareness of your automatic reaction patterns is therefore the key, along with a sense of commitment to yourself.

6. Discover What has not Come and Gone during your Overwhelm.

The last step is to focus on all the different states you've found in yourself during this process; first you were in overwhelming emotional pain; then you were relatively calm and serene; then you were involved in thought processes in your mind; and now you are experiencing whatever is currently present for you.

Look at all these different "you's". See that they've all come and gone. Take the time now to tune into what has *not* come and gone – the YOU that was there throughout all of that drama, constant and unchanging. Move into that Awareness now, that silent, constant Awareness that is always present – no matter what changes are happening in your inner landscape, no matter what emotional "weather" is occurring at the moment. And rest there. Know that this is who you are.

You are not the suffering. You are not your emotions. You are not the thoughts about the suffering. You are not even the person dealing with emotions. You are that silent abiding Consciousness within which all of this is occurring.

Surrendering to the Emotion

The second approach you can take when you find yourself in emotional overwhelm may take some courage, but it can have quite spectacular results. It is to simply surrender to the emotion you are feeling – to totally and completely give yourself to it, experience it, holding nothing back, with *all* of yourself.

Surrendering to an emotion like this may sound like indulging it and getting lost in it, but it's actually quite different. Indulging an emotion is a reaction of giving up and passively letting it take over, falling into all the thoughts and stories about it. Surrendering to an emotion is an active, purposeful, and courageous decision to consciously dive into the middle of the emotion and totally experience it head-on. It's to ruthlessly let go of any resistance you have to it, and experientially investigate the emotion. Another way to put it is that indulging an emotion entails diving into your mind; surrendering to it involves diving within your body into the emotion itself.

I gave an example of this process in Chapter 11, when I described working with the woman who dove into her fear of death. She wasn't quite in overwhelm at the time, but she was quite strongly feeling the fear. When you're in a state of overwhelm, you have all the more energy with which to dive in and explore what's there.

Paradoxically, the process entails taking just enough control of yourself – so that you can completely let go of all control. It involves making the conscious decision to jump into the very core of the pain, without thoughts, judgments, or analysis. As you completely surrender to what presents itself, your mind must be left behind. And you must be willing to face the fear you may have of being consumed by it. Only with this kind of commitment can you truly discover the freedom that exists at the very core of the emotion.

As I've said, this process can take some courage – or maybe just a large dose of desperation. But if you are truly sick and tired of feeling bullied by an emotion, this may be the step to take. Face it squarely; call its bluff. See for yourself if it can annihilate or devour you as it's threatening to do. The results may startle and amaze you.

An Experience with the Surrendering to the Emotion Exercise

Many years ago, I tried this approach with myself for the first time. I was in the throes of a gut-wrenching reaction to something my boyfriend had just said to me. I had abruptly left him sitting there and gone into another room; feelings of rejection and abandonment were so overwhelming, I knew I needed to be alone.

As I sat there alone, tears streamed down my face. As always, my mind was chasing around in circles, panicked, trying desperately to think of something I could do to put an end to my unbearable suffering. Surely there was some way I could fix or change these emotions, so I could find some respite! But I could think of nothing. As enormous fear spread more and more deeply through my consciousness, a feeling of paralysis threatened to take hold of me.

I had felt all of this countless times before. Each time I'd just wanted to die. It seemed the only way out. Even with all the ways I had learned to deal with emotions, I could never find anything that would even begin to dissolve the pain of this familiar profound sense of rejection and abandonment. The best I could ever do was push it underground for a while by distracting myself with something else. And, inevitably, the next time it was triggered, it reappeared.

As I sat struggling with the unbelievable pain of these emotions, a new idea nudged its way into my awareness: What if I could just let go of my resistance to the pain and see what would happen? What if I just stopped trying to fix or change it and instead just let it be? Inwardly I heard from my inner guidance, "Dive into it – consciously and purposefully. See for yourself what is actually there. You may be surprised."

Dive into it? I thought. *You've got to be kidding.* Terror immediately arose in hearing this, terror of either being totally consumed by my emotions, or of going insane. I wrestled with this idea for a few minutes; then, exhausted, I just decided to do it. I was finally so weary of these emotions that I realized I had to do the only thing I'd never tried before.

With my eyes closed, I became aware of where the emotional pain was in my body – in the center of my gut. An image immediately came to me: something that looked like the mouth of a cavernous black hole. I knew that deep within this hole was dark fear, rejection, and abandonment. In my mind, I carefully inched my way over to it. Terror truly took hold of me; I was physically shaking. But I knew it was either dive into the pain and really see what it was or face a lifetime of running from it. I was desperate.

Without another thought, thrusting myself into the jaws of the beast, I quickly dove in. Immediately, my mind began grabbing at me: "No, no, don't jump – come back, we can figure this one out. You're going to die! You'll go crazy!"

There was a struggle for a while, as, in my mind's eye, I'd put my hand halfway up for something to grasp and pull me out. But then I became resolved. Either I was going to do this all the way, or forget it. Finally, I plunged into the center of the black hole in my gut, into the fear and experience of absolute abandonment. I completely let go and sank into its depths.

Profound blackness surrounded me. Nothing was there – just complete and overwhelming darkness. I was quivering as I held myself there and then did what I could to plunge ever more deeply into it. Surprisingly, I soon found a sense of profound anger beginning to rise in me. I was yelling inside myself, "Show yourself, Abandonment! Damn you! Show me your teeth! What's the worst you can do to me?" It appeared like a snarling beast. Snakes and scorpions were writhing around inside its mouth. Naturally this was frightening; but somehow my facing up to this beast and demanding that it show itself had surprisingly strengthened me.

My anger began building. I was shaking now with rage rather than terror. And yet I could still hear my mind doing new numbers: "You know, you should be expressing this rage to your boyfriend. Look at what he said to you!" Or "This is silly. It's like a grade B horror movie here. What are you doing?" Or "Let's stop here. It feels good to be angry. Let's not go any further with this."

After following these thoughts for a few moments – and almost becoming convinced by them – I again pulled my attention back to the beast and simply surrendered to it, letting go of all resistance. As I did this, much to my amazement, the beast disappeared. I had plunged into the middle of it, only to discover that nothing was there.

Indeed, nothing *at all* was there. Absolutely nothing. It was utterly depressing. Slowly a landscape began to appear. All around me was a desert – the ground was gray sand stretching on forever in every direction. The sky was gray, as well. Tears welled up inside me again. It felt as if this were really how my whole life had been: barren and empty. But I stayed alert with this; I was determined not to fall into a habitual state of self-pity. I kept hearing, "Dive even deeper." So I now dove into what was there in front of me – the barren sands of depression.

A few moments later, I emerged in a place that looked like a desolate moonscape, complete with craters and scraggly hard ground. It was all black, as if a fire had once raged there but had burned out and left cold, solid-packed dirt. Compared to this landscape, the desert had been a warm and friendly place. It was as bleak and God-forsaken a place as I'd ever seen. I sat there, unable to move. Profound despair had a hold on me. And yet, I knew I had to do something. I certainly couldn't stay there. Sighing, I finally summoned up what little courage and energy I could and dove down into one of the craters.

For a few moments, I felt almost suffocated. But then, much to my surprise and delight, I suddenly saw clear blue skies above me – beautiful, bright and friendly skies, with puffy white clouds floating through them. I let out a long sigh of relief. As I looked around, I found I was in a garden, the most incredibly lush garden I had ever seen. Brilliant flowers bloomed everywhere in bright color. Trees rose into the sky, with chirping birds flying back and forth through them. Colorful butterflies played among the flowers. Squirrels ran up and down the trees. Rabbits hopped around, chasing each other. I laughed, for this was the land of Bambi—in vivid technicolor. Such joy arose in me as I gazed around!

I walked along a path through the garden and eventually came to a beautiful, serene, turquoise lake. I sat down on a log next to it, gazing into its depths. I felt as if I could stay there forever. Amazingly, my feelings of fear, rage, and abandonment had been left far behind. A profound peace and contentment now filled me. I was ecstatic.

And yet, something kept pulling at me. The voice was again calling to me, "Come deeper. Come deeper still." Somewhat reluctantly, I decided to see if indeed I could go any more deeply into what I was experiencing. I got up and dove into the middle of the lake.

As I slowly let myself fall ever more profoundly into its depths, I soon realized I could breathe underwater. And as I relaxed more and more into it, a serenity began flowing into me – one even surpassing the one I had experienced sitting by the lake. It began rippling through me with tremendous power. In a strange way, it felt as if it were pulling me apart – and yet it was an exquisitely pleasant and sensuous experience.

As I gave into it more and more profoundly, I soon found myself experiencing a sense of enormous vastness. I realized I was everywhere. I extended in all directions. The entire universe was inside of *me*. I was the Mother – the Source of all that is. Tears began streaming down my face again. As I vibrated with the tremendous power and elation of this realization, I quickly dove in even deeper.

I began remembering the feelings of rejection and abandonment I had been experiencing so profoundly just a short while before, and they were like mist – unreal – so insignificant in the whole scheme of things. They so obviously had no power whatsoever over who I now knew myself to be, it was a joke! I began laughing, then began to rock. Soon it felt as if the entire universe were rocking.

I sat there for almost an hour, blissfully marveling at what I was experiencing – and at what I had discovered. By finally facing the demons inside me, and fully surrendering to them, I had discovered what truly lay at the core of them: my eternal Self.

When I finally got up and walked into the other room where my boyfriend sat, I could see he was obviously still angry and sullen from our argument. I simply smiled at him and told him I was leaving and that we'd talk later. I could see he was puzzled. The last time he'd seen me, I had been raging with helpless anger and pain. Now I was obviously calm and fully in charge of myself.

I knew that something had definitely cleared in me. I was no longer terrified of feeling emotionally or physically abandoned by him – or by anyone. Such incredible freedom! I have never again experienced the kind of fear of abandonment that, up until that point, had haunted me. Sometimes a ghost of it appears in my awareness. But it has no power over me anymore. Since I finally saw it for what it was, it can no longer do anything to me. By courageously diving directly into the dreaded emotion, I had discovered there was nothing there – except the true nature of my deepest Self.

I have gone into such detail in recounting my experience because it's important to understand that this process can take you to many surprising places which may not seem at first to have much to do with your initial motivation to dive in. The important thing is to follow where this process takes you. Trust yourself, rely on your higher guidance.

Emotions as Gateways into your 5D Self

As is clear, this process of surrendering to an emotion can take courage, persistence, and patience. But the value you can derive from it is beyond words. At the very least, you will have faced your fear of the emotion and will no longer need to feel bullied by it in the future. More importantly, you will likely discover who you truly are, beyond the emotion. You will find that you have indeed survived surrendering to it completely; you have not been annihilated or devoured. Indeed, you have found that who you are is much larger and more powerful than any emotion you could ever experience.

The extraordinary discovery is that you can actually use your emotions – the very emotions that threaten to overwhelm and annihilate you – as gateways into the experience of your 5D Self. Although seemingly hidden at times, if you simply take the time and the courage to look for this Self, it can be found and experienced.

There are probably many ways in which you can handle overwhelming emotions. Most of them will likely give you a sense of relief. Some of them may even offer a healing of the emotion. However, what I am suggesting is that you take it one step further and go to the core of the pain, to the cause of *all* emotional suffering: your belief that you are a small individual being who is subject to the power of emotions. If this is what you identify with, then you are doomed to suffer. Dragging you back and forth, inside out and upside down, emotions will run you ragged. They'll feed you horror stories. At times, they'll overwhelm and drown you in third-dimensional sorrow.

The only way out of this is to know that who you are is the essence of Life itself. You are the very *Source* of all emotions. Without you, they have no life. An effective way to discover this is through understanding that there is no reason to try to control, manipulate, or get rid of emotions. Simply see them clearly for what they are – forms of energy that are visiting your consciousness. They have no inherent power except that which you give them.

It's helpful to remember too that not only are you not your emotions – you are not even the person who is experiencing them. This person is just a temporary expression that is currently appearing within the vast field of Divine Light that is YOU. Even when this person is gone, YOU will remain.

Of course, because of all the years of emotional conditioning you've had while living in the Third Dimension, treating emotions like this may be easier said than done. So, in order to help you get your arms ever more securely around this animal of emotional suffering so you can eventually release it it for good, I will come at it in the next chapter from another direction. I will address the ways in which you can be trapped in your emotions by holding onto your "story of suffering".

Chapter 15

Letting Go of Your 3D Story of Suffering

Aside from anything else, the Third Dimension is certainly about suffering. There's no way around it. Suffering is inherent in this controlled dimension's structure. Yet, it is possible to step free of it. One thing necessary is to be willing to let go of your personal story of that suffering and stop defining yourself through that story. You cannot release the suffering while remaining attached to the story about it. It just doesn't work. And very importantly, you can't take this story with you into the Fifth Dimension.

However, letting go of the story of your suffering may not be an easy thing to do. Without even being aware of it, you may tend to give a great deal of energy to it. Perhaps you think often about it, talk about it, ask people's advice about it, and try to figure out ways to stop it. With all this, it's easy to begin believing this story somehow defines you.

If you're familiar with the Law of Attraction, you're aware that the more we focus our energy on something, the more we continue to create it in our lives. This is especially true in how we perpetuate suffering in our lives: the more energy we put into our stories about our suffering, the more we perpetuate them. In fact, if we look closely, we can find that, because we have focused so much on our stories, we have actually created "broken records" in our lives: the same painful events and situations keep repeating themselves over and over again.

You may feel you have good reason to put energy into your story of suffering. Perhaps you have worked hard in getting in touch with all the pain and hardship you've endured and in learning how to deeply experience your emotions. You have talked about your story to many people, analyzing it over and over again – believing that, if you can just figure it all out, the suffering will be relieved. You may protest that you're not trying to perpetuate your suffering with all of this; you're trying to understand it so as to alleviate it.

It is true that getting in touch with your story of suffering is indeed an important step toward emotional freedom. You need to know what has been keeping you in bondage. Attempting to fix the story by changing behaviors, attitudes and beliefs can also be helpful. But if you've been at this process for some time and are still deeply caught in the suffering, you might want to honestly ask yourself: Do I truly want to be free of my suffering?

Motivations for Keeping the Story Going

One thing to be aware of is that there is a common and often unconscious belief in compassionate lightworkers that if they're not suffering, they aren't being a "good" person. There's a conviction that because there are people in the world who are suffering, they need to be suffering too. In other words, it's not okay to be happy and free when there are so many others who are not. This can be very subtle, so it is important to reflect on this to see if this belief may be something you are holding onto on some level.

For other people, a personal story of suffering is an important way in which they can feel special; their stories are a way they can feel valuable, special, and interesting. In fact, in some circles, the more juicy a person's story of suffering is, the more interesting and well-respected they are. I've listened while people actually try to one-up each other with their stories, as if to say, "You think *you've* suffered – wait till you hear *my* story!"

To be clear, nothing is inherently wrong with 3D stories of suffering. They are, actually, often what has given color to life. Sometimes people have incredibly fascinating stories; they're exciting, dramatic, tragically humorous. They can all be entertaining in their own way. And, if there has been a lot learned and accomplished through all the suffering, they can be instructive and motivating, as well. But it's what we *do* with these stories that causes us further suffering. It's how we use them to perpetuate the pain that gets us in trouble and how we stay attached to them, building our identity around them.

Throughout the earlier years of my counseling practice, I had a number of "drama queen" clients. In some ways, these women were the most difficult to help. So often their whole identity was caught up in the stories of all the suffering they had endured. Whenever I would finally suggest that perhaps they were attached to their stories of suffering, they always protested that of course they weren't – they wanted to put an end to them.

Diana was one such woman. She did, indeed, have a tragic story to tell. From the very beginning of her life, she seemed doomed: a harsh, alcoholic father and a schizophrenic mother; criticism, abuse, and abandonment all through childhood; one dysfunctional relationship after another throughout adulthood; accidents and abortions and children out of wedlock. You name it – she had experienced it. It was understandable that she held onto her story of suffering – what else did she have in her life? Because of her early wounding, she had never been able to discover anything besides her suffering to help her feel important.

At first she could not even hear the suggestion that making her story so important was precisely what was perpetuating it. It took many long months of counseling before she could even begin to look at this possibility. But when she finally did and began stepping out of her identity with her story, her life finally began turning around in monumental ways. For the first time, she was able to attract a partner in her life who was kind and loving toward her.

Trying to Fix the Story

As we've seen earlier, anyone on a self-improvement path can make the erroneous detour of falling into worshiping their wounding. Usually, after some therapy or reading certain self-help books, people will begin to look closely at how their story of suffering came into being. This usually takes them on a journey of exploration of all facets of their story of wounding.

Then, often, the next step is trying to fix the story in some way. This is a fourth-dimensional healing approach which can definitely produce some relief. Positive changes can be made and greater freedom can be experienced. However, the problem usually begins when the attempts at fixing the emotions in the story no longer have the truly desired results. At this point, people generally decide they just haven't found the right techniques or insights to fix the suffering, and they go back and rehash the story again. At some point, the story finally becomes fully ingrained in their identity. And, to make things worse, the efforts to alleviate their suffering end up being woven into the story, itself, strengthening it even further.

After feeling unsuccessful in stopping their suffering, the next step people will often take is to see their suffering as "spiritual lessons" they are here to learn. They adopt the belief that all their pain has a purpose: they are "growing and learning" through it. Although this new age perspective has the flavor of archonic infiltration running through it – with the subscript that suffering has a purpose, that it is necessary for humanity to learn and grow – it is true that people often do tend to learn and awaken through their suffering.

Yet, in the end, the solace this perspective offers is limited. No matter how much reframing we do about experiences of emotional suffering – if we're honest about it, the suffering is still there. Neither our philosophy about it nor our analysis of it truly alleviates it. As we've seen in the last few chapters, emotional freedom can only really come about when we detach our identity from the emotions themselves and simply let them be. And to let them go, we also have to let go of the story we have about them.

Do You Really Want to Let it Go?

What it comes down to is asking yourself: Am I really ready to give up my 3D story of suffering? Think about it honestly. Are you ready to not take it so seriously, to not make it of such primary importance in your life?

Are you ready to stop talking about it to people so often? Are you willing to stop thinking about it so much, analyzing it to death? Once you've done all this, are you willing to see what might be left of you, without your story?

If you think you might be ready for this, here are some steps you can take to begin letting go of your story.

Exercise: *Letting Go of the Story*

1. **Understand that your story of suffering is about your 3D self; it's not about YOU.** It's the story that your 3D self has created about its painful reactions to the events and situations that have come its way since childhood (and perhaps also from past lives). This story, in reality, has nothing to do with YOU. The true YOU has simply stood by and watched the whole drama the little self has created. It has been compassionate and loving; yet, being utterly free, it has not been touched by the suffering.

Even if you can't yet see the story from this detached viewpoint, just understanding on the intellectual level that this story is about your 3D self and not the true YOU can be a start.

2. **See your life as a story.** The next step is to begin seeing your 3D life of suffering as a story – or perhaps a movie. While you are watching it, you engage with the story for a while, probably identifying with the main character in the drama, totally engrossed in how the story will resolve itself. But, once it's over and you leave the theater, you easily let it go.

This can be a fun process, one that can bring in humor and a sense of relief. Become the objective observer of this drama. Take time to look over the long expanse of your life, assuming a neutral attitude about it, as if it were the story of someone else's life.

Now attempt to determine the important themes of suffering that have been woven into the story throughout the years. Look at the painful experiences that have happened over and over again; note the emotions and thoughts that have gotten triggered each time. Also become aware of who the main players in the story have been, the ones who have helped you to play your role as the tragic hero or heroine of the story.

3. **Write a summary of your life**. Compose a short summary of your 3D life of suffering. Here are two examples:

a. *This is a story about a woman who has felt misunderstood and unloved most of her life. Even when love is offered to her, she always manages to reject it, because she feels undeserving of love. She has felt lonely and unhappy most of her life.*

b. *This story is about a man who has rebelled against authority figures all of his life. This has gotten him into trouble time and time again – first with his parents, then with teachers at school, then with bosses and superintendents at work. He has also automatically rebelled against anyone he feels is smarter than he is. He has experienced enormous rage and suffering because of all this. He has never really felt loved, because he's always pushed the most important people in his life away.*

4. **Find a broken record**. Now choose a particular theme within your story, a painful event that happens over and over – and determine specifically how the dynamics of this "broken-record" work. Let's use the example above of the woman who felt misunderstood and unloved most of her life. The woman who came up with this story wrote the following broken record scenario:

It all starts when I see someone I find attractive and think I want to get to know them. Pretty soon I start feeling like I really want them to love me. So I begin doing everything I can to try to win this person's love. I do great things for them. I take care of them when they're sick. I give them support and nurturing when they need it.

Quite often, as time goes on, the person will start showing signs of loving me. They become affectionate and warm. They do caring things for me. They even tell me they love me. But as soon as all this begins, I start feeling turned off by them. I think, if this person loves ME, how attractive or smart can they be? And I no longer want to be with with them. I leave.

5. **See how you perpetuate the story**. Now that you understand better what your 3D story of suffering boils down to, and how the dynamics of a broken-record scenario work, it is time to ask yourself what you do to perpetuate this story. By this I do *not* mean for you to continue analyzing what happens in the story so you can fix it or change it in some way.

I am suggesting you step outside the story and see what you do with it that perpetuates it. For instance, what attitudes do you hold about yourself as the hero or heroine in the story? Do you judge yourself for what you do in your story? Judging yourself or your story will certainly keep the story going strong. Perhaps, out of shame, you try to hide your story from people.

Similarly, feeling pride or sentimental pity for yourself will perpetuate the story as well. When you tell your story to people, do they tend to respond with awe toward you for how much suffering you have to deal with on a daily basis? Do you talk endlessly to people about it? Do you think about it constantly? All of these actions and attitudes about your story give energy to it and keep you attached to it, perpetuating it in your life. In other words, it is not the story per se, but your attachment to it that guarantees its reenactment in your life.

6. **Let go of the story.** After becoming aware of all you are doing to perpetuate the story, the final step is to give up doing these things. You will probably see how habitual some of the attitudes and actions are and find them difficult to release. Persistent vigilance may be necessary at first. The attitude toward your story needs to be an objective, dispassionate one, but with also a great deal of compassion for yourself.

Starving Your 3D Story

Giving your story this new treatment probably won't immediately stop the broken-record scenarios from playing out in your life. They will likely continue for a while, simply because they are so familiar and habitual. However, you can begin robbing them of their vitality and pain by observing yourself while you're playing them out. Watch them as if they are episodes in a TV series. See how boring, repetitive, and predictable they really are. Given no energy, they will eventually disappear from your life.

The important thing to remember is that your story of suffering is not a story about YOU. It's something your 3D self has invented. Have the courage to let go of it – even for a short time – and find out what is left of you, without a story of suffering to define you.

To begin with, you can try an experiment in doing this for just a day. During the entire day, watch both your thoughts and what you talk about to other people. Watch for any thoughts that have to do with what's wrong with your life and how you're suffering because of it. Catch all thoughts that have to do with how bad these things make you feel, all the times in the past they have happened, how they might happen again in the future – and how you need to fix any of it in any way.

Note these thoughts, and the feelings that go with them, without rejecting any of them. Then turn your attention toward something else. Act similarly with any urge you have to talk to other people about your story: when the impulse arises, simply decide to talk about something else.

In other words, give your 3D story of suffering a starvation diet for the entire day. See what happens. You may be amazed at the peace and freedom that are waiting for you, once you spend even a short period of time without this tired, old, familiar story. And then think about what it might be like to drop it for good!

Ashley's Story

I once set up a psychodrama situation in a class I was giving, in order to demonstrate how to let go of the story of suffering. It turned out to be a fun and powerful learning experience for all of us.

First of all, everyone in the class wrote out their stories of suffering and then the dynamics of one broken-record theme within their stories. After all of them shared what they'd written, I chose a woman, Ashley, to be our subject in the psychodrama. I could see she was very clear about what her story was and that she was also eager to learn how to let go of it.

Ashley had been coming to individual counseling for a number of months, during which time she had been working hard to discover why she kept getting caught up in feelings of anger and resentment. We saw that she had developed many patterns of overextending herself to please others and then becoming resentful when they were not as considerate and kind to her in return.

We began working on how she could take responsibility for creating this situation and turn it around. As a bright young woman and also very motivated, she began focusing on giving to herself more than had been her practice and habit, not giving to others from an "empty cup", and not expecting others to fill the needs that she "by all rights" needed to fill herself. She was empowered through this work, and over all, more happy in her life.

Yet she realized that, no matter how much she'd changed and how vigilant she'd become, the same situations were still happening. She wasn't as reactive in these situations, nor did she experience quite as much suffering in them, but they were still occurring. And she was getting truly sick and tired of them.

At this point, she was very ready in this class setting to try a new approach. I asked her to read to us again her broken-record scenario. Here's what she told us:

> "First I decide to do something really nice for someone. Sometimes I actually bend over backwards to please them even

when it means I don't take care of my own needs in the process. But, at the time of doing these nice things, I'm usually feeling loving and warm toward the person.

"Then the person either ignores what I've done or they actually criticize me for doing it; they get angry at me, or feel hurt and resentful about what I've done. I am amazed and incredulous. I can't believe they aren't feeling appreciative about what I've done for them. I try explaining why I've done what I've done and end up getting defensive about it.

"Then they get angry and even more critical. Finally, I get furious, yell at them, and leave – vowing never again to do anything for them."

After outlining this broken record so clearly, she described three people in her life with whom she was currently playing out the story in one form or another. She told us about her brother, her husband, and her cousin, describing the situations she was in with each of them, what their personalities were, and what their basic messages to her were.

I had her choose someone in the class to play the part of herself, the heroine, in the psychodrama and explained that she would simply be observing it as part of the "audience". I had her then choose three other people to play the roles of her brother, her husband and her cousin. I explained that the rest of us in the class were going to be people who would be watching the TV series called "Ashley's Life".

As the "audience", we acted as if we were all very familiar with the story in the "series"; we'd seen previous episodes and we knew the plot and themes very well. Before the show began, in our roles as the "audience", we talked about the story. We mourned how Ashley was always being misunderstood and unappreciated. She was such a good person, so nice and good to everyone – and look at how she is always treated! We passed popcorn and soft drinks to each other, as we sat and chatted among ourselves about Ashley's story, waiting for the show to begin.

Then it started. The actress playing "Ashley" immediately fell into the role with great authenticity. Her anger and her tears were very real and palpable. The other players in the drama were also playing their roles quite convincingly. As is so delightfully common in psychodrama, all the players discovered they'd been given perfect roles. In one way or another, they could relate only too well to them.

As the different scenes unfolded, and "Ashley" in the show began truly to become embroiled in her emotional struggle, we in the audience began to talk among ourselves:

"Oh, here comes the part where she gets hurt and angry!"

"Oh, poor Ashley – people just don't understand her. She tries so hard to be nice to them, and look what they do!"

"Ashley is such a good person – I feel so sorry for her."

It was apparent by this time how uncomfortable the real Ashley in the room was beginning to feel. Although she was laughing and joking about the story with the rest of us, she was beginning to see clearly how her story looked from the outside. She was, in effect, able to see it objectively, perhaps for the first time.

What really struck her was how boring the story was, how repetitious and predictable. She was shaking her head, unable to believe that this was the story she had been putting so much effort into all her life – and that she had come to identify herself as the disempowered heroine of this story.

At one point, I stepped outside the psychodrama role I'd been playing as part of the "audience" and said to her "Remember, Ashley – this woman in the movie is not who YOU are. She's just a little 3D self that goes around in the world believing herself to be a separate, individual little being who has to figure out how to run her life. She doesn't know that you, as her Higher 5D Self, are here to do that job. And with this very limiting ignorance, she's doing her best to cope with what life is handing her. It's not easy! Have love and compassion for her. And, at the same time, don't get caught up in the illusion that she is who YOU are."

I could see the light in Ashley's eyes brighten, as what I was saying registered. She knew what I was talking about; she had had some important experiences of her 5D Self in the past. All she needed to make the shift in awareness at this point, even in the midst of her pain, was a reminder of the Truth. She smiled and nodded. I could see her body relax, as the final scene concluded.

At the end, the players bowed, and we all clapped and lauded them. They briefly shared their experiences in playing their roles. I then turned my attention to Ashley and asked her to share what her experience had been. She told us how painful it was to see her story enacted so clearly – but also how elated she felt. Something had shifted inside her, she said; a decision that it was definitely time to drop this whole story had been made on a profound level. Although she had thought in the past that she had made this same decision, she realized now that she never really had. She had still wanted to cling to the story of the mistreated, unappreciated victim. Now she was utterly nauseated by it.

I told her I understood her reaction and I knew she could no longer play out this scenario in the same way. She now knew this was just a script she had developed somewhere along the way throughout her 3D life but no longer needed to follow. I also cautioned her that this wasn't necessarily an easy thing to do; she would probably find that broken-record scenarios seem to have a life of their own. The process is similar to when a ceiling fan has been switched off; it takes a little while for it to completely come to a stop.

I added that, at any time in the future, when she found herself in the same situation, she could step back and watch it as a movie – just as she'd done in class. She could become the observer of the show, as well as the heroine on the screen. In doing this, she would inevitably discover that the scenarios happened less often. More importantly, she would discover that she was really not touched by the suffering going on in them.

Observing a Story of Suffering

I described to the class how I had experienced this with my own story in a number of situations, and interesting things had happened. One time I was on the phone with a colleague with whom I had had difficulty over and over again; we always seemed to miscommunicate about about one thing or another. Typically, she would get angry – and I would assume all the blame and then end up feeling defensive and hurt. I had tried numerous times to change this pattern – by not assuming the blame, not getting defensive, staying "neutral" in my explanations. I had also tried talking to her about our "problem" in hopes of resolving it together.

Although the situation seemed to get a little better for a while, it was never really resolved. The pattern continued in one form or another, and I kept getting pulled into it. It seemed I had put so much energy into my role of suffering in this particular scenario that the pattern would not break. My identity was still hooked into that of the misunderstood victim.

Finally, I began to loosen my identity with this victim-self; I distanced myself enough to just watch her as she thought her tiresome thoughts and went through her predictable defensive behaviors and explanations with this woman. Little by little, an almost visceral "unhooking" took place, along with the direct realization that this victim was not who I was, but just a product of conditioning that had occurred numerous times, throughout not only this life but many past lives as well. In later years, I would have recognized that this kind of pattern of self-blame was stemming from the inner critic implant; but at the time, it was enough to simply realize it was not a part of who I actually was.

A short while later, as I was on the phone once again with the woman with whom I'd been having trouble, I started observing myself as the whole dynamic once again began to unfold. I observed what I was saying, what I was feeling, how I was reacting. Suddenly, I found myself becoming very bored with the whole scene, without the energy to even continue it. I stopped mid-sentence and was silent for a few moments. Then I said to her,

"You know, I don't want to do this anymore. It's old, it's tiresome, it's a waste of time. I'll call you later." And I hung up.

Amazingly, we never entered into that dynamic again. Our miscommunications even diminished. The few times they did occur, the dynamic between us was very different. We each assumed responsibility for our part in it, and we very quickly cleared it up and moved on. I had had to see it very clearly, objectively, in order to get so bored with the story, that I could finally let it go.

Developing Boredom with your Story

Ashley reported to me a week later that the same old dynamic with her cousin had happened again. However, she said that throughout the scene, she had been able to watch it. Although it continued much as it always had, her emotional discomfort about it was greatly diminished. She knew she had finally seen her story of suffering so clearly and had become so bored with it, that it could no longer grab her as it had in the past. She'd also been able to see the pathetic humor in it all; her poor little 3D self was just doing what it had been conditioned to do.

I could see she was finally beginning to feel at peace about her story. She said she was no longer interested in even talking about it to anyone anymore. Nor did she feel she needed to do anything to fix it. She just needed to continue viewing it as a movie that was playing over and over again, and not give it much thought. She could just let it die a quiet death and put her attention into something more exciting and productive. She laughed with relief. After so many years of trying to fix her story of suffering, she was finally letting go of it.

As time went on, Ashley realized something else very important, something I, too, had realized about myself: once you begin letting go of your 3D story of suffering – aside from experiencing the relief of letting go of something so negative and painful – you also realize that you have made room for your 5D Self to begin shining through into your awareness. Without the clutter of all the emotions and thoughts about the suffering, there is suddenly space, an openness, for something else to come present. You find a peacefulness, a harmony, begin to pervade your consciousness. You realize that this is for you to rest in, to drop into ever more deeply – and to see where it takes you.

You may find that, even after you have begun truly to let your story of suffering go, your story starts finding new ways in which to allure you once again into following it. Don't worry; just let that be. Give it no energy. Just keep focusing on the peace and the spaciousness in your consciousness. When ignored long enough – and when seen clearly for what it really is –

the story of suffering eventually begins to evaporate. It becomes clear what it was made of all along: a story your own mind, influenced by the inner critic implant, had created and believed.

Chapter 16

Surviving Relationship Challenges in the 4th Dimension

Letting go of the story of suffering has been especially challenging in recent times due to conflicts that have occurred between family members, spouses and friends around the vaccines and politics. Many people continue to suffer from broken ties with loved ones.

However, these kinds of conflicts between people would probably be occurring anyway, due to the ever-more powerful 5D frequencies now flooding the Earth. These energies are forcing to the surface all hidden conflicts, imbalances and unhealthy agendas within relationships – situations that can't be taken into the Fifth Dimension. The conflicts either need to be resolved – or the relationships need somehow to end.

Although perhaps good news in the end, this process of clearing out unhealthy relationships is understandably challenging if certain relationships are important to you; any disruption in them can be extremely distressing. This is especially so if it is one that has been long-term. You may be finding that old, painful patterns that have never been clearly resolved are coming to the surface. Perhaps communication between you has become more difficult, old unhealed traumas are resurfacing, and you're finding your emotions are more difficult to hide than ever before.

If you're not aware of what is occurring on the deeper levels of Ascension, it can be very unsettling. And, furthermore, you can more easily get lost in both your story of suffering and your identification with your emotional self – once again re-identifying basically with your third-dimensional self.

Change Must Occur

Again, many people are having similar experiences in their relationships. In some cases, it is apparent that, if they are are going to continue on in those relationships, things are going to have to change rather dramatically.

Some are discovering that no matter what they do or say, it's evident the relationship cannot last. A number of marriages have become quite rocky; others, even after long years of being together, are actually breaking up. Business partnerships are also splitting up. People are having to learn how to let go of loved ones and friends who have been in their lives for a long time.

In other relationships, people are managing to maintain the relationship, but it's become clear that certain changes in their behaviors and relating patterns must occur. For example, if a couple has been playing out an enabler/abuser scenario in the relationship, it becomes clear this can no longer continue. Or, if both people have been holding onto past hurts, betrayals or anger – and especially if there has been a great deal of blaming of each other – these patterns also can no longer persist in the relationship.

In other cases, people are discovering that, if they're to stay together, they can no longer hide things from each other. If either person has not been expressing his or her true feelings, if they've been dishonest in any way, the truth must come out. And, at the same time, if the two people are too emotionally dependent on each other, this too is no longer working. Everyone is now being compelled to be responsible for creating their own happiness and their own sense of feeling valuable and lovable.

In general, people are discovering that, in order to stay in a relationship, all of the patterns they've developed in the old 3D reality that are not based in love and respect must now change to match the new frequencies.

Positive Aspects of the 5D Frequencies on Relationships

If any of this is happening in your life, it's important to realize that, as challenging as these disruptive high-energy frequencies may be to your relationships, they have a very important and positive purpose: they are here to assist you in your evolutionary process. They are serving to help awaken you to who you truly are beyond your third-dimensional ideas of your identity. They are also offering profound opportunities for creating greater honesty, integrity and freedom in your relationships.

In addition, there is also the opportunity now, both for yourself and for those you are in relationship with, to experience a much deeper love – and to see how your commitment to each other can be greatly strengthened.

The 5D frequencies are ultimately coming in to "set right" all relationships that are destined to remain in the coming years of Ascension into the Fifth Dimension. No dysfunctional pattern can survive this shift and must be resolved in one way or another.

In certain cases, in order for a relationship to heal and rise in vibration, a drastic event, such as a death or a severe medical diagnosis, may occur. A lot of fear and upset may ensue; but when the people involved can take responsibility for themselves and are motivated to emotionally mature, their relationship can not only survive, but actually greatly deepen. They can experience a more profound love connection than ever before with their loved one, as well as greater respect.

Ending of Karmic Contracts

There is an interesting type of relationship change that is also occurring for some that has less to do with conflict, and more to do with simply feeling an energetic shift in the relationship.

It can feel like something has somehow changed – sometimes rather abruptly – or that something that has always been present in the relationship has disappeared. There's somehow more freedom, less struggle occurring. There's more space for reflection, greater clarity, and surprising ease in communicating.

If this is happening for you in an important relationship, it is likely you are experiencing the ending of a karmic contract with the person. This may come about simply due to the fact that you have completed the karma you came in to resolve with the other person – or it may be happening because the whole corrupted karmic structure humanity has struggled under for eons is finally collapsing and karma everywhere is dissolving. Whatever the case, the feeling is that you have completed some conflict that was there between you and the other person and you are now free to determine if there is any reason to continue staying together.

This can be a greatly freeing experience, but it can also be disorienting. If it is with a family member or a long-term relationship with a friend or partner, it can also be greatly disturbing. There can be a sense of *What now? Where do we go from here? Do we still want to be in relationship with each other?*.

When this feeling of completion occurs, it may mean that you will choose to stay together, but you will likely be engaged in a freer way of relating to each other. New agreements, whether acknowledged or not, will probably be made. As you get to see each other more clearly and come to know each other in new ways without the familiar knot of karmic connection present, you will likely go through a period of awkwardness. But you will find a new and freer rhythm with each other.

However, the ending of a karmic contract can also mean that it's time to terminate the relationship. The karma is complete, so it feels like there is no need to be together anymore. As scary as this may initially be for both people, they will probably eventually find that the sense of freedom they feel from no longer being tied to someone in this karmic way is greatly uplifting.

Different Paths of Ascension

One of the most obvious ways we have seen relationships break up in recent times has been around the choices people have made about taking the vaccine. Family members have battled with each other over this issue. Spouses have been amazed in finding they are on opposite sides of the question. And, after years of feeling so similarly about all things in life, friends are disappointed to find how they do not agree on the issue. As a result, we have seen a clear split taking place in humanity as a whole – between those taking the shot and those who are adamantly opposed to it. Similar issues arose in the US during the last presidential election – in that arena, as well, hard and fast lines were drawn between family members and friends.

It's common to think that it's just politics or fears about the pandemic that are causing these strong breaks in relationships that are occurring. But, in reality, as earlier described, these issues are just bringing into greater focus the splits that, due to the 5D frequencies of light that are flooding the planet, would be occurring anyhow in one way or another.

In truth, what is happening is that people are making their decisions to go in whichever direction is right for them at this time. As Souls, we are each being inwardly directed onto the path that will best serve our own unique evolutionary growth. It can be painful to see loved ones going in a different direction than we are; but as sovereign Beings, we must all make our own choices. And, if it is clear we are headed in different directions, we must be able to let go of the old ties we've had with them.

Sometimes, when we feel doubt about which relationships to hold onto and which to let go, it can be helpful to tune into our body to see what it is telling us. So often, our mind and emotions can muddle our sense of knowing what is right for us. But, speaking through sensations and energetic shifts, our body can tell us the truth quite clearly.

In the end, we need to be courageous in trusting that if love truly is there between us and another person, at some point we will be reunited again. And, in truth, no matter what occurs, the love we feel for them will still remain in our hearts.

Finding New Relationships

If you're having a difficult time letting go of old familiar relationships with people who seem to be traveling in a different direction at this point, it can be helpful to see your situation from a higher perspective. You can become aware that a space is opening up for new people to come into your life, people more like yourself, people who perhaps have a similar spiritual mission as you, people who more harmoniously resonate with your worldview.

Be aware that a new life is actually appearing in front of you during these times; and, in order to enter into your life, everyone and everything new coming in needs a clear and open space without old 3D energies in it. So it's important to look around you and see who does seem to be on the same path with you and tune into them energetically. Feel into them with your body, as well as with your mind and emotions. Is there an energetic resonance between you?

Some of these people you may already know but you have not thought about getting to know more deeply. Others may be brand new in your acquaintance – or the only connection you can have with them at this time is online.

Nonetheless, it can be important now to try to deepen these relationships. These people are likely part of your Soul Tribe – those you will be traveling together with on your continuing Ascension path into 5D. You may be destined to work with them on humanitarian projects together. You may share similar passions you never knew about before.

New Phase of Ascension

Since the beginning of 2021, we have definitely been in a new phase of Ascension — a much more rapid one. The tensions will likely be heightening as we ride through the next few years to come. But remember to keep in mind that this is all due to the Ascension energies coming in: everything in your life, including your relationships, must now come into alignment with these energies.

In order to shift more clearly into your 5D identity, you need to be wise in letting go of what is leaving your life and to welcome what is coming into being. Truly, all is perfect; you are now being guided more closely and lovingly than ever before on your path to 5D freedom.

If you can just trust this and allow the Ascension energies to have their way with you, it can be so much easier.

Chapter 17

Experiencing Freedom in Intimate Relationships

Clearly, these times we are living in are truly testing us in all of our relationships. But perhaps the relationships that are most challenging are those that are intimate, the ones with spouses, partners and lovers. Emotions run especially high in these relationships and, therefore, it is easy to fall into 3D identity within them. Even before the Ascension process really started amping up, these relationships had generally been the most difficult to navigate, simply because of childhood woundings that seem to naturally get wound into them.

Therefore, this chapter will be devoted to exploring intimate relationships and how you can understand the challenges in them when functioning from third-dimensional consciousness. Then we will focus on how you can shift your relationship into a more fifth-dimensional one, with its promise of greater emotional freedom. Most of what will be discussed can also be applied to any other important relationship you may have.

As noted, creating and maintaining a fulfilling relationship with another human being hasn't always been easy, mainly because we've approached it while identified with our 3D selves. Some people undertake valiant efforts to make their relationships work; yet, all too often, they fail. Always there is something not quite right or satisfactory in what they create.

"Good" and "Healthy" Relationships

I think most of us can look around at the marriages and partnerships with which we are familiar and see few we might call "good" or "healthy". Often we think some are healthy and happy, only to learn later that, just to keep the relationship going, painful compromises have been endured by one or both partners.

The fact that people have stayed together in a marriage for many years does not automatically make these marriages "good" or "successful" relationships. It *is* possible that it signifies a healthy, mature quality the partners share: knowing how to "hang in there" through the difficult times they have together.

But it can just as easily signify an unhealthy dependence and fear they each have of being alone. Think of all the marriages you know in which the partners, while obviously disliking each other and making each other miserable, have unbelievably stayed together for years. Or the ones in which one person in the relationship has "sold out". In order to hold onto the other person, they've decided they'll do anything – including letting go of what is most important to them. It seems that as unhappy and unfulfilled as the people in these relationships may be, facing the fear of living alone feels like a worse alternative.

Many relationships, of course, have beautiful aspects to them. Deep love, acceptance, support, respect, and appreciation are all profoundly present. But these have generally come about through many years of hard work, compromise and sacrifice. And inevitably, this isn't the whole story. Often other aspects of these relationships aren't so rosy.

One Catch that Cannot be Avoided in Relationships

Furthermore, even the most positive and loving relationships usually have one catch that cannot be transcended as long as the people in the relationship look to it as a main source of their happiness, security, and love. This is that there is no guarantee that the relationship will continue past the present moment. No matter how many promises people in a partnership may make to each other about staying together forever, forces beyond their control can come in at any time and challenge these promises.

Life brings all sorts of surprises – accidents, unexpected situations, and unsolicited attractions – that can change a fulfilling and seemingly secure relationship overnight. Often the most devastating event is death. Whether conscious or not, when in 3D consciousness, the fear is always present that an important relationship could end at any moment through the death of a partner. With this death, the person would be alone again, without the source of love, security, and fulfillment they once had. This realization can bring such immense fear that it is usually kept unconscious, but it is always there.

Hundreds of books have been written on how to be happy in relationships, books that tell us how to stay in them, how to leave them, how to fix them to make them more fulfilling. I think it's safe to say that most people who seek therapy end up (if not begin by) talking about their intimate relationships. Either they are having problems in the one they're in, or they're not in one and would like to be. People obviously find relationships very important – but are continually dissatisfied with what is going on in that area of their lives. No matter how full of love and trust their primary relationship may be, they always want something more.

Addressing the Real Issue

In such relationships, dissatisfaction is inevitable because the basic issue in relationships based in 3D consciousness is rarely ever addressed. And this is the fact that what most people are looking for in a relationship is a guarantee of love, security, and a sense of being desirable and valuable – and this cannot truly be given by another person.

Often, at the onset of a romantic relationship, there is the illusion that this guarantee is, indeed, being given by the other person. Believing they have finally found the person who will fulfill their important needs, people in love float around in sheer bliss. But ultimately this illusion bursts. It is discovered that this person is not, after all, giving all that has been promised. This is when many relationships break up: when people realize that the partner they've chosen isn't going to give them the love, security, and fulfillment they were hoping to receive.

This would be an important insight, except that, unfortunately, most people experiencing this type of disillusionment believe they have simply chosen the wrong partner. They still insist that all they need is to find the right one who will give them what they want. *They don't realize that no one else can actually fulfill their basic emotional needs for them.*

Some people in relationship, either through therapy or simply through personal insight, discover this truth. They realize that they have to fulfill their own basic needs for love, security, and emotional fulfillment. They can accept whatever their partner may be able to offer in these areas, but they know it is up to them to find the true fulfillment of these needs within themselves. Coming to this insight is an important step toward a truly healthy and mature relationship, and it can bring about tremendously rewarding changes.

However, this still does not go far enough. Most people, unaware of their own true divine nature, attempt to find the love, security and wholeness they desire from within the meager resources of their 3D self. They learn to be good to themselves; they learn to love themselves as unconditionally as possible; they develop rewarding relationships with other people; they develop new interests and new talents and skills. All of these things can be immensely fulfilling and take a lot of pressure off of a primary relationship.

If you have done such things in your own life, you have probably experienced this. However, even so – if you're honest, you may realize that there is still an empty hole of desire and need that has not been filled by all these changes. There is still something missing. You have not, after all, truly fulfilled the need for feeling completely and wholly loved, the need to feel safe and secure in the universe, or the need for fulfillment and a sense of wholeness.

Perhaps, out of habit and frustration, you have again turned to your partner and your relationship to get these things that still elude you. And you are back to square one, attempting to get from another 3D self what you have not been able to give yourself.

An Attempt to Improve a Relationship

I once had a client, Joanne, who had been miserably married for almost fifteen years. Although unhappy almost from the beginning, she had never been able to leave her husband. In order to improve her relationship, she had spent many of the years in therapy and in reading self-help books about relationships. But she was as miserable as ever.

She finally came to the realization that, after all this time that she had been focusing on trying to improve her relationship, she was still feeling helpless about it all. And she saw that this helplessness had evolved into a constant resentment and rage she carried around with her.

When she realized all this, it became clear to her that, since her husband wasn't fulfilling her needs, she needed to focus on herself and attempt to fulfill them herself. I remember that she became hell-bent at this point in wanting finally to resolve the turmoil she had created in her life around her relationship.

It wasn't easy, but she began turning around some old, ingrained habits in her marriage. She decided she was no longer going to bend over backwards to "keep the relationship together". She essentially stopped pursuing her husband and demanding his attention. She developed her own interests which didn't happen to include him and, in the process, developed a number of new and fulfilling relationships with other people. She decided to take the risk of finding a more interesting and challenging job.

She also began taking care of her body as never before; she joined a gym, took saunas and steam baths, and got weekly massages. Her focus in therapy was no longer on fixing her relationship; it now centered on herself and, in particular, on her spiritual growth. She began meditating every day and felt more and more balanced in every activity in her life.

Predictably, her husband began taking notice of this new woman in his life. He began missing all the attention she had formerly given him and the tremendous effort she had put into keeping their relationship going. As a result, he found it necessary to put his own attention and energy into this task for a change. Joanne, of course, loved this. All she was doing for herself was lending new life to the relationship and was making her a much more attractive mate for her husband.

For a couple of months, I heard nothing but glowing reports about the state of her marriage, along with all she was doing to enjoy life more on her own. Then, eventually, I began noticing a slight sense of flatness about her and, not much later, the familiar old depression made an appearance.

It seemed she was backsliding into her old habit of looking to her husband for fulfillment, but that wasn't all that that was happening. She was simply finding that this new program of self-improvement was not really doing it for her. Sometimes, late at night when everything was still, the old emptiness would still creep into her awareness. Despite all the attention her husband was now giving her, and the fun they were having for the first time, she still sensed the lack of true fulfillment deep within. She still didn't feel totally loved and cared about. She came to therapy one afternoon in desperate tears, telling me all this. "After all I've done, I've still missed the mark. I'm still not happy. What's wrong with me?"

What she had discovered, of course, was that her 3D self could not give her a true sense of love, security, and wholeness. When we are identified with our 3D selves, we are simply not capable of it. In 3D consciousness, our understanding of reality is based on illusion; except perhaps intellectually, we cannot even grasp the true nature of it. This is because our 3D self perceives itself as a separate, individual little being, operating within a vast, often unpredictable universe.

Your 3D Self Cannot Give You the Fulfillment You Seek

It's important to understand that, when fully identified with this self, you believe that the only tool you have to combat this sense of helplessness is your rational mind. And when it comes to understanding reality and the forces of the universe, this mind is hopelessly limited. Thus, the whole notion that, when in 3D consciousness, you can provide yourself with a true sense of security and fulfillment is absurd.

No matter how much you may "improve" your 3D self – by healing traumas, changing attitudes, expectations, beliefs, and behaviors – it will never be quite enough. And, in addition, no matter how much you may demand that another person give you what you want and need, you will never really get it – especially not on an on-going basis. No one operating from their 3D self can give you the love, security and sense of wholeness you seek, because 3D selves are incapable of doing this.

Although it might sound simplistic, underneath all other issues, the basic strife that occurs within intimate relationships stems from this one unrealistic notion – that two people are capable of fulfilling each other's needs for love, security and fulfillment. Because of this, no matter how much two people may wish to do this for each other, the capacity to do so simply is not there.

So what is the answer to this? As always, it lies in the realization that you are not the small, limited 3D self form that cannot fulfill its own emotional needs – but the true 5D Self *which has no emotional needs*. Who you are, in reality, IS Love, IS Wholeness, IS Fulfillment. You have no need to seek these qualities anywhere from anyone or anything. Issues of insecurity, loneliness, and lack of self-worth don't even arise; they're irrelevant. When functioning from within 5D consciousness, you know yourself to already be complete, whole, and fulfilled. There is no need to find someone else to give you these qualities.

If two people come together in partnership, truly realizing themselves as their 5D Selves, there can be no strife due to unfulfillable demands. They simply give each other the freedom to be as they are. They can be loving companions, supporting each other to continue in their ever-deepening awakening to their true nature. They can assist each other on the physical level to make life in the world easier and more comfortable. They can have fun and share adventures together. They can even have exciting, passionate sex together. But that is basically it – no demands or expectation that the other cannot fulfill.

The need for emotional security, happiness, and a sense of wholeness is already naturally taken care of through their awakened consciousness of who they really are. In addition, because respecting boundaries is naturally part of how people with 5D consciousness live, there are no issues around creating such boundaries or needing to make it known what is okay or not okay to do.

This may not sound very appealing to you; it may not even sound like a "real" relationship. Where is the blissful romance? Where is the emotional attachment? These, for better or worse, have disappeared, along with the heartache, the loneliness, the dependence, and the insecurity of believing yourself to be a small, separate self.

There actually *can* be some sense of "romance" in a relationship between people who are living in 5D consciousness, but it is not the ordinary kind that is rooted in the illusion that the other person is going to fill all one's emotional needs. It's a carefree, playful response to the magnetism felt between the two people. It's a light and whimsical courtship that is experienced as a dance, a delightful game – and therefore does not ultimately produce the disillusionment and disappointment that so often occurs when people finally fall out of love.

Commitment Agreements

And yet, it must be added that relationship in 5D consciousness does not entail absolutely no commitments to each other. At some point when two people get together and have spent enough time with each other to know they wish to make the relationship important in their lives, certain subjects must be discussed and agreed upon. The first might be the nature of how they imagine their ongoing relationship to be down the line.

As discussed earlier, no absolute promises can ever be made – there is no knowing what unpredictable circumstances may occur as time goes on. But there must at least be some discussion and agreement about what their intention might be at the present time, about whether the relationship will be a primary one – or not. The question must be addressed: "Is this a relationship both partners see to be a committed type of relationship, leading to a more firm and committed partnership in the future?"

This is not about giving unrealistic promises to each other; it's about intention, based on what each one is experiencing at the present time. If one partner expresses they want to just "live in the moment" and "go with the flow", and the other is not comfortable with this, then this issue must be resolved.

Very important, too, are the questions of sexual and emotional monogamy. What is comfortable for each partner? First, there are, of course, health-safety reasons to consider around sexuality; both partners must agree to what extent they are each free to interact with other people on this intimate level. And, if they are in agreement about having other sexual partners, then certain measures to ensure safety must be agreed upon.

But if one person wants to be free to develop other sexual relationships and the other does not, honesty and transparency about this issue is essential; otherwise, it will inevitably draw the partners into conflict down the line. Too often, one person will agree to their partner's desire for sex with other people, but not really feel comfortable with this.

Further, the extent of emotional intimacy with others that each person is comfortable with must also be expressed. There needs to be freedom given to each partner to find others with whom they wish to share details of their life. But what are the agreements for how much each one might discuss the details of the relationship? And with whom would this occur?

As is clear, creating and continuing an intimate relationship within 5D consciousness is a tricky dance – at least now as we are all still existing in a 3D/4D world. There's a great deal of freedom each partner needs to give to each other; and yet, if certain agreements are not made and certain commitments are not given, the relationship is liable to fall into the type of loose and unhappy relationship all too common stemming out of 3D consciousness.

There's a level of integrity with which both people need to stay in. And there is also a need to totally know oneself and one's preference for how a relationship is to be, and to be honest about it. Both people as individuals may be generally functioning in 5D consciousness, when on their own, but they might not agree on the type of commitment they wish to enjoy in a primary relationship.

Moving into a 5D Relationship

Once a couple can reach the point of agreement about these various aspects of their relationship, the next question is how to maintain the kind of relationship in which both partners can truly experience a 5D sense of inner freedom with each other. If you're currently in an intimate relationship, how can you shift from the ordinary, run-of-the-mill, somewhat satisfactory relationship to one that enhances your ascension into 5D consciousness?

One way is to focus on creating a deeper and deeper realization of who you really are. You can also take steps to deal with your relationship directly. Below are some steps that might be helpful to you in this regard. Please note that they aren't strictly sequential. Some can be done simultaneously with others; others may have to be done over and over again. But all of them can help to free you from your unhealthy attachment to your intimate partner, your dependence on him or her for your emotional needs, and your identification with your 3D self.

1. **Focus on loving yourself.** As discussed earlier, this is where you need to begin. If you are not able to truly love yourself, you will not be able to create a conscious, free, and loving relationship with your partner. Ask yourself if you are being as loving toward yourself as you could be. If not, what can you do to be so? Sometimes, especially if you have been conditioned for a long time to be hard on yourself, it can be difficult to know how to be more loving. You may really want to learn how to love yourself, but you don't know how to begin turning all your old habit patterns around.

As you have likely discovered, there are many, many books and classes offered on how to do this. If you need some help in learning how to love yourself, it might be good to read a few. Books on how to heal your 'inner child" are especially helpful. Naturally, the simple message offered in most of these books and classes is to stop doing those things that are unkind and harsh to yourself and to begin doing those things that reflect love, gentleness, and understanding.

You can often find advice on how to stop allowing the critical parent voice inside your head to beat you up. As discussed in Chapter 2, it can be helpful to understand something that few authors realize: that this voice is not even a natural part of you. It is actually an implant containing negative programming designed to create fear, guilt, shame, self-doubt, and a sense of not being fully connected to Source. It was inserted in the frontal lobe of your brain by the controlling forces that have created the distorted 3D experience for humanity.

If you tune in, you may sense how alien this judgmental voice is to you, how it's never really belonged inside your head. It's just a programming telling you in one way or another, over and over again, how you are not okay, and how you should feel guilt and shame for who you are and what you do. In realizing that self degradation does not arise from your Essence but is an alien programming imposed upon you, you can find it much easier to stop listening to it. (While you're at it, keep aware that any sexual conflicts you may be having with your partner may be due to the sexual implant, also described in Chapter 2. If you are experiencing guilt or shame around your sexuality or feeling tension around your sexual relationship, question this; what is actually causing it?)

Of course, other ways to act with love toward yourself involve taking care of your body: Eat well, get exercise and be gentle and nurturing toward your body. Own and feel your emotions, so they do not get stuck in your unconscious – and eventually in your body. Do what you can to heal yourself on all levels. Take responsibility for your own well-being; make it a priority. Don't give to others from an empty cup. And most importantly, accept yourself exactly as you are.

2. **Begin focusing on all the positive aspects of your relationship.** Rather than focusing on what's wrong with it and what's missing, begin looking at the positive aspects. Become aware of all the positive qualities your partner has, and focus on your love for him or her. Become aware of all you have to feel grateful for. Let your love and your gratitude flow through all your communications with your partner, and watch the miracles that can occur in the environment you are creating together.

3. **Stop blaming your partner for your own unhappiness.** Once you experience more love for yourself and focus on your love and gratitude for your relationship, it is time to take the next essential step: Stop looking at the things your partner is or is not doing that are "making" you unhappy. Blaming keeps you in a helpless position. If you expect your partner to be or to act in a certain way so that you can be happy, you have given the power over your happiness to him/her. Since you essentially have no control over your partner, you feel helpless – and this produces anger and resentment. It is therefore necessary to take back the power you have given awayr and to use it to begin creating your own happiness.

Be careful, however, when you remove the blame from your partner, that you do not then place the blame for your unhappiness on yourself. In 3D consciousness, we are all conditioned to believe that if there is something "wrong," then blame must be placed somewhere for it. This is not so. No blame at all needs to be placed anywhere. Blaming anyone, including yourself, is counterproductive. It keeps you in victim mode.

What *is* productive is to step outside the blame paradigm altogether. Understand that taking responsibility for something is not the same as taking blame for it. Taking responsibility is claiming the empowerment to do something about it.

4. **Pull back your demands and expectations.** Become aware of how you may have been expecting your partner to fill certain needs you have, such as happiness, security, and a sense of being lovable and valuable. Realize that doing this for you is not part of your partner's job. He or she actually *cannot* do it – only you can.

The love you are undoubtedly looking for is unconditional love – which assures you that you are loved simply for who you are, no matter what you do or what may happen. It's a love you don't, in any way, have to earn; you are loved simply because you are you.

This kind of love cannot come from someone's 3D self. The love of that self is always fraught with subtle or not-so-subtle demands. When functioning within that consciousness, for you to "earn" the love you want, there are conditions that you must be a certain way and do certain things. If you don't, then the love is threatened. At the very least, the demonstration of the love is removed until your behavior changes. 3D love is also typically entwined with a sense of possessiveness, which brings its own conditions and demands.

Unconditional love is what everyone really wants. In rare situations, a person is actually able to give this to a partner in an ongoing way. It's important to distinguish, however, between unconditional love that emanates from a true awakening of the 5D Self – and a feeling that may seem the same but is actually a co-dependent attachment that says, "You can do anything to me, even abuse me – but I will always love you." This isn't truly free, unconditional love. It is a needy, emotional attachment to a person, rooted in self-denial. Attachment and need are often mistaken for love.

At the same time, it's important to understand that unconditional love does not mean the loved one can abuse you in any way. If you are feeling unconditional love for someone else, it means you have already developed that kind of love for yourself. And this means you will not allow abusive and disrespectful actions toward yourself. It means you have naturally developed clear boundaries to protect yourself. Because you are clear about your boundaries, you feel free within them. If your loved one tries to push past your boundaries, you don't react emotionally; you stay strong, and at the same time, loving. If you can develop that kind of love with natural boundaries, you'll find that people will not even try to push past them.

Of course, most people in a healthy and mature relationship experience a 5D type of love for their partner from time to time that is truly unconditional. When attuned to 5D consciousness, this true love flows forth naturally toward the loved one. Generally, however, people are not able to sustain and attunement to their 5D Self all the time; thus the unconditional love they feel for their partner comes and goes. If you are depending on this kind of love from your partner, especially all of the time, you are bound to experience disappointment and resentment.

Also, the sense of security and safety you may be seeking from your relationship cannot be given to you by your partner, simply because no one can have any real control over future events. The best that can be given are expressions of feelings and commitments felt in the present moment.

For example, rather than a promise of "I will never leave you," you can more accurately say something like, "Right now, I feel I never want to leave you. I certainly do not ever want to hurt you." However, as accurate and realistic as even these kinds of statements may be, they still do not take care of a person's basic need to feel secure and safe in the world. The fulfillment of this need, too, must be sought from within.

Seeking a sense of wholeness from your partner must ultimately remain unfulfilled. Your partner cannot give this to you; you must find it within yourself. You may have experienced what seemed like a sense of wholeness with your partner. Perhaps it has come as a feeling of "merging" with him or her. This can be a very blissful experience. But has it ever lasted? Do you actually have any control over "making" it happen again? And did it truly give you the feeling, deep within yourself, of finally feeling completely whole and free?

The merging of two 3D selves, no matter how profound and fulfilling it may be at the time, cannot provide the true feeling of wholeness each partner seeks, because, by their very nature, 3D selves are limited and imperfect.

You may believe that the merging you have experienced with your partner wasn't one of 3D selves coming together, that a higher spiritual consciousness was present. This may well be so. But the problem still remains of controlling the process of merging and making it on-going. These experiences cannot be controlled; and therefore, to depend on them for a sense of wholeness is bound to bring disappointment and frustration. Another more reliable source must be sought.

Letting go of these expectations of your partner may not be easy at first. So much of our conditioning in 3D has told us that a partner in an intimate relationship is "supposed" to provide us with happiness, security, fulfillment, and wholeness. And yet, as we've seen, not only is it not our partner's job to do this, he or she, no matter what they might wish or intend, is ultimately incapable of doing it.

So it is important to be realistic. Don't have expectations that are doomed to be unfulfilled. Know that your needs can only be fulfilled by awakening to your own true nature, and focus your attention on that. Then if your partner happens to be tuning into 5D consciousness at certain times and is able to bring a sense of happiness or fulfillment to you, this will be the "icing" on your "cake" – the cake you yourself have made. Icing makes a cake more delicious, but it is not necessary for the cake's existence.

5. **Stop trying to fix or change your relationship.** At this point, at least for a while, see if you can take your focus off trying to do anything at all about your relationship. Allow things to be the way they are; allow your partner to be the way he or she is. Ignore the urge to have to fix or change anything.

Of course, if simple, obvious things occur to you that will improve something between you and your partner – things that come easily and naturally – then, by all means, do these things. But if the problems require much thought, if you find yourself getting involved in blame and hurt and anger about them, or if there are issues that you've gone around and around with in the past, then abandon all thoughts for now about trying to resolve these problems. They'll just get you back on the merry-go-round of dissatisfaction about your partnership. Begin, instead, to center your awareness on yourself.

6. **Explore your emotional attachment to your partner.** It's now time to begin exploring more deeply within yourself to find the more

subtle ways in which you are creating attachment – and therefore suffering – in your relationship.

First ask yourself the question: "What does being in this relationship mean to me?" How attached are you to being in this role? What does being in this role mean about you? What would being out of the relationship mean about you? Would you somehow feel less of a person if you were not in this relationship? Become aware in general of all the judgments and values you place around being in relationship (and in the particular relationship you're in). Answering these questions will help you see the attachment you have to the relationship and how much your sense of identity is wrapped up in it. It will also reveal to you how much of your happiness is dependent on your relationship and on how things are going in it.

Next, face your worst fears about your relationship: Ask yourself: "What if my partner were to leave me?" Face this possibility squarely; don't push it away. What would this really mean for you? Without dwelling morbidly or sentimentally on it, and without falling into self-pity about it, just look at what feelings it brings up. Observe them objectively, as described in Chapter 13. If there is fear, allow yourself to feel it, without resisting or rejecting it. Find out honestly what the worst thing could be if your partner were to leave you.

Now ask yourself, "What if my partner were to die before I did?" Again, have the courage to face this possibility. Just sit quietly for a while with this question, and allow your feelings and inner truth about the issue to surface. What would it mean? What would you feel? What would you do? Where would you go? Then answer the question honestly: would you be able to go on without him or her? Would you be truly devastated?

What about the possibility that your partner might choose to continue being with you, but he or she decides to have affairs with other people? Again, this is not something to dwell on in a morbid, fearful way. Staying still within yourself, simply ask yourself the questions: "What would I feel and think about this? What would I feel this means about me? What would I do? How would I handle it? Could I stand to stay in the relationship?"

Now face any fears you may have about possibly wanting to leave your partner. Although you may think at this point you'll probably never want to leave, certainly you have had thoughts at one time or another of wanting to leave. Maybe at times, the challenges you've experienced in the relationship have gotten too difficult. Perhaps you occasionally feel bored with your partner. Maybe you've felt attracted to someone else.

Or maybe you'll be the one to die first. How would your partner react to any of these situations – and how would you feel about his or her reactions? Would you feel responsible for his or her feelings? Explore all these these questions. They will reveal a lot to you about your attachment to the relationship and your partner and show you the degree of emotional freedom you have in this whole area.

If you are finding these questions difficult to face and your inclination is just to pass them by without exploring them, this may be an indication of your general fear of being alone. This is, then, where you may want to start. Ask yourself, "What does being alone, without an intimate relationship, mean about me?" Discover what judgments and values you have about people who are single, without a romantic relationship. In particular, what would this mean about you? Face whatever fears you have about being alone.

Do you know if you could make it on your own, should you have to – physically, financially, emotionally? How dependent are you on your partner in these areas? How does feeling dependent feel to you? You may believe that you have no choice except to be dependent in one way or another; but, if you're honest, you'll see that you always have a choice. There may come a day when you'll have to be independent, whether you want to be or not. And you will see that you can be.

Facing the fears that asking all these questions can evoke is very important. It does no good to keep them hidden in your subconscious mind. You are probably going to have to face some of them sooner or later, anyway. You might as well do it now, so the fears don't run you.

Perhaps more importantly, facing these fears can also take you out of your immediate situation and give you a view of the larger picture of your life. In this larger picture, you can see that all events, situations, and relationships in your life come and go – and yet, YOU remain. With or without a partner, in or out of a relationship, YOU continue on. Experiencing this perspective can bring a peaceful sense of spaciousness and timelessness, as well as a knowing beyond all issues or questions around relationship of who you are in Reality.

7. **Focus on awakening into your 5D Self.** Once you have done all the preliminary healing work of balancing your 3D self, you can then focus on awakening more deeply into your 5D Self. You can, of course, have this focus throughout your explorations of your 3D self attachments; indeed, it is always helpful while you explore your identity with your 3D self to keep your higher Self in mind. But once you begin to get clear about how your 3D self operates, it is easier to turn more fully to your awakening into 5D consciousness.

There are many ways in which you can do this. Everything described thus far (and in subsequent chapters) can be helpful. Focusing on experiencing glimpses of your 5D Self is a start. Review how to recognize your 5D Self in your everyday life. Take the time to prolong the glimpses you do have of it. Cultivate an environment and a lifestyle that are conducive to becoming more and more familiar with your 5D Self. Create and be faithful to a meditation practice. Attend spiritual gatherings or classes – whatever will "light your fire" spiritually.

Begin to observe how attached you are to the roles you play in life, and learn how to become more detached from them. See how you identify with your body and with your emotions, and begin detaching yourself from these identities. Take steps to become more of an observer. Open yourself to experiencing yourself as pure Awareness.

See if, as time goes on, you can begin trusting your 5D Self more to take care of you. Do your best to surrender your sense of control over your life. Try accepting your life as it is. See what happens.

As you begin doing all these things, your relationship with your partner will undoubtedly be affected. Wonderful new experiences between the two of you may begin happening. You may inspire your partner to begin doing some of the same things you have been doing. There may develop a greater closeness and alignment between you than ever before.

However, other changes may also happen. If your partner is not open to growing and expanding his or her awareness into greater awakening in the way that you are, your doing this may at first cause some strife in the relationship, especially now as the frequency of Ascension is growing ever-stronger on the planet. Your awakening into greater freedom can't help but upset the status quo. But if your relationship has its foundation in Truth, it will weather this rocking and become stronger.

If you are fearful that your awakening process may destroy or break up your relationship, and you find yourself closing down your own inner process because of this, you might really want to look at this. What are you choosing? What are your priorities? Is staying in your relationship at all costs worth it to you, even if it means shutting down the speed of your own Ascension process?

It's important to ask yourself these questions. But do be careful not to fall into an unnecessary "either-or" position about it, thinking you have to immediately choose either your own Ascension process or your relationship. Sometimes it just takes time for a relationship to catch up to the awakening process of one of the partners. Wait and see. Don't put pressure on your partner or on your relationship to conform to some new concept you have about what a relationship should be like. Give your partner freedom to be who she or he is. Focus on love and acceptance. Focus on your own awakening.

Your partner may soon be making his or her own awakening just as much a priority as you're making your own. You can then become companions along the road of Ascension into 5D, giving each other support in your explorations. If this doesn't happen, so be it. Either way, if you are on your way to emotional and spiritual freedom, you can't lose. You are becoming more and more aware of who you truly are. And you will continue to benefit from this, whether you happen to be in or out of an intimate relationship.

The True Value of Relationships

There is no doubt that intimate relationships are challenging. They can show us only too well in what ways we are not free emotionally and how attached we are to our emotional identity. But, for that very reason, they are tremendously valuable. We can use our relationship as a forum in which to become progressively more free; we can use it to help us learn to detach from our emotions and the suffering they can bring when we identify with them.

Experiencing greater and greater emotional freedom in general is immensely rewarding. As we've seen, learning to simply observe our emotions and let them be – without resisting them, indulging them, or trying to fix them – is an important step toward this freedom. Letting go of our story of emotional suffering is another. And gaining freedom within our relationships is yet a further key. As we gain a detachment and freedom with our emotions in these ways, our awareness becomes less and less cluttered. With this clarity, we can then begin to deeply experience our 5D Self as it shines through into our consciousness more and more clearly.

Chapter 18

Shifting your Identity from your Mind

Identification with our mind is probably the most difficult identification of all to see clearly, and it is therefore the most challenging from which to detach. It may be especially difficult if you have a strong intellect that you have spent years developing; you are naturally going to be hesitant to give up your identification with something into which you have put much effort and about which you have developed pride. But to attain true 5D freedom, it is ultimately necessary to see clearly that you are not your mind and to be willing to give up your identification with it.

At the same time, it's important to understand that there is nothing inherently wrong with the mind. As you become aware of the hazards of identifying with it, be careful not to make it into an enemy, something you have to guard against. Assuming this attitude would actually be falling prey to one of the many tricks that the mind, itself, performs: dividing itself up into separate parts and then creating battles between these parts. You don't have to get caught up in this game. You can learn to simply watch the mind – and the myriad tricks and cartwheels it performs – without identifying with any of them.

The mind is actually an amazing and wondrous thing to observe and study. And when used properly, it is an extremely effective tool. Its ability to create and traverse multiple realms, many of which remain mysterious and uncharted, is vast beyond measure. It creates thought in countless different varieties: concepts, ideals, images, memories, projections, beliefs, values, opinions, morality systems, judgments. Like a super-computer, the mind receives information from the senses and instantaneously analyzes, categorizes, labels, cross-indexes, stores, and downloads. Indeed, it is an indispensable tool, helping us negotiate this three-dimensional physical world.

However, if you identity with this tool – if you believe that it is who you are – this will keep you trapped in 3D consciousness and prevent you from clearly experiencing your 5D Self. It is therefore important to be aware of this identification with your mind and to focus on releasing yourself from it.

Confusing the Mind with 5D Consciousness

One of the challenging qualities of the mind is the very subtle nature of thought. It is so subtle that it can be very easy to believe a thought you may have about 5D to be a direct experience of 5D itself. At times you may have very lofty thoughts about spiritual matters that can give you a sense of freedom and joy. These thoughts are undoubtedly infused with the grace of 5D energies that can give you this sense. But it is important to remember that if you are involved in thinking thoughts with your rational mind – no matter how beautiful they may be – you are not fully experiencing 5D, which is an experience that is beyond conceptual thought.

Part of the difficulty in knowing the difference between a thought about 5D and the direct experience of it stems from the fact that many spiritual paths do not address this difference. In fact, their teachings only deal with the "spiritualizing" of the mind, without much reference to the direct experience of a consciousness that is beyond thought.

It's true that the process of spiritualizing the mind can be an important step on the road to true 5D freedom; the mind must become clear and focused positively before authentic and frequent glimpses of 5D become possible. However, ultimately, it must be understood that thought about 5D consciousness is not the same as directly experiencing it. And it is this direct experience that must be pursued.

I was once sitting with a group of friends in a meditation circle. We had just meditated together and were sharing the experiences we had during the meditation. A good friend of mine, Jim, began speaking. Immediately the whole group came to rapt attention about what he was saying. He described in simple yet eloquent terms an exquisite experience he had just had of his 5D Self. His eyes were shining, and his face was suffused with a bright glow. The energy of love was radiating from him toward every one of us, as he described the quality of unimaginably blissful peace and the rapturous joy that had pervaded his whole being.

As usually happens when someone is directly transmitting the energy of an experience of 5D consciousness, the rest of us were soon feeling a quickening of our own awareness of 5D. Because his very presence was fully suffused with the grace of his 5D Self, it was causing an experience of awakening within each of us sitting with him.

Then something very subtle began happening. It was hard to put a finger on just when it began; but, at some point, I felt a slight shift in the energy in the room and noticed that everyone's attention was beginning to drift away from him, as he continued to speak. The feeling of rapt attention was gone, and people seemed to be in their own worlds, thinking their own thoughts. The "magic" that had been present just moments before had very subtly dissipated.

Perplexed by this, I began listening very closely to Jim as he continued to speak about his experience. Suddenly, it became clear to me what had happened: he was no longer directly describing his experience from where it had happened; he was now analyzing it from within his mind. It was a very subtle shift. He was using many of the same terms and phrases he'd been using previously, but the energy was different. It was now mental. He had slipped through the very subtle doorway from the experience of 5D into the realm of the 3D mind.

Just as I realized this, Jim seemed to, as well. His voice drifted off in the middle of a sentence and then he was silent. Everyone's attention was immediately back with him. Somewhat puzzled and sad, he said, "I lost it, didn't I? I'm back in my mind. I'm thinking about my experience, rather than just being it." He closed his eyes at this point, and the rest of us did also, attempting to call back the Silence we had "lost" by falling into the mind. Although we were somewhat able to recapture the exquisite sense of stillness his expression of 5D had brought to us, it was not quite the same.

When we began speaking again a while later, we realized that, as disappointing as this experience had been in one way, we had all learned something very important about the subtle and tricky nature of thought and how it can masquerade so clearly as pure consciousness. The dead giveaway, we realized, is the mental energy that an expression of the mind brings and the lack of true inner stillness. We realized how important it is to pay attention to the subtle energetic shift the mind brings when it begins to analyze an experience of 5D consciousness, rather than allowing the experience itself to speak directly.

What is important in seeking the experience of 5D is to realize that it is much closer to you than your mind is. As close as your thoughts may seem, you need to look more clearly; your 5D Self is not as far away as your thoughts are. Indeed, there is no distance at all – it IS you. To discover this, you can look inside to where the thoughts are coming from; find their source. Ask yourself: "Who is it that is thinking these thoughts?" See what you discover.

Another "gateway" into 5D through using the mind is to realize that you can perceive the mind. You can watch it, you can talk about it as something you *have*, something that is separate from who you are. Therefore, it stands to reason that your mind cannot be who you are; you are the perceiver of it. So ask yourself: "Who or what is it that is perceiving my mind?"

The Mind Creates the Illusion of Duality

If you have had profound glimpses of 5D reality, you have likely experienced a blissful sense of oneness with all that is – a knowing that everything that exists is of the same essence, that it is all one unified Consciousness.

The 3D world that the rational mind lives in, on the other hand, is one of duality: there's "me" – and there's everything else. In fact, the mind perceives reality as an infinite number of pieces; everything is defined and separate from each other. It does not see, and cannot truly comprehend, the oneness that exists for the 5D Self, except as a mental concept.

The mind's basic misperception of Reality can cause a number of problems. Perhaps most importantly, it can cause feelings of separation, lack, fear, and loneliness. If you believe yourself to be a separate, individual being in the world, something apart from all other people and things, and separate from Source, there can be enormous suffering. Especially when people or things you believe you need are taken from you, you can experience an unbearable sense of loss and helplessness.

Other times, if you are feeling that you don't have what you need in order to be happy, the sense of separateness may bring up deep anger and hostility. Especially if you see others who have those things you need or want, you may experience greed, envy, and conflict with them. These feelings in some people, in turn, might even push them toward crime, violence, and war. This is very important to understand: all these negative emotions are based on an erroneous understanding of the nature of existence. They arise from a third-dimensional belief in the illusion that we are separate beings, existing apart from everyone and everything else.

Another difficulty within the experience of duality arises when the mind takes the pieces it sees in the world – all people, objects, ideas, emotions – and creates divisions between them. Some of these polarized concepts are useful to us in communicating with each other and the world: for example, such terms as "big" and "little", "cold" and "hot", "up" and "down" are quite essential in our everyday communication. However, other polarized concepts are much less useful and, indeed, often cause many problems. Some of the worst of these concepts are "good" and "bad" and "right and "wrong". Polarities like these tend to cause conflict because people have formed beliefs around them and find it necessary to oppose other people, things, and events that do not agree with the beliefs they have adopted.

Other polarities that people often create in their minds and cause themselves distress over are "spirituality" vs "money", "spirituality" vs "sex", and "spirituality" vs "the world." Neither money, sex, nor the world is opposed to spirituality, and none is inherently wrong. All of these concepts, including "spirituality", are simply concepts, emanating from the rational mind. Yet people tend to believe they are real and experience guilt, shame and confusion due to this belief.

Of course, to live and function in this 3D/4D world effectively, it is still necessary to act as if duality exists. We generally need to treat the things the mind perceives as if they are separate and defined objects. However, this can be done while at the same time holding the knowing inside that, in Reality, there is no actual separation between anything that exists. When in 5D consciousness, this is what you naturally know and experience.

The Mind Gets Caught in Time

Another way in which the mind can prevent you from clearly experiencing 5D consciousness is the way in which it lives in linear time. The 5D Self essentially lives outside of time. Indeed, an important aspect of many glimpses of this Self is the sense of timelessness. The 5D Self lives in a dimension where time as we know it simply does not exist. There is the knowing that everything is taking place in the Eternal Now, the present moment; there is no past, future – and really no present, either.

In fact, when experiencing 5D consciousness, you can become aware that linear time is something the 3D mind has simply made up. It might be difficult at first to see it as an invention of the mind. Most people assume that time has its own inherent reality. But a direct experience of 5D will give you the understanding that it does not; it is simply an idea that has been created by the mind existing in the Third Dimension.

Time itself is not a problem. It has its useful purposes; it is certainly helpful to us in functioning while we're still existing in the 3rd and 4th Dimensions. Indeed, coordinating events among all of us on the planet would probably be impossible at this point without the idea of time.

However, we can get into trouble when we allow our minds to get caught in focusing too much on time. Too often, we become so involved in our memories of the past that we bring them forward to create the same situations over and over again. And, if we spend too much time focusing on the imagined future – especially if there is any fear present – we end up missing out on what is actually happening in the present moment. Because we're living in our minds, there's little space for new and spontaneous experiences to happen in the present moment.

Most importantly, by getting so involved in time in general, we aren't able to experience the Eternal Now. We cannot get there from the past or from the future. We actually can't even get there from the present, if this "present" is just another place on the continuum of linear time.

So how can we, while living in this 3D/4D world so dominated by the concept of time, get to the Home of the 5D Self – with its exquisite sense of timelessness? If you feel stuck in this time-focused world and find yourself swinging back and forth between the past and the future and experiencing the subtle suffering this circular and exhausting ride can produce, here are some steps that might help you get off of that ride.

Exercise: Accessing Timelessness

1. **Come into the present.** First of all, bring your attention completely into the present and observe your physical surroundings. Look all around you at the objects in your field of vision. Observe the details of these objects, their colors, their sizes, how they occupy space.

2. **Be aware of your body, thoughts and feelings:** Now become aware of your body. How is it feeling? Notice how it is occupying space. Take some deep breaths, and feel them in your body. Observe your thoughts and your feelings; don't follow or resist them – simply observe that they are present.

3. **Observe yourself.** Take in the whole gestalt of where you are and what is happening at this moment in time to this mind-body organism with which you currently identify. See it objectively, as if you were standing outside of it. See it sitting, lying down, standing, or moving through space – whatever it is doing. See it turning its head and taking other things into its field of vision. Watch it moving its hands. Observe its thoughts and feelings as they float through the mind.

4. **Watch yourself moving through time.** Now see this entity as it moves through time. From moment to moment, see how it continues to exist, but somewhat differently in each moment. Physical, emotional, and mental changes are constantly happening.

5. **Contemplate the phenomenon of time.** Become aware of how strange a phenomenon time actually is. The present continuously becomes the past, and the future continuously becomes the present and then the past – all in just an instant. Quietly observe how time is doing this. Is there truly any difference between the past, the present, and the future? Are

they perhaps all the same thing? Do these concepts even have an inherent reality of their own?

6. **Ask who is observing all this.** Become aware of who you are as the observer of this thing called time. Who or what are you? Where are you existing? Does time exist there?

Finding a doorway into the experience of timelessness can be an important step in having a direct experience of your 5D Self. It can bring a sense of restful, and even blissful, peace. Because linear time itself is only present in the Third Dimension, you can realize that the stressful pressures you create in your life around time are totally unnecessary.

In fact, the more you can live your life from within the realm of 5D timelessness – and learn to trust it – the more you can realize that things in life have a way of working out smoothly, synchronistically, without any intervention on your part. Time is never an issue. You neither have too much nor too little of it. Even when others are involved in what you're doing, you're somehow always right on time. There is always enough time for everything that really needs to happen. All events flow spontaneously in a natural way.

The Mind Claims Spiritual Experiences as Its Own

Yet another thing the mind tends to do that can create distress is to take an experience you have in 5D Consciousness and claim it for its own glory. Quite often, if allowed, the mind will look at an experience you have with your 5D Self and begin to think, "Wow, see how spiritual/evolved I am." Although the mind actually had nothing to do with the experience, it can move in to claim ownership of it. Indeed, it can actually begin believing it has created the experience itself. This, of course, is what would be called the "ego" aspect of the mind.

It's therefore necessary to stay aware of the mind's tendency to take over that which is completely out of its realm of understanding. It really is incapable of understanding 5D consciousness. It can be aware of itself and of other objects; but, except as a concept, it cannot be aware of what its own Source is. This is not true understanding.

Remember, the next time your mind begins analyzing 5D consciousness or an experience of your 5D Self, that it can only know any of this as ideas. Don't be satisfied with this. An idea cannot give you the true peace and fulfillment you are seeking. Only a direct experience of 5D consciousness can.

Thinking with your Heart

You may be wondering that, if it's important to essentially give up thinking with your mind except in certain limited ways, how you can then make important decisions in your life. When you shift into 5D consciousness, one thing you can become aware of is that your deep thinking is actually coming out of the area of your chest, rather than your head. Your brain is functioning to assist you in sifting through information and analyzing data, when necessary. But you discover that it is your Heart that has become your guide for important decisions you need to make and for guidance in general.

You have likely experienced this way of receiving information before, and probably called it your "intuition" – something that occurs occasionally, usually at random times. What you maybe haven't practiced is the intentional use of this inherent faculty you have in finding answers to all dilemmas or decisions you need to make in life. You may not have made listening to your Heart a daily practice in everything you do.

You can begin to practice this the next time you have to make an important decision in your life. Rather than sifting information continually through your mind, weighing the pros and cons back and forth, or looking for information in external sources to assist you, try focusing on your Heart with your question. By "Heart", I am not referring to your emotional heart; I am speaking about what could be called your "Spiritual Heart". This is something that resides much deeper within you in a place of deep silence. It's a space of deep knowing and wisdom.

To reach this part of you, you can try sitting quietly with the decision you need to make and and take time to sink into this profound space within your body. And then, while contemplating your question, allow yourself to deeply listen. Be sincere in your intention to be open to whatever you may hear or feel.

The Heart speaks quietly, but it is generally very clear in its messages. It may speak in words, or it may be a sensation, an image, or simply a knowing that emerges. You can sense a feeling of unconditional love and support with it. You can know the truth of what it is conveying to you, whether it is something you might want to hear or not.

If you follow what your Heart is telling you, future messages will become even more clear and often bring with them other important information you haven't even known to ask.

* * *

There are two other important aspects of the mind that tend to get us in trouble and can keep us identified with it. The first is its chattering nature, its tendency to be repetitious and over-analyzing. The second is its tendency to create and follow desires, believing these will bring it happiness.

Since both of these tendencies of the mind are rather complex, we will explore them in the next two chapters.

Chapter 19

Stilling the Chattering Monkey

Have you ever noticed how many repetitious, boring and unnecessary thoughts you think every day? There was once a group of scientists studying the mind that concluded that on the average, we think about 60,000 thoughts a day. This statistic alone is somewhat startling. But what is really interesting is that they also concluded that almost all of these 60,000 thoughts are thoughts we have previously thought!

As you become more aware of your own thought processes, you will probably find you can corroborate the conclusions of these scientists. In fact, you may find that most of the thoughts you think are actually useless, habitual distractions that aren't helpful or purposeful in any way. They're just noisy, irritating chatter. Although many of the thoughts may revolve around a problem you're trying to resolve, you'll undoubtedly find they do not generally resolve anything; they are simply recycled thoughts.

Much to your embarrassment, there may be times you find that some of these chattering thoughts are simply habitual, defensive reactions to ancient criticisms. Maybe when you're leaving dirty dishes in the sink overnight, feeling guilty, you'll find yourself explaining to your mother why you need to do this. Or when you're not wanting to take care of your personal bookkeeping, you're defensively explaining to your ex-husband how you're not lazy, just tired.

Although you may not realize it, much of this useless, boring and irritating mind chatter stems from the programming of the primary implant in your brain described in Chapter 2. It is designed to keep you hooked into a state of inner noise to prevent you from easily dropping into the deep silence and peacefulness of Source within you. It keeps you stuck in a subtle (or not so subtle) state of mental unrest. Although, as described earlier, this implant is slowly becoming less and less powerful within us as we rise in vibration, it is still quite active in most people and needs to be seen for what it is and what it creates within us.

For example, you may notice that, especially when there is an obsessive, out-of-control quality to your thinking, your mind can become actually painful at times. Quite often, a variety of distressful emotions may weave their way through this obsessive thinking, pulling you into a morass of inescapable psychic sludge. The silence of 5D consciousness feels a million miles away.

A woman in a class I once gave complained about her noisy, chattering mind. In order for us to hear what her chattering mind could sound like, I asked if she would get up in front of the class and speak her thoughts out loud. Here's what she came up with:

> "Oh God, how am I going to pay the bills this month? I never have enough money, I've got to get a new job. Oh, but I don't want to get a new job. But I've got to get some more money somehow. How am I going to pay the bills? I've got that doctor bill, and my car insurance is due. Should I get a new job? I can't get a new job, I can't afford to get a new job at this time. Maybe I should go back to school. No, I can't afford to go back to school. I need to get a new job. But I need to pay the bills first. How am going to pay my car insurance? Without a car, I can't even go to work. I have to go to work. But I hate my job. I wish it paid me more money. I'm going to get sick, worrying like this. Then I'll have to go to the doctor and I'll owe him even more. God, I can't even pay my present bill. How am I going to pay my bills this month?"

By the time she finally wound down, the rest of us were laughing. It all sounded so familiar. What a waste of time and energy this kind of thinking is!

If you have ever become aware of the pointlessness and the pain of this type of thinking in your own mind, you may have attempted to do what many people do: You tried to make your mind shut up. But you likely had little success, at least not for very long. Someone once said that trying to force the mind to be quiet is like holding a dog's tail in an attempt to straighten it: as soon as you let go, it curls upward again. The mind cannot be forcibly held in a quiet place for long.

Learning to Quiet the Mind

If your mind is caught in a noisy pattern, the thing to realize is that it's generally not possible to simply force it into being quiet. But a number of things can be done to coax it into becoming quieter, so you then have a chance to slip past it into the Silence. A quiet mind is much easier to ignore than a noisy one.

1. **Body Relaxation Exercises:** There are a number of body relaxation exercises you can do. One is to focus on relaxing the muscles in your body. Somehow, turning your attention to your body helps to pull your focus away from thoughts in your mind.

Start by closing your eyes and taking a few deep breaths. Then begin focusing on one part of your body at a time, consciously relaxing and breathing into the muscles in that area. You can start with your head and neck and work your way down, one part of your body at a time – or vice-versa. As you do this, you can use the imagery of calling in white light or energy from the earth into each group of muscles.

Another way is to briefly tense each set of muscles very tightly for about five seconds and then let the tension out; this allows the relaxation to flow in. These exercises not only relax your body, they also help your mind to become still.

2. **Physical Exercise:** Physical exercise or sports can also relax the body and the mind. It pulls your energy and attention away from your conditioned mind and focuses it on your body and movement, releasing it from the chattering "ticker tapes".

3. **Changing your Environment:** Sometimes all it takes to move your mind out of habitual thinking is to physically go somewhere else more conducive to a quiet, meditative state of mind. This may be obvious, but when repetitive habitual thinking has you hooked, it might be surprising how the obvious doesn't always occur to you.

4. **Focusing on Something Physical:** Something that can be done immediately, wherever you are, is to focus your attention on some object close at hand and look closely at the details of it. If you can, pick it up in your hands and feel it, smell it, listen to it. Observe how it occupies space. Focus on the space around it, the space between it and other objects close by. Concentrating on something concrete, even for a short period of time, can quite effectively break conditioned thinking by bringing your attention into the physical world.

5. **Listening to Music:** Sometimes you can find music that will help to quiet your mind or jog it out of its circular ruts. This could be quiet meditation music, or it might be loud, rhythmic music that invites you to

start moving or dancing. Either way, it's shifting the energy out of your conditioned mind and freeing it.

6. **Working with Your Hands:** Finding something to do with your hands that requires mental concentration can be still another way to break free of habitual, circular thinking. This can involve working on a creative project that brings you joy and a sense of accomplishment, or it can simply be attempting to fix something physical that is broken. What is important is to choose something that demands your concentration.

Redirecting the Mind

The second group of suggestions involves inwardly redirecting your mind in some way, to coax it into a quieter space.

1. **Focusing on Rational Problem-Solving:** Finding a problem that needs to be thought through in a rational way can be helpful. This might include figuring out how you're going to get your car to the mechanic's tomorrow and then negotiate the rest of the day without a car. Something practical like this can redirect your mind out of painful habitual thinking about an emotional problem into functional thinking, such as deciding whom to call to take you to work when you need to leave in the morning and so forth.

Another example of redirecting your mind might be planning a vacation: deciding where you want to go, when you'll be leaving, where you'll be staying. In other words, you're still using your mind, but you're directing it into new and fresh areas of thinking that are not laden with heavy emotion and involve issues that are relatively easy to resolve. Just switching the mind's focus like this can be a great relief.

2. **Listening to Visualization Tracks:** There are a great variety of tracks and videos online designed to assist people to relax and become more mentally still. Many of them include suggestions or music to induce an alpha, theta or delta state in the brain, which naturally relaxes both the body and the mind. Others contain positive affirmations about different situations in life to assist in changing limited thought patterns. Without demanding a lot of effort on your part, playing these tracks can calm and quiet your mind.

3. **Meditations that Require Concentration:** Doing any type of meditation that requires concentration can be a very effective way to quiet the mind. Some that work especially well are various meditations found in

yogic traditions, Qi Gong, T'ai Ch'i and chakra visualization. Many of these are not only designed to quiet the mind, but also to direct you beyond the mind into silence.

4. **Witnessing Thoughts:** This is a meditation much like the one described earlier of observing your emotions. It involves simply watching thoughts as they come into your mind, without following them and without resisting them – and just letting them be. You can become aware of how thoughts, like emotions, are simply a form of energy. You can realize they are not even inherently "your" thoughts. There's no need to claim them and make them your own.

This can be an especially powerful exercise when you're feeling caught in painful habitual thoughts. By moving into the observer perspective, you immediately take power from them. You're not following them on their old, familiar pathways into further thoughts; you're not resisting or judging them; you're not getting caught up in the emotions the thoughts evoke. You're simply watching them, letting them float by in your awareness. It might take five or ten minutes of focusing on your thoughts like this; but you begin finding that you have effectively stopped the broken record of thinking.

5. **Opening Your Mind:** Yet another method to shift out of habitual thoughts is to take a moment to close your eyes and visualize your mind opening up wide to the whole universe. In this new, vast space, you can become aware of all the energy forms – the thoughts, emotions, concepts, memories, and emotions – that are floating around within it. And you can see how the thought you have been caught in is just one small bit of energy floating through this space. You can choose to focus in on it, if you wish – or you can choose to focus on any other energy form that is floating around in this open, expanded space you call your mind.

You can then focus on all the spaces that exist in between these energy forms and feel the draw of these quiet, empty spaces and allow yourself to be pulled into one of them. If you relax into this long enough, you may find yourself floating through one of the doorways into 5D consciousness.

All of these exercises are designed to quiet the mind. They distract it just long enough to get it out of a habitual, conditioned rut, so that you can then redirect it into a quieter space. When done with attention and sincerity, they can be quite effective and bring great relief from the chattering mind. However, I encourage you not to stop here simply with a quieter mind. Instead, take the opportunity you now have to slip past the mind, beyond it, through it – to where you really ultimately want to go: to the true Silence within you.

Experiencing the Silence Within

With practice, there is a state you may reach in which you can suddenly find yourself beyond where your mind operates and all thinking actually stops. It's almost as if you have broken through a barrier in your consciousness, and you're just in what could be called a "flow state" of being. There is no more mind chatter; yet you are fully awake and aware.

You might find this space by initially focusing your awareness on your body, and specifically on your chest, where you sense your Spiritual Heart to be. As you focus your attention on your Heart, a quiet energy will likely begin to sift through you, a letting go. And then, as you take time to fall more deeply into it, you may discover a deep silent space that pulls you in, welcoming you.

The Silence you discover is profoundly peaceful, warm, and safe – you can feel yourself wrapped in a soft blanket of deep security here – it is so relaxing, your whole body just begins letting go. This Silence is way deeper than the space in which your mind and your emotions reside – it's within your body, and yet it is where you can drop into a completely different dimension, a whole different reality, in which thoughts, concerns and body pain are but a faint echo. It's a feeling of being *Home* – your true connection to Source.

There's a clarity here in this Silence – it's where you discover the real YOU – the eternal, changeless YOU that is always present, always awake, knowing what is going on. It is silent and still — and yet vibrant and alive.

There is a deep and clear understanding of Reality, of what life is. There is no need for words here; and yet, you can come to understand everything you need to know within this deep place. There is no need to make decisions here – they make themselves, and they emerge clear and definite and right.

As you settle ever more deeply into this sacred Silence, you can feel your body relax more and more; your breath becomes slow and quiet. And as you open to the Silence, it saturates every cell in your body, and you drink in the deep and pure love that resides here. The Silence nourishes you and feeds you – it resets you on your path, where you need to go. It pervades your entire being. Everything you need is here.

There is a profound Love here in the Silence – love for yourself, love for others, love for all of life. You can be aware of the suffering that is increasingly happening for others in the world, and you experience great compassion for them – and yet you yourself are not caught in suffering. You are like the great Mother, powerful, able to embrace all of humanity with empathic love and understanding.

Within this place of deep Silence in you, you experience the huge expansiveness of who you are – you can feel yourself stretch way out from your body – past the energetic fields of your mental, emotional and spiritual bodies – out into the universe.

You come to know that you are not only a part of the universe – the essence of you *is* that very essence of the universe. You are Source. What you are is in all of creation – in all Beings, animals, all trees, plants, and rocks – even the Earth herself. And the stars and planets, the sun. You are everywhere in everything.

You realize that you are ancient — an ancient Soul who has known, experienced and learned so much throughout millennia of time. You have traveled through the universe, been a part of so many experiences throughout the ages. And you are here now, very purposely, to assist humanity through these times of momentous transformation and ascension into an entirely new reality that's been called the Fifth Dimension.

You come to know all this when dwelling within this deep, deep Silence within you. Maybe the memories aren't clear, but there's a knowing inside you of this truth of who you are – and how important you are to be simply living here during these times. Your consciousness of love, understanding, and knowing of Reality is weaving itself into the collective consciousness of humanity.

And you know that you can begin to live your life from within this deep Silence. You can begin to think and feel emotions and make choices from this place – you can relate to others, you can work, play, and relax. You can create all you wish to create.

Indeed, you can live your life *as* this sacred Silence – free, powerful, and deeply loving – and know you are impacting the entire world.

This experience of the deep Silence within you can be so overwhelmingly peaceful and filled with such light, it may bring tears of joy. But even if you cannot reach into this delicious state of being, you may ultimately discover that it really doesn't matter if your mind is chattering or not. The key is not to focus on the chattering, but to look beyond it – to the stillness that exists, no matter what the mind is doing. This stillness is no more bothered by the mind-chatter than the ocean is bothered by the waves. You can just let the chattering be, while seeking more deeply beyond it to discover what is always still, peaceful, and never-changing – the vast and silent space that is YOU.

Once in this silent Consciousness, you will find that any thinking that appears is fresh, inspired, and creative, springing directly from 5D Consciousness. Such a joy this kind of thinking can bring – and how entirely different from the old, stale, conditioned thinking your mind so often produces!

Chapter 20

Rejecting the 3D Self's Game Plan for Happiness

Have you ever noticed that, no matter how many desires you fulfill, you are never quite satisfied? How many times have you believed that if you could just have that one more important thing in your life, you would finally be happy? Maybe it's more money, a bigger home, a relationship with a partner, a more exciting job, a beautiful vacation – or any of the millions of things that look like they can finally give you the happiness that always feels just out of reach. But then, when you've finally received that thing or attained a wished-for goal, the initial sense of contentment and fulfillment somehow just doesn't last. There is always something more that occurs to you that you need before you can *truly* be happy.

Perhaps at some point along the road of pursuing desires, you realized that the happiness you were seeking wouldn't ever be satisfied by material things. So you began desiring the more subtle things in life, such as more harmonious relationships, a deeper sense of security, or a greater sense of personal power. Maybe you even became aware that what you really needed to attain these more insubstantial things was to improve *yourself* in some way. So you began reading self-help books, seeing a therapist or healer, taking workshops and trainings. And perhaps in doing these activities, you did begin to experience a greater sense of happiness.

But maybe you still weren't satisfied. Your life was better, but you still weren't feeling a lasting sense of fulfillment; you were still yearning for more. So then perhaps, thinking that what you were really yearning for was even more subtle than empowerment, harmonious relationships, or fulfilling work, you turned to spirituality. You began learning to meditate and practice certain spiritual rituals. Again, these probably proved helpful; at least some of the time, a deeper sense of contentment arose within you.

Maybe you have even experienced some profound glimpses of your true Self or peak experiences of bliss and freedom. Yet perhaps you are now discovering that your desires still haven't ceased. You now want more of this peace, bliss, and fulfillment. You want more glimpses of your true Essence – longer and more profound ones. And your desire for these things is now driving you just as hard as it ever did for all those other things in the past. In fact, you may be actually feeling even more unrest, dissatisfaction, and lack of fulfillment than ever before.

Perhaps you are now wondering: Why is this? Why hasn't my pursuit of fulfilling my spiritual desires finally brought me the peace I am seeking? If you have traveled this far along the path of pursuing desires, sometimes you undoubtedly feel frustrated, angry, or despairing.

Believe it or not, feeling all this is actually good news. As distressing as it may be, you are now likely ready to begin seeing the incredible lie that your 3D self has been feeding you all along: that the way to happiness and fulfillment is through following your desires.

Understanding the Nature of Desire

The truth is that *fulfilling desires cannot bring lasting happiness, peace, and fulfillment; on the contrary, it actually produces more suffering.* It does this through continually creating more never-ending desires. Desire feeds on itself. Fulfilling desires breeds more desire.

Contrary to what your 3D self may believe, grasping after what feels good and trying to avoid what feels painful is not only an endless task, it is also a fruitless one. It can never be done successfully for any length of time. This is because, as we've seen before, pleasure and pain come in the same package. You can't have one without the other. The Buddha gave us this very message, stating very simply that desire creates attachment, and attachment creates suffering. Do away with desire and attachment, and peace and contentment naturally appear.

Although this message may not be readily understandable, you can learn to see it clearly for yourself. If you take some time to examine closely the suffering in your life, you will see that, in the midst of the suffering, desire is always present – desire that things be somehow different from how they are. You'll also see how, because of the desire, attachment, expectation, demand, and fear are also present. When you are caught in any of these experiences, there can be no true inner peace.

In fact, true peace only happens when we are completely empty of desire. It is true that happiness can appear when we finally fulfill a desire. It may last a moment, or perhaps an extended period of time. But it always comes to an end. The happiness we experienced in fulfilling our desire was not really due to what we gained; it was due to the state of desirelessness we had finally achieved. *It is the lack of desire that gives us the feeling of peace.*

Desire is a hungry ghost. It's always after MORE – more things, more power, more security, more knowledge, more love. It's never satisfied. If we continue to give in to these demands, desire only gets stronger and continues to want even more. We need to realize that nothing in form will ever satisfy this ghost and bring us true peace. All things, however gross or subtle in substance, are merely reflections of what we all ultimately want: true inner freedom, peace, oneness, love. And only waking up to 5D consciousness will give us all this.

Finding Freedom from Desire

Of course, it is one thing to intellectually understand the whole dynamic of desire and to see the lie we've accepted about it, and an entirely different thing to be able to let go of desires and the endless pursuit of them. This habit of chasing after desires must be one of the most deeply ingrained habits we all have. Yet there are some things you can do to begin the process of freeing yourself from your fruitless pursuit of happiness in this wrong direction. The following are suggestions that may help get you started in this process.

Exercise: *Experiencing the Feeling of Desire*

The first suggestion is to become fully aware of exactly what holding desire in your consciousness can do to you. You can do this by closing your eyes and focusing inward for a few moments. Tune into an important desire you have – perhaps one you've had for quite a while. Feel the sense of lack and the feeling of discomfort or pain you generally experience when thinking about this thing you want so badly. Don't go off into all the stories about it – simply feel the sense of need and the feeling of lack that are present.

Now step back slightly from this and see more clearly just what this energy of desire is creating in you. Be aware of the discomfort, the unrest, the irritation it produces. See the distress that comes from this sense of not feeling full, whole, and complete. Be aware of your body. Note how having this feeling of desire actually prevents you from being totally relaxed. It keeps wanting to drag you into the future when you hope to have this thing you don't currently have; or it's dragging you into the past, searching your memory in an attempt to discover something, anything by which you might fulfill this desire. You'll see that desire won't let you be; it keeps gnawing at you, demanding to be fulfilled. Experience this painful sense of discontentment and see clearly how desire is causing it.

Seeing desire for what it is is never easy. You may be tempted to believe that the suffering you are experiencing is coming from not having what you desire. But investigate closely. This is the lie you've bought; it is not what is true. It is the desire itself that causes you the suffering. To truly see this, it takes a ruthless resolve, born of utter weariness with your persistent pursuit of happiness.

Becoming Fully Aware of Your Desires

After experiencing the true nature of desire and the trouble it causes you, take an inventory of what your important desires are by making a list of them. You might wish to list them in categories, such as desires around your job, your primary relationships, your material possessions, traveling, money, etc. Take time with this list. Allow your mind to empty all of its desires onto the paper. When you feel complete with this, sit back and look over your list. Become aware to what degree you are caught in the trap of desire.

Exercise: *If Only...*

Look carefully at each of these things you desire. Be aware of the happiness you believe you might create in fulfilling them by completing the sentence: "If I only had ____, then I'd be happy."

Then think carefully about the situation. Would having that thing alone do it – or, once you had it, would there just be more desires that would crop up? Remembering times when you finally obtained what you'd been desiring can be helpful. How soon did dissatisfaction set in again after you'd fulfilled those desires?

Example: Nola was someone who often felt depressed. She complained that she and her family lived in too small an apartment. She believed that if she and her husband could only afford to move into a house, all her problems would be solved.

She had dreamed for a number of years about moving into a house in a particular neighborhood. Finally, an opportunity to buy a house there arose. It was a house that looked perfect, like one in which she had always pictured herself living. Beside herself with hope and anticipation, she was absolutely elated. Her desire might finally be fulfilled. After a number of weeks of offers and counter-offers, she and her husband finally signed a contract for it.

When that happened, Nola could talk about nothing else. Her entire life revolved around this house, and about how wonderful life was finally going to be. For weeks she was entirely wrapped up in all the details of the move.

After they'd been moved in for about two weeks, I received a call from her. I was amazed at the depressed sound of her voice. "The upstairs tub leaks, and it looks like we have to retile the whole bathroom. And our next door neighbors are so noisy – we had no idea. And the house is so big. I realize that cleaning it is going to take me a good hour longer than our apartment ever did. I'm feeling a little overwhelmed. I really want to get a housekeeper, but Ted doesn't know if we can afford it."

The scenario, of course, is familiar. Whenever we get something we've asked for, we always have to be prepared to accept whatever goes with it. Nola had spent years desiring something and had finally gotten it. She may have had a few days of enjoying the state of desirelessness she had finally attained around her living situation – but then a whole new set of desires began to besiege her, once again dragging her down into the state of restless discontent and depression she'd been in before. Like most people, she didn't realize that this was because of the new desires that had moved in with her. She kept believing that she simply needed to fulfill these new desires.

Exercise: *What Do You Really Want?*

This exercise helps you see through the desire you think you have. Using your list of desires, pick an important one and answer these questions about it:

- What do you want?
- If you had that, what would you gain?
- If you had that, what would you gain?
- If you had that, what would you gain?

Keep asking this, until you feel you've hit a bottom line with it.

Example: Here's how a woman responded when I asked her these questions:

- *What do you want?* An intimate relationship with a man.
- *What would you gain, if you had that?* I guess I would feel loved, special.
- *If you had that, what would you gain?* (with a sigh) Then I could relax, really relax.

- *If you had that, what would you gain?* I could feel safe. I would finally feel safe. (Her voice wavered some with this one.)
- *If you had that, what would you gain?* (pause, as she started crying) I could finally experience peace – total peace. God, that's all I want. Just deep, inner peace.

We did this exercise with a few other desires she had – all very different desires. To her surprise, each time her bottom line turned out to be inner peace, or something very close to it. You may find you have a similar experience. Perhaps your bottom line might be feeling joy or freedom or love. The point is to become aware of what it is you *really* desire, what it is you are truly searching for through pursuing these things you believe yourself to be desiring.

Are you Effectively Pursuing What you Really Long for?

So now look closely at how you are going about trying to fulfill this true desire that resides beneath all your others. Ask yourself honestly: *Is pursuing these desires really going to give me what I actually long for*? Again think back into your past for a moment. How many times have you fulfilled similar desires, hoping to gain your true desire? How many times has this plan failed in the end? When will you finally be weary enough to see clearly that it doesn't work? When will you be convinced that something else must be tried?

I realize these questions may not be easy to answer. Some part of you may still be convinced that fulfilling desires – even just a few important ones – will give you what you really are yearning for. For example, if you are someone who has never had fulfilling work and have been yearning for this for a long time, it might be difficult for you to be convinced that finally finding fulfilling work isn't going to bring you the kind of happiness you seek. Or you may be someone who has never really experienced a close, intimate relationship with someone and very much would like to have one. You might believe that finding this kind of relationship would finally give you what you've been looking for your whole life.

If there are areas of your life like this, it is understandable that you would believe that following an important desire would bring the fulfillment you seek. And, if this is the case, it may be necessary for you to follow these desires further until you can fulfill them – and then see what you experience.

Some deep desires do need to be followed in order to bring you certain experiences for your spiritual awakening and for completing karmic patterns. You may need to follow them through to their end, to see for yourself where they lead you. In addition, learning to manifest things and create positive experiences for yourself through consciousness techniques can be an important learning experience as you journey through the higher Fourth Dimension.

However, if you have already had successful manifestation experiences and have followed and attained many desires in your life – and you realize that you are still feeling unsatisfied, restless, and unhappy – then perhaps you are ready to try some suggestions designed to help free you from the whole trap of desire itself.

Exercise: *Looking for the Block*

Close your eyes and relax. Breathe a few deep breaths. Bring into your awareness the desire for deep joy, peace and love in your life. The desire may bring up some discomfort as you experience the feeling of lack. Get in touch with that discomfort. And then become aware of what you believe fulfilling this desire would bring you.

Find the Block. See if you can find something within you that prevents you from having your desire filled. It might be a belief, an emotion, a particular fear, or a past experience. When it comes to you, don't analyze it – just see if it will appear in your mind's eye as a type of wall that separates you from that which you desire. Be aware of yourself where you are now, feeling unfulfilled and unhappy, and then see yourself in the distance, happy and fulfilled. And then see the wall that separates these two versions of yourself.

Investigate it closely. Now look closely at this wall. What is it made of? Does it really have any substance? Is it anything more than a mental or emotional concept – an idea or a belief or a memory? Is anything real actually preventing you from experiencing joy, peace, or happiness at this moment? Take an honest look to see if you can just let go of any ideas that prevent you from experiencing what you wish for.

What you may discover is that nothing of any substance is actually preventing you from experiencing the peace, joy, and love you wish to experience – because, inherently, you ARE these qualities.

How can anything prevent you from experiencing who you already naturally are? You are the very essence of joy and peace and love. All you need to do is drop any ideas you have about not being these things, and let go of the desires you've created about them – and discover immediately what is already there, waiting to be experienced.

Example: A lovely girl of seventeen, Amanda, came to see me due to problems she was having with her mother. Amanda had always experienced her mother as harsh and critical, and she longed desperately for someone to understand and love her. She had never known her father and there didn't seem to be many relatives around who spent much time with her. Despite having some friends at school, she was in many ways a very lonely girl.

About a month after she'd started seeing me, she met a boy with whom she immediately became emotionally involved. However, he soon left her and began dating a friend of hers. Amanda was devastated. She had thought she had finally found someone who could love and understand her.

She came to a session the day after her boyfriend had left her. The weight of her depression and despair was palpable. She talked and cried for a while, expressing the pain she was feeling, but that didn't help her feel much better. She finally said, "All I want is to feel loved. That is all I want...I just want to feel loved...."

I nodded with compassion. Gently, I suggested she close her eyes and attune herself to her body to see what she was physically feeling. She immediately told me about the constriction in her chest and solar plexus and the heaviness she felt throughout her body.

Then I asked about the emotions she was feeling. With tears, she told me she was feeling lonely and sad. Then she added, "I feel totally abandoned by God. So alone...and unloved...."

"What you want to feel is that you are loved?"

"Yes! Really loved. I want to feel it all through me, really know it. I want to feel safe and warm...and that I will always be taken care of...." Quiet tears streamed down her face.

"Of course. You want to feel entirely loved, protected, and safe. I understand. (pause) What I'd like you to do, Amanda, is to first of all see yourself standing alone, really feeling the sense of being unloved."

Tearfully, she said, "Okay, I am."

"Now see if you can imagine yourself, some distance away, feeling fully loved – and step into that imagined you."

She hestated and looked confused. But after a few moments, she said, "Okay I guess I can do that". After a minute or so, she suddenly exclaimed, "Oh! It feels so good..."

I let her experience this for a bit. Then I said, "Okay, now step back into the unloved you, looking over at the loved you in the distance – and see if you can see what is in between the two of you. Is there some kind of a wall that separates you?"

She looked puzzled for a moment. And then she said, "Well there's nobody to really love me. I mean, I'd feel loved if there were somebody I knew who really loved me."

"Okay, so what's separating you from the feeling of being loved is the idea that someone needs to be with you who is loving you. That's what is standing between you and feeling loved – kind of like a wall?"

"Yes, I guess."

"Try to see this clearly. There's you with this feeling of being unloved – and then there's another you that you can see somewhere away from you, one who feels loved. And in between you and this feeling is this idea, this thought, that you need someone to love you in order to feel loved that is kind of like a wall."

"Yeah, that's right. I can see it. It's more like a mist – not really solid, but it's in my way. God, I can almost feel the feeling of being loved…I want it so badly. But it's over there. Like in a land I'm not allowed to go to, or something."

"Why don't you see what happens if you try to walk through that mist toward the you that is feeling loved?"

A few moments passed, and then I saw a sweetness appear on her face. Very softly, she whimpered.

"What's happening?"

"Oh," she sighed. "I'm in it. I'm in the feeling. Oh my God…it's so sweet. I feel like I'm being rocked like a baby in God's arms…."

Tears flooded her eyes. Her face indeed had transformed into that of a baby. "It feels so warm and safe…there's so much love. It's like I don't have to do anything…I can just be loved for who I am…." She was now sobbing and could say no more.

After a while her crying subsided, and she said softly, "You know what's so amazing is that it isn't even like I'm being loved anymore. It's kind of crazy, but I've kind of disappeared into God…it's more like I AM love. I don't have to BE loved. I feel so full. My heart – you should feel my heart. There's like this pressure all around it – but good pressure. It's soft and vibrating and kind of filled with this light…."

It was amazing to me. By simply looking closely to see what appeared to be blocking her from feeling loved, in a matter of minutes, Amanda had gone from total despair to a deeper knowing of who she really was.

This experience, of course, did not entirely eradicate her yearning to find someone to love her. Being so young and without the experience of being truly loved by someone, she was still going to pursue that desire. But what she had experienced in our session became a powerful reference point for her in discovering the true source of the love that she yearned for.

She now knew she could contact this source inside herself – and that her own true nature was Love, itself.

Exercise: *Observing Your Desires*

This exercise is the same basic practice described before when it was suggested to observe emotions and thoughts as they enter your mind. This one involves simply observing desires as they come into your awareness – and doing nothing about them. It means not indulging or pursing them; and it means not resisting, judging, or suppressing them in any way. It's just a matter of letting them be.

Like thoughts and emotions that come into your mind, desires are just forms of energy that you have given attention to in the past. At first, as you give them this new treatment of simply observing them, they will undoubtedly pull on you even harder. Do not react. Eventually, as you give no energy to them, they will begin to lose their strength and power over you.

Redirecting Energy From Desires

You may discover that there is one desire that can actually be beneficial – and that's the desire for true freedom, for full awakening to your true Self. Although, ultimately, this desire too needs to be released, it can be used at first to propel you toward the experience of awakening.

When this desire first appears powerfully within you, it is an important signpost telling you that you are headed toward full awakening into 5D Consciousness. This is indeed a blessed event. When you discover that this desire for true freedom is your only true desire – that freedom is all you really want – this is definitely a happy day! This is when freedom will begin pulling you Home. At this point, all you need do is completely surrender to this divine pull.

To get to this place, it's important to focus your attention and love on your desire to fully realize who you truly are. When it appears in your awareness, give lots of energy to it. See it as a flame you are fanning. Do everything you can to build this flame, to make it burn more brightly. When suffering appears, throw it into the flames. When desire for anything else comes, throw this on the flames as well. Redirect the energy of the desire into your desire for freedom. Then watch the flames of this one desire burn away the desire for anything transient and illusory. It can be truly liberating.

Example: Milana found herself in dire financial straits. She was recently separated from her husband, and she was attempting to build a real estate business from scratch. Money was already very tight, when she suddenly found she had many large expenses she needed to pay almost immediately. A sense of panic about this threatened to take hold.

I had been coaching her to simply observe feelings as they arose, and I now encouraged her to observe the panic. This was successful to a degree; but after a while, she began speaking about a deep desire to be financially free. She believed that, if only she could attain financial freedom, so many problems could be solved.

I asked her to become aware of the power she was giving this desire every time she gave it attention. She exclaimed, "You're right! Whenever I think about it, it then comes into my mind more often, and soon it's monopolizing my attention. It's all I can think about. I give it an inch; it takes a mile." She added that sometimes, along with the thoughts, came such a deep longing and such a sense of suffering that she felt she was going crazy. It was as if she were drowning in her feeling of need and lack and helplessness.

I suggested that she become aware of her desire to fully awaken to who she was. I knew this desire was very strong within her. I suggested she see it as brightly-burning flame inside her. She closed her eyes, and almost immediately, she said, "It's like a bonfire inside me – my longing to be done with it all and just be free. God, I just want to be free of all lack and longing and suffering! Wow, I can really see and feel the fire!"

"Okay, see if you can allow it to grow, to intensify."

She was silent for a moment and then moaned, "It's so huge already; it's eating away at my insides."

"Okay, now focus for a moment on your desire for financial security. Find that inside you."

"All right...yeah, I'm back to that."

"Good. Now take that longing and throw it on the fire."

I could see for a moment that she might be drawn into giving that longing some energy and attention again. Then her face suddenly changed. It's hard to describe her expression – surprise, pain, joy, all at once. And then tears. I sat quietly with her for about five minutes as she wept. I could see her whole body trembling with release.

When she was finally able to speak, she told me that an incredible burning for true freedom had occurred at the moment of throwing the desire for financial security onto the fire – that it was like throwing gasoline onto it. Her whole body felt an actual burning; heat was coursing through her veins.

She was still stunned by what had happened. Then she said, "This yearning for my true Self is so intense and so painful – and yet it's so sweet. All I can do is surrender to it."

We sat together for a while, not saying much. She continued to report that the fire was still burning inside her. I suggested that she could simply observe the fire, rather than feeling consumed by it. She fell into a gentle, quiet, relaxed state of being. "The fire's out," she finally reported. "I feel just warm and tingly."

I suggested she look around inside her for the desire for financial security. She said she could only feel a kind of "ghost" of it. All that was really there was peace. "You know, it's strange. I just have this knowing now that I will always be taken care of....I really don't have to worry anymore."

Of course, this wasn't the end of worry thoughts about finances for Milana. But she was handling them very differently now. They didn't grab hold of her so furiously as before. She didn't pay as much attention to them. She said they kind of flitted though her mind, like pieces of tissue paper floating on the breeze, but did not stay long.

This process of throwing all desires into the one true desire for full and final realization of your true 5D Self can be a very powerful experience. You can realize that the yearning itself – as painful as it can be at times – is simply your true Self calling you Home.

It Takes Some Time

Desires will probably always be with you. Like thoughts and emotions, they're simply part of the human psyche. There's no need to make them wrong or feel weak when they arise within you. But what can change is your response to them. You have no obligation to follow them or put energy into fulfilling them. You need not obsess about them until they are satisfied. You can simply let them be. You can even follow them to some extent, so long as you don't fall again into the belief that fulfilling them is necessary for your state of happiness and peace.

It does no good to try to suppress them. But you can understand them and continue to realize how they function. You can begin to see clearly how trying to satisfy them simply continues your misery, disappointment, and discontent. This is the first step in becoming free from desire.

From there on, it's simply a matter of not giving them much attention when they arise –except to watch them or redirect their energy into your desire for total awakening to your 5D Self. Given this treatment, they will eventually fade and weaken and become no more than part of the passing show within your consciousness.

You will begin to see that, no matter what desires are fulfilled or what you have or haven't achieved, you can be happy no matter what is going on in your life. You'll find that you can experience true inner peace, no matter whether pleasure or pain is present in your life; you'll see that both of them are actually irrelevant to your experience of peace and contentment. They are merely phenomena passing through your awareness. They come and they go. You need not resist or grab onto them. The peaceful, joyful fulfillment that you are experiencing – in fact, that you ARE – is untouched by it all.

And surprisingly, in finally realizing this, certain other things you have been desiring and longing for may also suddenly appear in your life. Certainly, you'll see that your basic needs will always be taken care of – but even many of your desires may also begin to show up. It is just what happens when you shift into 5D consciousness.

* * *

In the last few chapters, we have explored a number of ways in which the mind can keep us in delusion, convincing us that it is who we are. We saw how the subtle nature of thought can make it easy for us to confuse it with the nature of pure Consciousness. We explored how the mind's creation of time tends to keep us out of the Now, where we can experience our true Self. We also saw how the mind tends to claim spiritual experiences as its own, deluding us into thinking that it has control over them.

We then explored the chattering nature of the mind to see how its constant flow of thought can keep us from experiencing the peace of the 5D Self. And finally, we explored how following the desires our mind creates can produce a profound trap that keeps us in continual dissatisfaction and unrest, preventing us from experiencing the peace and happiness that inherently reside within us as our essence.

It is important to stay aware of all these potential traps your mind is constantly setting for you. You have fallen into them over and over again – and will continue to do so, even knowing what they are. Deeply-ingrained habits can be hard to break. But, with persistent vigilance and practice, they can be weakened and broken. As these habits are broken, little by little, your identification with the mind will begin to weaken and eventually fall away.

When you can begin to see your 3D self clearly and attain a degree of detachment from it, your 5D Self can begin to shine forth naturally and become self-evident. In one way, the 3D self can be seen as simply a lot of clutter that needs to be cleaned up and put aside, so that the 5D Self you really are can be clearly seen and experienced. This Self is always present; you just can't always see it because you are focusing on all the clutter.

As you earnestly seek this higher Self and detach your identity from your 3D self, you will discover this lower self slowly becoming a pale shadow of what it was, a translucent presence that you can simply ignore. As this happens, you realize the humorous paradox in the whole process of "letting go of the 3D self: that, on one level, this self never even existed. All there has been all along is the 5D Self. The 3D identity has been a finely-wrought illusion that you've mistakenly believed to be real. In Truth, it's all been a type of dream.

Chapter 21

Releasing Your Identity from your "Spiritual Self"

What you may have come to regard as your "spiritual self" is likely another difficult aspect of your 3D self to recognize. This is the part of you that has been a spiritual seeker for some time, perhaps hoping through spiritual practices to become enlightened or awakened into your 5D Self. Or maybe it's the aspect of you that is focused on healing and becoming more whole and happy – or perhaps the one who is focused on "being of service to others".

It might be hard to see that this aspect of yourself is part of your 3D identity, because it has felt to be a higher aspect of yourself, a happier, more empowered part of who you are. And that is true; when you're identified with this spiritually-focused aspect of yourself, you are certainly functioning from a higher vibration, and you're probably at least aware of 5D consciousness. But identifying with even this aspect of yourself can still be holding you back from truly experiencing who you fundamentally are – that One who does not need to awaken to anything, that One who is already awake and living in 5D and beyond, that multi-dimensional YOU that is totally free.

The Trap of Spiritual Identification

It may be especially disheartening to realize this if you've spent many years meditating and conscientiously performing other spiritual techniques. Such practices may have awakened you more and more to your true spiritual nature – perhaps you've even experienced 5D consciousness during times of doing one of these spiritual practices. Think about it, however: the one doing this has been focused on becoming something else, something more, something different. This is the part of you who feels you must *do* something in order to become who you really are.

Is that really your 5D Self? When you are actually identified with your 5D Self, do you feel any need to do anything to become something different?

The distinction between your 5D Self and the one who is attempting to change itself to be that Self is very subtle. But this is perhaps the last distinction you need to make to fully shift into identification with your 5D Self. The 5D Self is not actually "spiritual" – it simply *is*. Spirituality and all the practices you can do to shift into 5D consciousness are the *bridge* to this identification – and the one who is crossing that bridge is not the One at the other end of the bridge. It's your 3D self. When you are experiencing your 5D Self, you're not doing anything, going anywhere, to become anything else or anything more – you just *are*. Nothing is missing and therefore nothing is being sought.

Now, this isn't to say that it's not valuable to meditate or do other spiritual practices. And it doesn't mean that, even when you're identified with your 5D Self, you wouldn't decide to do them. Of course, you might. It's just that, when in 5D consciousness, you meditate because it happens to feel good; it's perhaps a way you can experience an even deeper Silence within you, or maybe it helps to more fully relax your body. But you're not trying to achieve anything "spiritual", tune into anything that will awaken you, or bring you closer to being enlightened. It's just something you naturally choose to do when it feels natural to do it.

When identified with your 3D self, meditation and other practices are generally methods of getting somewhere, doing something to change or improve yourself. As such, when you're identified with what you might regard as your "spiritual self" doing these things, it's not really different from when you're identified with your body, your mind, your emotions, or the self that is playing a role in your life. When identified with it, it's one more aspect of your 3D self that can waylay you in your shift to full identification with your 5D Self.

An Even More Subtle Trap

If you are someone who has been trained to assist others to spiritually awaken, the misidentification can become even more subtle. Perhaps you have become a healer, a yoga teacher, a t'ai ch'i instructor, a Reiki master, a new age minister, a channel or some other kind of spiritual teacher. Or you are simply a natural conflict mediator or problem-solver. Maybe an animal communicator. Or an impassioned activist involved in creating the New Earth. These are all valuable roles to play, and you may be very effective in what you have to offer to others.

The tricky part is if you begin believing that the role you're playing is who you actually *are* – when, in fact, this identity is still simply an aspect of your 3D self playing a role, a part of you that may have a need to feel important or valuable. If you are not careful, you can fall into one or more of these "traps" on your Ascension journey into 5D consciousness.

Again, this is not to say that you can't serve in these kinds of roles and actually be functioning from 5D consciousness. Of course, this is possible. But unless you've truly made the transition from identifying with your 3D self to your 5D Self, you can be side-tracked onto a path of illusion for a while. It's important to be aware of this possibility.

Differences between 4D and 5D Identification

Very simply, if you identify yourself to be a someone in a body, doing something, thinking or feeling in a certain way, you may still be identifying with an aspect of your 3D self. When in 5D identification, you experience yourself more as a subtle essence of being – more as a field of energy or light. You are highly conscious of yourself functioning on many different dimensions, but there is generally nothing obvious about this. Doing, thinking and feeling all still occur, but there is no attachment to any of these activities, no identification with them. They are all just happening and you are observing them. You are aware of how temporary the manifestation of this human being form with you is. And you are aware of the simultaneous existence of many other dimensional manifestations of yourself.

One way to understand this more clearly is to liken it, for example, to when you might sprain your ankle. It would be natural to focus for a while on that as an important part of your identity; but once the pain has passed, you would no longer think of yourself as someone with a sprained ankle. So it is with all the self-identifications you might adopt in 3D consciousness. They can be your idea of who you really are for a while, but they all pass. They are impermanent and are not the reality of who you are.

It is also important to realize that, when identified with your spiritual self, there is still the possibility of feeling either successful or failing in some way; there is usually the desire to "be a good person" and feel yourself lifting up into another realm where you experience greater healing or clarity. Although you may be sincerely attempting to receive inner guidance, you still find yourself at times seeking outside help when you feel stuck. All these characteristics are of someone in high fourth-dimensional consciousness – a wonderful place to be; yet, you are still not quite functioning in 5D consciousness.

This is not to discourage you – far from it. If you are functioning quite steadily in 4D and dipping in and out of 5D, you are as close as almost any human being can be while living here on Earth at this time. The Earth is still not fully in 5D, herself. Once this shift occurs, it will be so much easier for you to ascend with her into the glorious new existence for which you have been yearning for so very long.

Surrendering to 5D

Chapter 22

Learning to Completely Trust Source to Guide You

Now that we have explored the ways in which it's possible to detach your identification from all aspects of your 3D self, it's time to look at the next step: doing your best to keep yourself in 5D consciousness in your everyday life. This involves learning to surrender to Source as much as possible, consistently trusting that it will take care of you and guide you in the best possible way.

Eventually, it entails giving up all attempts to control your life through the information you've gleaned from the external world and processed through your mind – and, instead, allowing the intuitive messages from your Heart and your body to guide you in your decisions and choices. Information from the outside world that has been processed through your mind can be helpful; but only when considered *after* you have chosen to follow the flow of the intuitive messages your Heart and your body are offering you. It can then help you to finetune your direction.

If you have devoted a great deal of your life to trying to control your life through your thoughts and intentions, this decision to surrender control may seem a frightening prospect. But it need not be. Through a process of testing and watching to see what happens, trust can naturally develop and the surrendering of control can be done gradually at a pace that is comfortable for you.

Remember that, when I speak of surrender, I'm not referring to an attitude of giving up or becoming passive and inactive. I'm referring, rather, to consciously and courageously choosing to allow Source to guide you in all your decisions. It entails an attitude of letting go and relaxing, one in which all struggle, resistance, and manipulation are released. In essence, it involves responding to life with a natural ease, trust, and flow.

Accepting Yourself Just as You Are

One of the important aspects of surrendering your life to Source is first fully accepting yourself, just as you are, and learning that there is truly nothing wrong with you. You are exactly how you should be. In 5D consciousness, you have a total acceptance of who you are at any given time; you understand that who you are is an aspect of Source, itself. And since this is true, Source is to be fully trusted to guide you.

Furthermore, there is no question of having to "improve" yourself in order to be okay or worthy of love or acceptance. There's an understanding that you are always naturally doing your very best, given what you know and understand living in a controlled 3D environment. There are no judgments or inner pushes to be better or different in any way; you understand that if something needs to change, you will be guided to do that and it will happen naturally and with ease. If necessary, you will also be assisted by outer sources that come synchronistically to your attention in just the right timing.

Here is an exercise that can assist you in learning how let go of any judgments and habitual programs you may have to improve yourself.

Exercise: *Practicing Acceptance of Yourself*

1. **Choose a Judgment.** Choose something about yourself you judge, something you spend energy either resisting or trying to change and improve. It can be something physical, mental, emotional or spiritual.

2. **Allow your usual reaction.** Allow your mind to begin its process with its worrying, analyzing, resisting, judging, and struggling to get control over it. Become aware of the energy you expend on this issue, trying to get control over it in order to fix it. See the effort it takes, how tiring it can be.

3. **What is attached to it?** Now see all the stuff that you have attached to it: all your judgments, beliefs, emotions, desires, fears, guilt, shame and projections into the future.

    For example, let's say you've chosen a behavior you call "overeating". In looking at your judgments about this behavior, you discover you have many: you consider it wrong, disgusting, and weak. You believe that because of this behavior, you are overweight and you look like a "slob". Because of these beliefs you also feel sadness, shame, anger, and hurt. Your fears and projections into the future are that you will never be able to stop this behavior and you will eventually become totally out of control and enormous. And so, of course, this all leads to a desire to get rid of the behavior, to somehow overcome it.

4. **Be aware of how it feels.** Feel the heaviness of all this, the clutter it creates in your mind, the pressure in your body. Become very clear about the fact that all this is stuff that you, yourself, have attached to this behavior or quality with which you have been struggling. See clearly that none of it is inherently, naturally there. The behavior or quality is simply what it is. Also keep in mind that none of it is YOU – it's all stuff you've picked up when traveling through the Third Dimension, while controlled by multiple forms of AI manipulation.

5. **Remove the clutter.** In realizing this, see if you can now begin to detach from the issue all the mental and emotional stuff you have attached to it. Pull away all the judgments, beliefs, desires, fears, and emotions you have about it, and simply see the behavior or quality as it is.

6. **Let go of the struggle.** In seeing this thing you judge about yourself with detachment, now try simply accepting it as a fact in your life – *at this time*. Take a deep breath, relax, and attempt to just let it be. Let go of the struggle to get rid of it or to improve or change it. Let go of your belief about what *should* be happening about it...and just allow it to be as it is. Know that this behavior or quality is simply a part of the personality structure of your 3D self at this time. It is not who you are. Your 3D self is not perfectible. Quit struggling under the illusion that you have the power to perfect yourself.

Feel the relaxation that can develop when allowing what-is to simply be. This doesn't mean you will never do anything about it or that nothing about it will ever change. It's simply giving up, at this point, the struggle you have created around it. It is also an allowance for the possibility that there is an important reason for this quality or behavior in your life at this time that you are not yet aware of.

Once you can simply be with yourself, completely as you are, you will find that the quality or behavior you had been judging will naturally begin to change to a more healthy expression of itself. New effective ways you can easily and naturally implement to change it will begin to occur to you. There will be no struggle attached to it. And a sense of greater freedom will start unfolding in your life.

Accepting your Life as it is – Just for Now

Once you have been able to more fully accept and love yourself, just as you are, it is then time to begin trusting Source to guide you in all other aspects of your life. Learning to do this involves two processes. As described above in dealing with your judgments about aspects of yourself, the first process is seeing clearly the situations present in your life without any added "clutter" of emotions, beliefs, desires, fears, judgments, resistance, or projections into the future about them.

The second is learning how to release the impulse to control the events in your life solely through your limited conscious mind, and truly begin trusting your intuition to guide you through your life. It's important to understand that accepting whatever comes into your life does not mean you have to *like* everything that happens or passively put up with it for the rest of your life; you simply need to initially *allow it to be, just for now* – without judgment or resistance. When you are able do this, you are in a clear place to see what – if anything – needs to be done with it and how to do it in the best way possible.

Letting Go of Trying to Control Your Life

In the West, two beliefs seem to generally be prevalent concerning life and the control we have over it. The first is that we do have control (at least some) over what occurs. The second is that by taking control of our life, we can find happiness. It is important to explore and question these beliefs, because they are often assumed to be facts about life or statements about the truth, rather than simply beliefs. And, like all beliefs, they may not, in fact, represent what is actually true.

If you hold the first belief – that we have at least some control over our lives – you might wish to explore the question: How much control do you really have over what happens in your life? Do you really know that what you do has a causal effect on what happens? How do you know that everything that happens isn't simply predestined to occur? Things may appear to go in a certain way because of what you do, but how do you know for sure it isn't the way things would have gone anyway? Perhaps you have simply aligned your will to that which was going to happen anyway, and it just looks as if you've caused it. Furthermore, do you even know that your decision to do something wasn't already destined to be made, even before you thought you were making it? What do you know for certain about any of this?

The answer to these questions, of course, is that you can't know. There is no way to know how much control, if any, we have over our lives. There is no way to prove it either way. This is the old debate between the ideas of "free-will" and "predestination" that can never be proven through any scientific or intellectual process. The assumption that we have control over our lives is simply a belief and therefore may or may not be true. To be clear, I am not saying we don't have control over anything in our lives – just that this is simply an assumption that must be seen clearly.

The second belief that is often assumed to be the Truth stems from the first belief. It is that by attempting to control our lives, we may be able to find happiness. It is important to explore and question this assumption as well. Do you know beyond a doubt that this is true? Has your attempt at controlling your life brought the happiness you've experienced? These questions also, of course, cannot be answered in any way that will satisfy the intellect. But again, it is important to see that the belief – like many beliefs we have – is not based on anything that can be proven, and therefore may not be true.

If you have been conscientious in practicing manifestation techniques, these questions may well be upsetting. Perhaps you've felt successful in manifesting a great deal more happiness and success in your life since you've been aware of how you have created all circumstances in your life through your thoughts and emotions. To be sure, there is likely some truth in the assumptions that you have indeed created new situations in your life, that you have, at least to some degree, controlled them.

And yet, are you successful with these techniques all the time? Do you ever get confused as to why you are apparently able to create what you want sometimes, but not other times? Do you fall into feelings of frustration, inadequacy and self-judgment when you seem to fail?

The answer may lie in the fact that, when you are not successful, you are attempting to use these manifestation techniques while identified with your controlled and distorted 3D self. When identified with this self, you really don't know how to control much of anything. And, even when you are apparently successful, and you feel a greater sense of power and happiness – how long does this frame of mind last? Isn't there always something more you then feel a need to try to manifest? As we saw earlier, desires are endless. Fulfilling them does not create a sense of fulfillment for long.

Learning to Trust your 5D Self

What you *can* learn through experience, however, is that you are being guided by your 5D Self and that you are in safe hands. With this trust, you may find that you are being guided into the situations that are exactly right for you, in the right timing. You are being brought to situations that will assist you to learn what you need to learn, and let go of what you need to let go of. You can see that you are presented with new opportunities to step into situations that will help you to awaken more and more into fifth-dimensional consciousness. In a way, this has always been true; but now, with the Ascension energies working so closely with you, it is easier to see more clearly how this is happening.

And you can perhaps decide to stop trying so hard to control your life and, instead, just sit back, relax, and enjoy the ride. Even when it tends to get a bit wild and bumpy, because trust has by now been firmly established, you can know that you're being guided perfectly toward the Fifth Dimension in the most rapid and successful way possible.

Feeling for the Flow

When considering the decision to release these controlling efforts in your life, you may well be asking: *So, if I'm not trying to control things, what do I do? Do I just become a passive observer, allowing anything to happen in my life?*

The answer is No. What you do is begin to intuitively feel for the "flow" in your life – what you are naturally and effortlessly being guided to do. And then cooperate with it. It involves being open and trusting, and being willing to do whatever you are being guided to do. Sometimes the message might actually be to use some manifestation techniques to bring something about; if so, you do that. But the message to do that comes from a place of flow and trust within your Heart – not from your rational mind. Remember that, in 5D consciousness, it is the Heart that guides you through life, no longer your rational mind.

This shift in how you make decisions in life entails maintaining a constant awareness of your inner guidance. As described earlier, inner guidance can come to you in many ways, and it is important to find the ways in which you best receive this help. It may come to you as words that you hear; you may sense or feel it energetically as sensations in your body; you may see images in your mind that point the way. Or you might somehow just receive a whole "download" of information into your awareness.

In a certain way, no matter how you receive the guidance, there's a sense of its coming from a deeper place within you than your mind. Your mind might then take the information and begin processing it; but be aware of the origin of the information. If it's coming from your inner guidance, it will be from your Heart.

You may also notice synchronicities in your external world that come at a time you're wondering about something regarding the situation. Perhaps a particular animal will suddenly appear in your space, or someone near you will surprisingly say something pertaining to your situation or question.

If you have difficulty discerning between what your mind might be telling you and what your intuition is guiding you to do, here is an exercise that might assist you. What you're essentially doing in this process is getting a sense in your body for where the flow is.

Exercise: *Finding the Flow*

1. **Write it all out.** Write out onto paper all that you have attempted to do about a problem situation in your life and all thoughts you have about it. This will serve to placate your mind and help it to rest. Be aware of what it feels like in your body when you are focused in your mind, attempting to work something out.

2. **Focus on your body.** Now close your eyes and take time to move deeply into the silence within you. Focus away from your mind and into your body. Completely relax every muscle. Breathe deeply and continue to keep focused on your body and how it is feeling. Especially be aware, as you do this, of sensations in the area of your Heart and the silence that begins to develop within you.

As described earlier, there is an experience you may have of suddenly finding yourself beyond your mind, and all thinking actually stops. It's as if you have broken through a barrier in your consciousness, and you find yourself in what could be called a "flow state" of being. There is no more mind chatter; yet you are fully awake and aware. When in this state, inner guidance comes in extremely clearly. But, even if you don't experience this and you can only reach a state of relative quiet within yourself, don't worry. This is enough to access your inner guidance.

3. **Ask clear questions.** From within this quiet space, now ask in a clear and unattached way: "Does anything need to be done about this situation? Do I need to do anything to change it at this time?" Be still and simply allow an answer to come naturally, peacefully to you. Be open to receive whatever it is, whether it's in words, sensations, ideas or images. If more questions occur to you, ask them, as well.

4. **Feel into the answers you receive.** As ideas or possible answers come to you, be aware of what feels most *effortless, natural,* and *flowing*.

What actions bring a sense of balance and peace, a warmth in your Heart, a light in your mind? Your body knows. You may get the message that there is something you need to do, or there may be nothing to do at that time. Simply be open to receive whatever comes to you from the place of deep stillness within you, without countering it or moving into analyzing it.

If something does need to be done about the situation, you will feel a clear and natural energy within you to do it. The action will be part of the flow. It will feel at least somewhat effortless; it will feel *right*. If there is nothing to do about it, at least not at this time, you will sense that clearly. There will be a knowing simply to let things be. Either way, there will be present a sense of peace, clarity, and relaxation. Your whole body and sense of being will feel aligned with this "felt-knowing".

If, in this process of opening to inner guidance, confusion appears – or if fears, desires, doubt, or analyzing slip in – you will know that you have moved back into your mind. Without judging yourself for this, once again drop deeply into the silence beyond your mind. Then begin again to ask what, if anything, needs to be done about the situation with which you've been struggling. Stay relaxed, unattached, and open. Be accepting of whatever comes forward into your awareness.

Bypassing the Traps of the Mind

On this path of letting go of your 3D identity, the art of going within to receive inner guidance is essential to practice and eventually master. However, inherent traps are involved in the process, and it is important to be on the outlook for them.

Old, habitual thoughts can feel flowing and natural: One of the major traps is listening to the guidance coming from your conditioned 3D mind, rather than from your 5D Self. The thoughts coming from your mind can often feel as if they are effortless and flowing and natural. In one way, they *are*, simply because they are so very familiar to you. You've thought them so often for so long, they feel flowing and natural to you.

If you investigate them closely, however, you will notice that these conditioned thoughts have an old, stale feeling to them. There's a dead energy about them – unlike the fresh, spontaneous, alive energy that ideas from the Heart of your 5D Self carry. Ideas from the programmed mind are furthermore often steeped in fear of some kind. Thoughts from within the Silence lack this fearful energy. The messages have a confident authority, as well as a sense of loving support.

For example, let's say you are standing in a room when an earthquake suddenly hits, and you panic, wondering what the best thing to do might be. You may immediately get the inner message: *Quick – leave! Run out the door!* This message might, on the surface, seem to be a fearful one. But if it is coming from from your 5D Self, while having a feeling of urgency, it will also have a sense of calm and firm authority, rather than fear. It will convey to you a sense that you are being loved and protected. For this reason, it will be easy to quickly obey.

Thus, the key to distinguishing between messages from your 5D Self and messages from your rational mind lies in the energy and feeling of the message. You can tell the difference, when you feel into what is behind the message: is there fear and an old, dead energy with it, or is there a fresh, alive energy that holds a loving authority?

Wishful, hopeful messages feel good. A second trap you can fall into when learning to distinguish between the messages coming from the 5D Self and those from the mind is falling prey to wishful, hopeful thinking. Certain messages can feel loving, joyful and positive, thereby causing you to believe they must be coming from your 5D Self. Of course, sometimes messages from this Self will match your hopes and wishes in a situation. This can create an incredible feeling because the plan that your 5D Self has for you is apparently in alignment with what you are personally hoping for.

The trap lies in believing that your wishful, hopeful thoughts are *always* coming from your attunement with your 5D Self, and sometimes this is not the case. You may hope that a certain path or action is the right one and try to make it happen, simply because it feels good; and yet, all the while, a small, still voice is telling you that a different situation needs to take place. You may feel compelled to ignore this quiet voice because it sounds "negative" – but in reality, all it is doing is telling you something different from what you want to hear. It can be very tricky.

Essentially, what you need to do when earnestly seeking true inner guidance is to be unattached to what you will receive when you ask a question. Leave all preconceived ideas and hopes behind, and simply be open to whatever guidance you receive. It demands a deep commitment to following the guidance of your 5D Self, wherever that may take you. You must also become sensitive to when it is your mind prompting you towards some action which it, your mind, and not your Heart prefers.

At the same time, if you are open to trusting your 5D Self and giving up your familiar habit of trying to control your life, you will find that the guidance you receive will feel right to ALL of you, including your mind, your emotions and your body. It will make sense. Even if you do not hear what you'd like to hear, if you're honest, you will know that it simply feels right.

Taking "Baby Steps"

Learning to tune into inner guidance is a very subtle art; it's a process of learning to trust your 5D Self as it communicates with you – and yet stay grounded and practical. It's an art that needs to be practiced and honed through testing and leaning into the guidance you believe you are receiving. And it's a skill that takes a while to develop.

In one way, as you have more experiences of 5D consciousness and become familiar with it, this trust happens naturally. But trust is also something you can consciously develop through taking "baby steps" in that direction.

The first step you can make is to look to see what is already present in your life – what situations, relationships, and "issues" you are living with – and move slowly into allowing all these things to be, just for the present, without adding resistance or judgment to them. Then you can begin to take small steps toward allowing your 5D Self to guide you in changing anything that feels wrong or uncomfortable to you.

Hold back on trying to change things, one day at a time. One way to do this would be to take it a day at a time, letting go of all conditioned urges to control what is happening. Simply go through the day watching this urge to change, manipulate, direct, or fix things – and not act on it.

As you simply allow everything to be as it is without trying to change anything, see what happens. Perhaps a whole new idea will come in, something you've never thought of before. Is there a sense of natural flow with it? Does it feel *right*? How does your body feel when you think of making the change?

If, after a while, it feels natural, effortless, and flowing to do something in particular, then gently move toward it. If it involves a struggle or resistance, don't do it. Don't act out of a belief that something is "wrong" or "bad" and needs to be changed; simply do it as a natural action emerging from the peace deep within you. There's a gracefulness with this; it's like doing a flowing, effortless dance with your 5D Self, following its lead, trusting it to take you where you need to go.

Work with one issue at a time. Another baby-step approach is to take one area or issue in your life you have been struggling with and begin a slow process of letting go of your attempts to control it. Develop an attitude of allowing it to be the way it is. Then become very alert to what your 5D Self may be guiding you to do about it, if anything.

If the action – or lack of it – that your 5D Self seems to be counseling you to take feels too drastic at first, then again, intuitively lean into it. Slowly follow what is emanating from the peaceful silence within you.

Watch closely what happens. If fear comes up for you in following the counsel you've received, drop back into the Silence, and be alert for messages.

Learning to trust this process takes some time. Start slowly. It is far less frightening if you begin with the less significant issues in your life.

Floating Down the River

The process of learning to trust your 5D Self is something like being in a boat on a river. Usually in life, in your attempt to guide your boat where you think you want to go, you are probably using your paddles to take you to this shore or that island. You're steering it away from rocks and trees and branches and, as needed, trying to go more quickly or more slowly. You may be somewhat anxious that, if you give up your vigilance and effort at paddling, you may get pulled someplace you don't wish to go. Sometimes that happens; the flow of the river is too strong, and you end up overshooting your desired destination. You end up getting snagged in branches, ramming into someone else's boat, or getting caught in a whirlpool.

If you don't get where you think you want to get, you might become angry, disappointed, or hurt. Maybe you blame the river and bemoan the fact that your boat and paddles are inadequate. Or you curse the other people who have somehow been lucky enough with their boats to have gotten to where you wanted to go. You feel victimized and helpless.

Maybe at some point, realizing this attitude is getting you nowhere, you'll renew your efforts to overcome the river's flow. Often after doing this over and over again, you likely just get worn out and, feeling defeated and apathetic, you let your boat drift for a while. Then maybe panic ensues, and you start madly paddling again, trying to force your boat back in the direction in which you wanted to go. All this can be so tiring!

The process of trust can begin when, at a time when it looks relatively safe to stop paddling for a while, you have the courage to do so. You simply put down your paddles and let the boat follow the flow of the river for a time. In doing this, you have the opportunity to feel the natural flow of the river; you can see clearly where it is taking you. Once you have quietly experienced the flow for a time, maybe you can then begin cooperating with it. While staying sensitive to any subtle changes in the course of the flow, you can gently paddle in the same direction.

There can be an incredible peace in this process of just floating down the river, barely paddling, trusting the flow. You can relax and enjoy the view and the gentle breezes. You can become aware that if your help in paddling is needed, you'll know. It is an automatic, effortless and natural action. Your ride down the river becomes pleasant and peaceful, as you fully experience the river and the views on either shore.

Surrender Doesn't Mean Doing Nothing

I wish to make it clear that surrendering to your 5D Self doesn't mean that you avoid taking any action when it feels right. It may involve less action than you are used to and more time simply *being*. But it does involve some action – action that is in accordance with the natural flow of things. What you will probably find is that the actions you do take in this approach to life are actually much more effective than those that spring from your conditioned mind and emotions.

Once, long ago, I had an experience that demonstrated this to me very clearly. I lived for a short time with several housemates. One of them was a man who was planning to live with us for just a few weeks. None of us knew him or really liked him much – but little did we know how disturbed a person he would turn out to be.

One day, when I happened to be home alone with him, he suddenly had what looked like a psychotic break and became violent with me. I had been sitting quietly at my desk in my room, when he charged in and began arguing about something with me. Because my response was not to engage him in arguing, he became enraged. He threw a chair at me and yelled, over and over, that he was going to bash in my face. I was shocked, aghast, and terrified. My conditioned mind was anxiously yelling two different messages to me: *Get up and run* and *stand up and fight back.* Things to yell back at him were also charging into my mind with an incredible force.

Thankfully, I had the awareness to do neither of those things. In retrospect, I think either of them might have only increased his rage. Instead, I very quickly dropped into a place of stillness in my body; and, focusing on my Heart, I silently pleaded for guidance. Immediately, I heard, "Just sit still and look him in the eyes". I did this, while also silently sending him love. I could see the expression on his face immediately become puzzled and uncertain. The longer I gazed at him silently like this, the more he backed up and seemed to lose momentum. He eventually stopped yelling, dropped the chair he had raised to throw at me again, and stalked out of the room.

Very thankful for this turn of events, I was able to reflect on what had happened. I felt such gratefulness! And how effective it had been to rely on my inner guidance to guide me in response to the violence being thrust in my direction – rather than on my mind and emotions.

Staying in the Now

In many ways, the process of trusting your life to your 5D Self simply involves staying in the Now as much as possible. This means avoiding dwelling on the past and projecting into the future with any thought about what might happen. It's amazing how much our conditioning can keep us dwelling on both the past and the future – and how we often we can miss out on what is actually happening in the present moment. For this reason, it is usually necessary to keep consciously alert to living in the moment as much as possible.

In one way, as time goes on, this is actually getting easier and easier to do, because, as we rise vibrationally in the Fourth Dimension, linear time is gradually collapsing. In the Fifth Dimension, it actually disappears. The way it can be best described is that all time frames, past, present and future, are happening all at once; and you can enter into any one of them you choose at any time. And at the same time, there is actually only the present moment – or what could be called the *eternal moment* – that is available.

But, while we're still traveling through the upper Fourth Dimension, there is still a tendency for us to focus on both the past and the future. There's still the automatic pull to one or the other focus. So there's a need to focus more consciously on the present moment and stay in it.

If you're someone who tends to dwell a lot on the past – either nostalgically on pleasant events and situations you are yearning to return to, or on fearful, unpleasant events you wish to avoid in the future – it's important to understand that dwelling on the past keeps you stuck there in your mind. It's difficult to move forward to allow for something new to enter into your life.

At the same time, it's important also to not focus so much on the future – either out of fear or in anticipation of what may happen – because you are then missing out on what is happening in each moment now. If you're someone who tends to constantly make plans, you might try living more spontaneously.

To some degree, plans do need to be made, just to map out a possible future, especially if certain actions include other people who have their own plans they need to juggle. However, when you feel you do need to plan for something that is somewhat complex or important, it may be wise to first move into the Silence within you, dropping past the mind with all its ideas and fears and beliefs, and become still and open. Then ask what needs to be planned and done to prepare the way. You will find that the plans that emerge are not only clear and to the point, they take little effort to accomplish.

And yet, you may be discovering more and more these days that it gets harder to predict what might happen on any day. With Ascension occurring so rapidly now, so many events and situations seem to appear "out of the blue" and are quite unpredictable. It's therefore wise to make plans, but to stay loose with them. Begin trusting that what you will need to know and do in the future for everything to turn out in the best way possible will come to you at the right moment.

You may also discover that nothing much actually needs to be planned, that the event you're foreseeing will just appear naturally, without your having to do anything about it. This approach to planning for the future allows for a great deal of spontaneity in life and a refreshing unpredictability. It allows you to experience a sense of "magic" as you watch everything working out just fine, without your interference. Synchronicities abound, perfectly orchestrated events occur, and everything seems to flow in an exciting, harmonious way.

To really allow this to happen, however, it is necessary to be unattached to outcome. It's necessary to step out of all expectations, demands, and anxieties about how things are going to work out, and begin to trust that there is a bigger picture you may not be able to see at the present time. It's a matter of seeing that a "divine hand" is guiding you through your life in the perfect way. This hand is bringing events, situations, and people forward in the way that will best help you awaken to the greater reality of who you are as quickly as possible. It may not look like it at the time, but later on, you will be able to see that this is so.

The Process of Surrender is On-Going

Once you begin surrendering your life to Source and trusting it to take care of you in the best possible way, you will find that this becomes an on-going process throughout your life. You will experience yourself surrendering to many situations each day; indeed, the feeling of surrender continues to happen in every moment. Again, this isn't a passive allowing of anything at all to occur; it's a conscious alertness to feeling into right action. And – unless you get a strong inner message to change something and that change is one that requires an action that feels flowing and natural – it involves an allowing of those things that are occurring to be as they are.

This approach is not simply a new attitude you bring into your life; it's the entire context in which your life can be lived. Surrender begins suffusing your consciousness with each breath you take. It's a sumptuous nectar that flows through your awareness, creating a sweet peace and serenity in all you do. Trusting all that comes to you, you begin floating through life, freely and naturally.

Chapter 23

Embodying 5D

A final step on this path of fully identifying with your 5D Self is learning to fully embody it. This entails constantly feeling its presence anchored deeply within you, all through your body, mind and emotions. You also sense it extending out all around and above you. It's when you are naturally identified with it all the time, without the need to "keep yourself there".

Most likely, this shift will be a gradual one that happens naturally, as you begin focusing more and more on your experiences of 5D, detaching your identity from your 3D self, and trusting what Source is bringing forward in your life. Gradually, this shift in identification will become increasingly apparent to you. You'll begin noticing more and more how smooth and easy your life has become and how peaceful you generally feel. And you'll be aware, when you tune in, of a sense of powerful bright light that emanates from your very being.

At times, you may experience a deep emptiness within you, or a sensation that you yourself are this emptiness. If this occurs, do not be distressed. By relaxing into this sensation of emptiness, and being curious, you can discover that the emptiness begins transitioning into a vast vista that is clear and open, steeped in profound peace and well-being. You experience yourself as pure Presence, a Consciousness that is everywhere, existing in all of creation.

At other times, you may also become aware of new aspects of yourself as a multidimensional Being. You discover there are other higher-dimensional selves that have always been with you – identities you've not been consciously in touch with for a long, long time. As a part of you, these selves have been dwelling in higher dimensions, even those higher than the Fifth Dimension, and have been guiding you all along. You may have been referring to them simply as your "Higher Self", not realizing that they are actual multiple selves living in different dimensions. Or perhaps you've assumed they were your "guides", but you realize now they've actually been a part of you. It's true that you have also had separate Beings who have served as your guides, as well, but some of them you've felt or heard have probably actually been a part of the greater YOU you are now discovering.

Paradoxical Experiences

Of course, the process of shifting identity to the 5D Self is different for everyone; we are all unique in our Ascension process. But it's probable you may be having some of the common experiences people have. These can be very strange. On the one hand, exquisitely beautiful experiences happen to you more often, as you are lifted up by the grace of your 5D Self and you begin to be carried along by it. On the other, some of the most difficult and challenging experiences can also occur.

At times, you can feel deeply steeped in a particular experience, and suddenly something very much the opposite occurs. For instance, you may find yourself in extreme grief about a painful situation – and then suddenly realize you're experiencing a profound love for someone that's welling up inside you. Or, you may be experiencing a sense of joyous freedom, relaxed and peaceful; and then, out of the blue, you're suddenly remembering a painful memory, and tears spring into your eyes. It's as if you are waking up, falling asleep, then waking up again.

Or, paradoxically, you may experience yourself to be both selves at the very same time. It can be rather crazy-making. All these strange experiences tend to occur at this stage of Ascension; it's what commonly happens in the higher Fourth Dimension. Your 3D identification is dissolving; yet it can still claim you, especially in certain situations. At the same time, slipping into 5D consciousness somehow becomes easier and easier. So there is this back-and-forth, up-and-down process that takes place. You begin to see that you're in a process in which a long-standing habit is being broken – the habit of feeling yourself to be a limited, small body/mind being. It takes some time to fully break this habit.

Experiencing Bliss

Aside from the somewhat confusing experiences you may be having as you begin to experience the embodiment of your 5D Self, you may also encounter extended times of sheer bliss. These experiences can be ineffably exquisite. As described earlier, when you begin surrendering your life to this Self, a magical quality can begin permeating your every experience. Delightful synchronicities happen daily; circumstances have a way of turning out even better than they might have, had you planned them yourself. Life takes on a charmed quality. You walk through your life with a sense of wonder, beauty, and awe.

Indeed, there are times when it seems that every moment is suffused with a golden joy: simple sensory experiences become excursions into exaltation. Colors somehow seem brighter. Nature is more alive than ever, and everything simply looks "happy". You can see that your whole life is woven with blessings, and gratitude permeates your entire being. You experience a true sense of wholeness and peace for the first time in your life, a sense that the deep, aching yearning you've always had has finally been fulfilled.

There's a knowing that everything is being taken care of for you, so there's less to worry or concern you. There's less doing and more simply *being*. The entire world is a promise of exciting adventure. You approach most events with a relaxed, yet curious attitude, wondering, as a child might, what life is about to bring forward for you to experience. And you trust that, whatever it is, it will be for the highest good of all concerned.

A greater sense of healthy detachment appears. The world becomes more like an entertaining show in which you are both participating and watching. As you begin seeing your story of suffering more clearly as the illusion it is, you may find that your sense of humor suddenly expands and breaks through, even within the direst of situations. It sometimes becomes delightfully difficult to take anything very seriously anymore.

In many ways, it's as if you've begun living in a whole new universe. A sense of timelessness moves into your experience. Every place you go, you feel at Home. There is a constant sense of peace, like a quiet hum or current, that runs through your awareness. Sometimes, when not much is going on, this hum is in the foreground of your awareness; other times, when you are engaged in some activity, it is more in the background. But it is always there, like a peaceful lake you can dip into at any time.

Riding the Waves of 3D Dissolution

However, as described earlier in this book, because Ascension is a bumpy ride, all of these exquisite experiences can be abruptly punctuated with those that are extremely challenging and demanding. There may be periods when you think you have "lost" your new identity and wonder if you were ever operating in 5D reality at all. You may realize that your life, as you once knew it, is in the worst shape you've ever experienced; in fact, it appears to be falling apart on you. Negative thoughts and feelings abound in your consciousness; depression moves in.

You experience periods which could be called "gray nights of the Soul" – in which everything becomes lackluster. You feel as if your life is going nowhere. It's totally bleak and uninteresting. This is when you are in the depths of the Ascension Void.

When you stop to realize what this process of shifting identification is all about – the "death" of your 3D self – it can all make sense. It's no surprise that it gets tough at times. As you see things that used to be so important to you either falling away or being ripped from you, it can be greatly disconcerting. Your old sense of who you are is no longer holding together; it's dissolving into the nothingness that it essentially is. It's like being someone who has jumped from one cliff, hoping to reach another one across a chasm – but is currently in no-man's land, without either foot on the ground. This can be terrifying at times.

To add to the confusion, this experience of shifting identification can also bring something else forward: the occasional onslaught of old, unhealthy patterns and tendencies you have in your subconscious mind that must also be brought into conscious awareness and then let go of. If you truly want freedom, all these things must surface to be released.

At times, it may feel like stuff is just coming out of the woodwork. Habitual reactions and unresolved traumas you haven't experienced for years suddenly reappear out of nowhere. This can bring great distress, if you're not prepared for them and if you take them seriously and think you have to do something with them – like changing or fixing them.

Yet, all you need do with them when they appear is to watch them. Be aware of them, identify them, but don't give them any energy. Don't judge yourself for them or fret about them. Just allow them to express and then let them go. You'll see that they can simply vanish, sometimes surprisingly quickly. With the new high-frequency waves of light now present on Earth, what might have taken weeks or months in the past to clear out of your consciousness might take only hours or days.

The whole process is as if the frequency of your 5D Self has been flowing into you over a period of time, like a trickle of clear water into a bucket, loosening up guck that has been stuck in there for centuries. The guck at the bottom is eventually bound to float to the surface. Just observe it as it does, until you become filled with this new frequency and your consciousness overflows, allowing the unwanted debris to spill out. That is really all that is happening.

It's important to remember too that another part of what may be happening is that the bliss you experienced so much in the first "honeymoon" days of awakening into 5D consciousness seems to be less present. This may be because what once felt like an extraordinary experience of bliss to you has now become your ordinary baseline of experience. You got used to the high your awakening gave you at first; but like all highs, it has dissipated somewhat.

As discussed earlier, you need to realize that the high is not IT. It's not truly what you're looking for. The state of true realization of 5D is not an on-going state of ecstatic bliss. It is rather a peaceful sense of profound well-being. States of bliss, although usually very important in your awakening process in the early stages, are not the reality of being in which true fulfillment occurs. Although they do continue to occur, even after full awakening into 5D, like all experiences, they come and go. Thus, if you have been expecting the ecstatic highs to remain, you will likely be disappointed or upset, believing you've "lost" your 5D awakening – when this is not at all true.

The World is Still in 3D

Something else that may be contributing to your hard times as your identification shifts into 5D is the belief that once you begin making this shift, difficulties in life will disappear. Unfortunately, this is not true. Since you are still living in a controlled world that is in transition from a very low frequency, all kinds of challenges remain, whether you're awake to 5D or not. The craziness in the external world is still playing out. And the AI implants in your body, although losing power, are still there, pulling at you.

The important difference, however, is that while all this is still going on, YOU can be free. You can stand amidst any situation you find yourself in and simply watch it dispassionately, knowing fully that none of it is happening to YOU. That is the monumental difference.

As time goes on, you will find that it becomes easier and easier to ride the waves of the 3D dissolution that are washing through you. And at the same time, the beauty and joy that flow into your life become so powerful that the rough times are experienced, at worst, simply as small irritants in your life.

Aside from this, your healthy detachment becomes such a natural, on-going state, that it really doesn't matter after awhile what is happening in your life or in the world. As the dance of life whirls around you, you're simply watching everything from within a center of peace.

In fact, you eventually find that you have actually never been bound at all. You have always been free.

Chapter 24

Keeping Focused on 5D Consciousness

Although the process of awakening into 5D consciousness is one that happens naturally and tends to have its own accelerating rhythm as time goes on, there are times when you might feel as if your awakening is losing momentum: you sense yourself unhappily drifting back into the trance-like dreamworld of 3D. This can definitely happen; the external reality can easily pull you out of your inner focus of awakening to who you are. But if this occurs after a time when you have been deeply enjoying your immersion in 5D energies, it can be distressing.

It's helpful at these times to know some things you can do to refocus your attention on 5D and the ultimate Freedom for which you yearn. The following are some suggestions that might be helpful to you.

Staying Vigilant

Even when the external world is relatively quiet, daily life has a way of constantly pulling us into the realm of habitual desires, thoughts, and emotions. If you're not vigilant, it's easy to succumb to your old conditioned ways of living. It's a trite saying that the price of freedom is eternal vigilance. But when it comes to the quest for true Freedom, at least at first, vigilance is indeed the necessary price. This path toward 5D identification has to be a very conscious one: it demands you be aware when you begin to passively allow your conditioned patterns, habits, and desires to run you. It calls for remembering to keep responding to life from a higher consciousness.

At the same time, the vigilance needed is not a wary, stressful one – but rather a free and almost effortless one. You need to be watchful and observant, but not tense – much like a cat watching a mouse: totally alert, yet gracefully relaxed. You watch for old tendencies to arise – conditioned desires, reactions, and thoughts – and you consciously refrain from acting on them. Or, if you do end up acting on them, you can then, without judgment or self-doubt, simply observe this and move back into relaxed vigilance. Developing this habit can be freeing and quite exciting.

Sometimes your sense of drifting away from 5D might come about due to a waning of your earnestness in your quest for experiencing it. It is important to watch out for this quality of indifference in your consciousness, as it is most likely an aspect of the Ascension Void. It can be helpful to ask yourself during times of diminishing interest: How serious am I about this quest? How much do I really want to experience the enhanced freedom of 5D consciousness?

Then see if you can discover if something you have been doing has pulled you away from the powerful intention you may have at one time felt. Have you been following other distracting desires? Have you settled for a temporary, watered-down version of happiness? Have you stopped taking time to be in the Silence every day? Stopped reading books that inspire you? And, very importantly: Have you been focusing too much on the unrest and chaos out in the world? Become aware of these things that have pulled you out of your earnestness in your quest, and begin reversing them. Start doing those things that will again light your fire for freedom.

Focusing on Being

Another way to get back on track when you feel yourself drifting is to focus on simply *being*. Catch yourself in your busyness, both outer and inner. Be aware of how much of your activity is really necessary and see if you can stop and simply *be* for a while. Rest your mind. Let go of all thoughts for a time and just bring your attention to simply being.

Just resting in beingness like this is true meditation. It's being still and quiet in your mind. The more you can do this throughout your day, the more you can naturally shift back into 5D consciousness.

Seeing Everything as Yourself

As you move through your day, approach everything and everyone you meet as simply another aspect of your Self. For example, rather than seeing another person as someone separate from you, see him or her as a part of YOU, a form that is interacting with the form with which you are identified. See how the two forms are actually both a part of the same Essence. They are coming together, then leaving each other – yet they remain two aspects of who YOU are. See that you are the Consciousness that animates both forms. Feel the love you have for them both equally, as aspects of YOU.

You can approach objects in the same way. See yourself – the form you generally identify with – approaching the other form, one that is perhaps less "sentient". Again, both forms are a part of YOU. You are the Consciousness within both forms, the Consciousness that animates them both.

Who is Experiencing This?

This is a variation on the question, "Who am I?". Whatever you are doing, you can ask these questions: "Who is walking?". "Who is thinking?". "Who is speaking?". Each time, pull your awareness back into yourself – back to where your mind originates. Go to the source of all your thoughts and look carefully. What do you find? What do you experience?

Listening to the Silence

This involves listening to the true Silence that exists, even in the midst of much noise or activity. You can start by listening to the Silence that occurs in between sounds that are being uttered. You can also listen to it in between breaths you are taking, or in between thoughts you are thinking. You'll see that it is always there, waiting to be heard and experienced. Then you can begin listening to it *behind* or *under* a sound itself. Silence permeates everything. By focusing on hearing it in these ways, you can begin to realize that not only is this Silence always present – it is who you actually are.

Staying Connected to the Earth

It's especially important during these times to stayed grounded and connected to the Earth and nature. Spending time outdoors and communing with the trees, the plants and the animals can help to keep you balanced and peaceful. It can assist you in clearing your mind of useless chatter and worry and remind you of the glorious creations of Source living on this planet.

Living Fully in 5D – Free

If there were ever a challenging time to fully make the transition into 5D Identification, it is certainly during this present time. It's difficult just to keep your sanity intact. It demands a great deal of courage and determination; it takes vision and deep soul-searching. And it requires, no matter what occurs, the desire to work through a myriad of challenges, losses, and to maintain trust in the process.

Yet, if you've read this far in this book, you are likely a Spiritual Warrior who has not only purposely chosen to live during these times on Earth and survive them – but also someone who is here to assist and lead others through the chaos and confusion of a world transitioning through a historical transformation. You're probably a Soul who has done this before, in ancient times, perhaps in other parts of the universe. And your awakening to your 5D Self is not something you are learning anew – it's something you're remembering how to do once again.

So the main thing to do at this point, no matter how difficult or dark it may become, is to just keep going, one step at a time, fully confident of your success. Keep remembering that humanity is now on a firm timeline into the Fifth Dimension. The New Earth is already emerging. Your freedom, and that of all of humanity remaining on this Earth in the times to come, *is* coming about. We are walking into a glorious future. And you are in the process of helping to create this future, not just for yourself, but for all of humanity.

**Vidya Frazier** has studied spiritual teachings from both western and eastern traditions for over 50 years. In 1993, she felt called to India to visit the spiritual master Papaji. Upon returning, she wrote *The Art of Letting Go: A Pathway to Inner Freedom* and began offering individual sessions, groups and workshops based on this book.

In 2007, she was invited to attend the Oneness University in India and was initiated as a Oneness Blessing Facilitator. She returned and offered the blessing to hundreds of people. Since then, she has studied with quantum healer Dell Morris, author Jim Self, and Jacqueline Hobbs.

In 2014, Vidya published her first book on the theme of Ascension, *Awakening to the Fifth Dimension—A Guide for Navigating the Global Shift* and gave a number of presentations and interviews on the subject. A year later, she published a second book, a more in-depth exploration on the same theme: *Ascension: Embracing the Transformation*. In 2017, she published a third book describing the Ascension process occurring on the global scale, entitled, *Triumph of the Light*. And, in 2020, her fourth book, *The Ascension Lightworker Guide* was published.

Currently offering sessions of remote Quantum Healing, Ascension Readings, and Ascension Coaching, Vidya assists people to find their way with clarity and ease through the powerful energies of the Shift of consciousness that is now occurring across the planet. She also assists people in discovering their spiritual purpose in life and stepping more fully into expressing it.

Drawing on forty-five years as a licensed psychotherapist, hypnotherapist, and spiritual guide, as well as on her own spiritual awakening experiences, Vidya serves as a unique bridge between the worlds of psychology and spiritual awakening.

You can contact Vidya at **www.vidyafrazier.com** at the bottom of the home page.

Printed in the USA
CPSIA information can be obtained
at www.ICGtesting.com
LVHW011728151023
761159LV00041B/570